ENGENDERING CURRICULUM HISTORY

"It is my pleasure, and indeed honor, to recommend Petra Hendry's *Engendering Curriculum History*. This book is much needed in the field of curriculum studies. The gendered viewpoint Hendry brings to issues of curriculum and teaching is extremely important. Her scholarship provides the reader with vignettes, drawn from many centuries, not found in other curriculum history books. Readers will be intrigued by the depth, breadth, and scope of Hendry's scholarship; her personal writing style with its clear and definite voice makes this book a joy to read. So I say to all, read and enjoy!"
William Doll, Emeritus Professor, Louisiana State University–Baton Rouge, and Adjunct Professor, University of Victoria, Canada

"*Engendering Curriculum History* introduces interesting narratives about women that are often excluded from traditional historical accounts of education. It is important to provide scholarship such as this that documents the knowledge that women have created and contributed to education."
Madeline Grumet, University of North Carolina–Chapel Hill

How can curriculum history be reinvisioned from a feminist, poststructuralist perspective? *Engendering Curriculum History* disrupts dominant notions of history as linear, as inevitable progress, and as embedded in the individual. This conversation requires a history that seeks *re-membrance* not representation, *reflexivity* not linearity, and *responsibility* not truth. Rejecting a compensatory approach to rewriting history, which leaves dominant historical categories and periodization intact, Hendry examines how the narrative structures of curriculum histories are implicated in the construction of gendered subjects. Five central chapters take up a particular discourse (wisdom, the body, colonization, progressivism, and pragmatism) to excavate the subject identities made possible across time and space. Curriculum history is understood as an emergent, not a finished, process—as an unending dialogue that creates spaces for conversation in which multiple, conflicting, paradoxical, and contradictory interpretations can be generated as a means to stimulate more questions, not grand narratives.

Petra Munro Hendry is St. Bernard Chapter of the LSU Alumni Endowed Professor, College of Education, Louisiana State University.

STUDIES IN CURRICULUM THEORY
William F. Pinar, Series Editor

For additional information on titles in the Studies in Curriculum Theory series visit
www.routledge.com/education

ENGENDERING CURRICULUM HISTORY

Petra Munro Hendry

LOUISIANA STATE UNIVERSITY

Routledge
Taylor & Francis Group

NEW YORK AND LONDON

First published 2011
by Routledge
711 Third Avenue, New York, NY 10017

Simultaneously published in the UK
by Routledge
2 Park Square, Milton Park, Abingdon, Oxon OX14 4RN

Routledge is an imprint of the Taylor & Francis Group, an informa business

Typeset in Bembo
by Keystroke, Station Road, Codsall, Wolverhampton
Printed and bound in the United States of America on acid-free paper
by Walsworth Publishing Company, Marceline, MO

Library of Congress Cataloging in Publication Data
Hendry, Petra Munro, 1958– , author.
Engendering curriculum history / Petra Munro Hendry.
p. cm. – (Studies in curriculum theory)
Includes bibliographical references and index.
1. Education--Curricula–History. 2. Feminist theory. I. Title.
LB1570.H455 2011
375'.0009–dc22
2010043230

ISBN 13: 978–0–415–88566–9 (hbk)
ISBN 13: 978–0–415–88567–6 (pbk)
ISBN 13: 978–0–203–83900–3 (ebk)

To my husband, John

CONTENTS

PREFACE

Bringing out the Dead:
The Future of the Past

> History deals with the past, but this past is the history of the present . . .
> The true starting point of history is always some present situation with its
> problems.
>
> *(John Dewey, 1916)*

> The thread that ran through my questions and my searching was an intuition
> that an understanding of the nature of time was essential for understanding
> the nature of education.
>
> *(Dwayne Huebner, 1975)*

> One of the disturbing characteristics of the curriculum field is its lack of
> historical perspective.
>
> *(Herbert Kliebard, 1992a)*

In his 1992 book, *Forging the American Curriculum: Essays in Curriculum History and
Theory*, Kliebard reminds us that until very recently there was "no such thing as
curriculum history as an identified area of scholarship" (1992b: xi). The history of
curriculum has generally dealt with the history of education and subsequently
focused on schooling. Schools are, of course, very recent inventions. To equate
education with schooling is to truncate curriculum history and sever it from its
past. Curriculum theory, a field that transcends "schools" examines the social,
political, and cultural dynamics of "knowledge" and "learning." Curriculum as a
discursive practice is understood as historical text. In shaping the field, Kliebard's
impact has been one of forging the relationship between curriculum theory and
history. He explains that his goal is to "use historical analysis as a way of disen-
tangling what we could possibly mean by a curriculum theory" (p. xi). This book

continues the conversation between curriculum theory and history through a gender analysis of the subjectivities made possible and impossible in particular historical moments. Unlike Kliebard, my intent is not to disentangle curriculum theory but to complicate the relationship between history and theory.

Complicating the relationship between curriculum history and theory is no easy task. The "ahistorical" nature of curriculum has been central to reinforcing conceptions of curriculum as neutral, universal (timeless), apolitical, and consequently a technical endeavor. In essence, "curriculum" has been constructed as devoid of history. Discourses central to curriculum—"the child," "reason," "the learner," "the teacher," and "knowledge"—are likewise constructed as static, fixed ideas that have no history. The reconceptualist movement and linguistic turn have challenged the ways in which these and other discourses have come to be understood as "normal." How subject identities have been "produced" as natural and unitary has been the critical work of reconceptualizing curriculum as poststructural text. Given the complex and contradictory ways in which subjectivity is constructed across time and place it follows that curriculum is not a coherent system but rather is the "almost chaotic interplay of forces, some rational and calculated, and a great deal that is instinctive or symbolic or ritualistic" (Kliebard, 1992a: 158). The symbolic nature of curriculum, and its history, is thus not concerned with representation as "truth." Instead, my concern in this book is the relationship between historical narrative, subjectivity, and curriculum. What is taken to be knowledge in certain times and places? Why are certain forms of knowledge validated and others excluded? What are the social effects of this inclusion and exclusion? Why and under what circumstances are certain forms of knowledge validated as official knowledge?

This book is a history of the present. The present situation is replete with many problems, not the least of which is the supposed "crisis in education." This book is an attempt to reframe this crisis by suggesting that the crisis is not one of education, but one of imagination or put another way, of reimagining education. By crisis, I refer not to failing schools, low test scores or America's loss of a competitive edge in the world economy due to poor math and science performance. While I do not mean to suggest that these are not serious issues, I would instead maintain that they are the consequence of a larger problem in which the insidious nature of "reform" demands a presentism that resists history and consequently limits our language for reimagining curriculum. Simply stated, the problem this book addresses is one of imagination. How can we begin to reimagine education as more than a technical, corporate enterprise?

To write curriculum history, as a curriculum theorist, is to enter into contested terrain. I consider myself first and foremost a curriculum theorist, whose research has increasingly focused on curriculum history. Bridging theory and history is like trying to paint a canvas with egg whites. The canvas shows only traces of luminescence and appears to be unchanged. Theory, when understood as an abstraction, appears to have little impact on history. Like the egg whites it remains invisible to the eye yet leaves clear traces. To trace this invisibility is the project I undertake. It is the invisible relation between theory and history in which I seek a third space to engage history as discourse in order to understand how our relation to the past is continually mediated by language and memory. This mediation is nowhere more apparent than in relation to the question of subjectivity.

A primary premise of this book is that women's subjectivity and modes of self-representation are largely unmapped, indeed unrecognizable, given the traditional maps of historical genre and periodization. Thus, the narratives of curriculum history in this book are those that have been refused an identity. Excavating histories of gendered subjectivities engages subject positions that have rendered genre and gender codes unintelligible and thus requires looking for other textual forms of self-representation and other geographies of identity.

This book began as a quest to situate women as curriculum theorists in the field of curriculum history. When I began my Masters in Education in the early 1980s I was stunned to find that although teaching was considered "women's true profession," the field of curriculum history was almost exclusively the terrain of men. My history of education course began with Socrates, Plato, Aristotle, moved on to St. Augustine and St. Thomas Aquinas, continued with Locke, Rousseau, Pestalozzi, and Froebel, culminated with Dewey and, as a footnote, mentioned Maria Montesorri. It was almost inconceivable for me to imagine that women were not present in the historical narrative of education. How could women not have thought deeply about education or contributed in any significant way to the history of curriculum?

As I continued my studies in the early 1990s, curriculum theory, feminist theory, and cultural anthropology made me leery of simple "add and stir" approaches to reconceptualizing history. "History" was not "out there" waiting to be discovered but was, like gender and culture, a social construction that was deeply embedded in power relations. I turned to the work of Michel Foucault, Hayden White, Raymond Williams, and the Popular Memory Group, as well as feminist historians Gerda Lerner, Denise Riley, and Joan Kelly to help me to deconstruct the hold that "history" had on representation.

While the poststructural, feminist, and linguistic turn raged in other disciplines, including curriculum theory, I did not find this to be the case in curriculum history. This project is an attempt to bridge history and theory as a means to complicate the relationship between past and present in order that curriculum histories might be engendered to speak to the complexity of our humanity. Bringing out the dead is a necessity in order that curriculum history may have life. When curriculum is our lived experience, history is always in our midst.

ACKNOWLEDGMENTS

This research would not have been possible without the support of many people and numerous institutions. My thanks go to the librarians and staff at the Chicago Historical Society and the University of Illinois Jane Addams Special Collections for their assistance. My research on medieval women religious was greatly enhanced by the opportunity to conduct research as a visiting scholar at University of East Anglia in Norwich, England. I am grateful to Ivor Goodson for the invitation and to the staff and faculty at the Center for Applied Research in Education for providing a space in which I could fully immerse myself in my research on Julian of Norwich. The staff at the Julian Center in Norwich was most helpful as were the sisters of "All Hallows" who shared their understandings of Julian. Most generous was Sheila Upjohn, author of several books on Julian, who was gracious to spend many hours in conversation with me regarding Julian.

In Germany, the sisters of the Abbey of St. Hildegard trusted that I was a serious scholar of Hildegard. Hildegard has become a popular "New Age" icon in Germany and is being quite commercialized and exploited in ways that are causing great consternation to the Benedictine sisters. After many appeals the sisters granted permission to visit with them at the Abbey. My many conversations with Sister Scholastika were extremely insightful as she is the resident scholar on Hildegard. I hope that I have done justice to the theological brilliance and spiritual insight of Hildegard. My research on Mechthild of Magdeburg was made possible by the Sisters of the "Begegnungs and Bildungshaus St. Gertrud" in Eisleben. Sisters Walburga and Gerburga were actively engaged in reestablishing a convent at Helfta after the reunification of East and West Germany. The convent at Helfta (in former East Germany) had become a socialist collective with the sanctuary used as a barn since World War II. Their dedication to reviving the abbey at Helfta as a great site of German learning and culture headed by generations of women religious was truly inspirational.

My thanks go to the many friends and colleagues who read drafts of chapters of the book and were generous in the time they spent discussing it with me: Nina Asher, Jackie Bach, Allan Block, Laura Choate, William Doll, Kate Jenson, William Pinar, Hillary Procknow, Molly Quinn, Becky Ropers-Huilman, Charna Rosenholtz, Ann Trousdale, and Donna Trueit. Without the insights and prodding questions of many students this work would be incomplete. I am particularly grateful to the graduate students of the Curriculum Theory Project at Louisiana State University whose own research has been critical to mine: Donna Porche-Frilot, Elecia Lathon, Sally Tyler, Soledad Smith, Emily De Moor, Douglas McKnight, Tayari Dar-Salam, Marla Morris, Nicholas Ng-A-Fook, Lavada Brandon-Taylor, Denise Taliaferro, Steve Triche, Hongyu Wang, and Ugena Whitlock. I am especially grateful to Jie Yu, Wei Guan, and Hillary Procknow who read the manuscript word for word and provided critical feedback.

This book was written over the course of what seems a lifetime. I have been sustained by a rich network of professional and personal colleagues whose belief in my work has been critical to sustaining the momentum in bringing this work to completion. They include: Terri Buchanan, Karen Callender, Claudia Eppert, Irene DiMiao, Wendy Kohli, Janet Miller, Craig Kridel, Margaret Crocco, Janice Jipson, Michelle Masse, Anna Nardo, Nancy Spivey, and Robbie McHardy.

The final stages of writing a book are often the most tedious and cumbersome. This work was made much more tolerable by the support of Naomi Silverman whose editorial guidance was invaluable from the start. Two anonymous reviewers provided generous feedback that was critical to fine-tuning the manuscript, I thank them now. I am also most grateful to William Pinar, Series Editor, whose close reading and insightful feedback made this a much better book. Over 15 years ago he encouraged me to pursue this line of intellectual work, his support and mentorship have been critical to its completion.

My parents are a source of never-ending support and I am grateful for all the opportunities they have provided me across a lifetime. It was my mother who first introduced me to Hildegard of Bingen when she spoke of the powerful role Hildegard had played in her own development as a young girl in Germany. My aunts "Tante Ulla" and "Tante Pip" also shared my enthusiasm in researching both Hildegard and Mechthild of Magdeburg by providing housing, transportation, and translation during my research in Germany. My cousin Birgit shared all she knew about the abbeys and famous medieval women she had researched in Herford, Germany and surrounding areas. Her own research confirmed my own emerging understandings of the powerful role women religious played in the medieval cultural development of ideas.

My husband John recently asked what I needed from him in order to finish writing this book (he is as ready as I am to have this 12-year project completed). Just asking the question was enough. I am forever indebted to his love and faith in me. While he does not always fully understand my work, I could not have finished this work without his presence in my life. He has been the anchor and the balance that has allowed me to venture into the past. It is to him that this book is dedicated.

The author and publishers would like to thank the following for permission to reproduce copyright material: Garland Press for Chapter 1, "Engendering Curriculum History," which originally appeared in a slightly modified form under the same title in W.F. Pinar (Ed.) (1998) *Curriculum: Toward New Identities*, New York: Garland Press. Caddo Gap Press and the *Journal of Curriculum Theorizing* for a portion of Chapter 3, "Embodying Curriculum," which originally appeared in a slightly modified form under the title "Disrupting the Subject: Julian of Norwich and Embodied Knowing," *Journal of Curriculum Theorizing*, 21(1) (Spring, 2005), 95–108. Rowman & Littlefield Publishers for a portion of Chapter 5, "Unsettling Curriculum," which originally appeared in a slightly modified form under the title "'Widening the Circle': Jane Addams, Gender, and the Re/Definition of Democracy," in M.S. Crocco & O.L. Davis (Eds.) (1999) *"Bending the Future to Their Will": Civic Women, Social Education and Democracy* (pp. 73–92), Lanham, MD: Rowman & Littlefield.

INTRODUCTION

Someone, I say, will remember us in the future.

(Sappho, 640 BCE)

"Effective" history deprives the self of the reassuring stability of life and nature, and it will not permit itself to be transported by a voiceless obstinacy toward a millenial ending. It will uproot its traditional foundations and relentlessly disrupt its pretended continuity. This is because knowledge is not made for understanding; it is made for cutting.

(Michel Foucault, 1977)

All history is an imaginative reconstruction based on an inevitably partial and interpreted record of the past.

(Ellen Lagemann, 2000)

If there is a direction that the history of curriculum has taken in the course of its short history, it has been mainly toward a multiplicity, if not a new complexity, in its interpretations.

(Herbert Kliebard, 1992a)

Curriculum history has been my passion for many years. Yet, my relationship with history has been complex. I have been suspicious of the "stable" nature of history—its ability to trick us, like Hermes, into a false sense of certainty, progress, and absolute truth. Perhaps my initial attraction to history was an illusion of certainty. I wanted to find my way and assumed the path would be clearly marked, traceable, taking me back to my origins and roots. Little did I know that this path would take me to places I had not yet conceived—to places that would hurt and cut. I had yet to understand that the power of history would not be one of certainty, but one of both rupture and rapture.

A significant rupture occurred as a graduate student when I first encountered Ellen Lagemann's "The Plural Worlds of Educational Research" in which she concluded that "one cannot understand the history of education in the United States during the twentieth century unless one realizes that Edward L. Thorndike won and John Dewey lost" (1989: 185). This "triumph" might be considered nothing short of a whole worldview that has shaped the culture of education, and most importantly, has determined the grand narrative of the history of curriculum theory. It signifies the privileging of modes of inquiry that are based in a technocratic, behaviorist, and positivist paradigm that reflect a particular modernist, industrial American view of success as dependent on efficiency, order, and control. Inquiry is reduced to research as a method, a closed system, in which science produces absolute truths. In contrast to this technocratic worldview, for Dewey, as well as for other pragmatists, science was understood as ongoing experimentation.[1] Science was not a "method," but the heart of an ethics in which the process of ongoing inquiry was critical to democratic thought.[2] The rigid dichotomization of these two educational theories as representing incompatible lines of thought as either "behaviorist" or "pragmatic" is one in which history functions to reduce the past to a singular representation. History is understood as the transmission of a complete and finished cultural narrative. To say that one ideology triumphed over the other is a misrepresentation. As Lagemann (2000) suggests, history is "an inevitably partial and interpreted record of the past" (p. 246). It is the partial and interpreted nature of history that invites us to engage in history as a site for embracing multiple, often contradictory worldviews as a means for enriching our understanding of the human condition.

Constructing history as the story of winners and losers, as triumphs and defeats satisfies the desire for tidy readings of events but obscures the complex ways in which history functions. At the time of my reading of Lagemann, I was conducting life histories with women teachers whose careers had spanned the 20th century (Munro, 1998a, b). Their stories as educators were ones that did not fit neatly into the history of education as a duel between two competing theorists, let alone a contest between conflicting ideologies. In their lived experience as teachers, they constructed understandings of pedagogy and curriculum in an ongoing fashion, one in which they often took up multiple and conflicting discourses. In essence, they sought to continually disrupt notions of a static philosophy or discourse of curriculum. Curriculum was a continual negotiation of their lived experiences within and against multiple ideologies/discourses of education. Their stories revealed an understanding of curriculum that was not as simple as choosing between Thorndike's behaviorism or Dewey's pragmatism, and suggested the complex ways in which we actually live history. This complexity provided not only a counter-narrative to the dominant curriculum histories that I had read but disrupted the very category of "history." Thus, I turned to examine the simply profound question of "What is history?"

Edward Carr began his 1961 lecture series at the University of Cambridge by asking "What is history?" He replied "our answer, consciously or unconsciously, reflects our own position in time, and forms part of our answer to the broader question what view we take of the society in which we live" (1962: 2). His explication focused on dismantling the theoretical conundrum of the day—"Was history the result of an objective compilation of facts or the equally untenable theory of history as the subjective product of the mind of the historian?" Drawing on the Oxford philosopher and historian Robin George Collingwood, Carr argued that the "philosophy of history is concerned neither with 'the past by itself' [facts] nor with 'the historian's thought about it by itself' [interpretation], but with 'the two things in their mutual relation.'" (p. 16). History is a *relationship* between the past and present. The past, which the historian studies, is not a dead past, but a past, which, in some sense is still living in the present. Carr ultimately answers the question "What is history?" by suggesting that it is "an unending dialogue between the present and the past" (p. 24). This dialogue is the project of "engendering" curriculum. To engender, from the Latin *ingenerare*, means to beget, or to bring into existence. Bringing into existence a dialogue between the past and the present is to rupture the "unknown immensity" (Winfield, 2007: 17) of history as a means to *remember* how the past is always implicated in the present and the present in the past.

This book seeks to reclaim and reinvision curriculum history. By disrupting dominant notions of history as linear, as inevitable progress, as embedded in the individual, engendering curriculum is an invitation to engage with history across time and space. History understood as an emergent process, not a finished product, is an unending dialogue that creates spaces for conversation in which multiple, conflicting, paradoxical, and contradictory interpretations can be generated as a means to stimulate more questions and inquiry. Historical inquiry, like education, is by its nature an endless conversation. By *engendering curriculum*, the *finality* of Thorndike's supposed triumph can be re-created to become an ongoing dialogue between Thorndike and Dewey, as well as open spaces for others (like Jane Addams, Carter G. Woodson, Anna Julia Cooper) whose exclusion is predicated on the construction of history as solid, stable, and certain. Engendering history seeks to rethink history in ways that allow for rupture, in which inquiry is grounded in endless questions that demand more thought, more complexity, and more multiplicity. It is a history that is comfortable with ambiguity and contingency, not dependent on a grand narrative (Cohen, 1999).

To bring history into existence, into the present, will require a rethinking of temporality. Julia Kristeva (in Moi, 1986) in her evocative essay "Women's Time" posits multiple modalities of time known throughout the history of civilization. *Cursive time*, the time of linear history and *monumental time*, the time of another history (both described by Nietzsche), produce subject identities that are dependent on historical sedimentation of supra-national, socio-cultural ensembles. History as "time," Kristeva suggests makes invisible female subjectivity. Female subjectivity, Kristeva argues, has less to do with time as linear since women's experience is grounded in repetition and cycles. *Cyclical* time understands history not as linear "time," but as a relational and recursive "space." From a modernist perspective time is linear; conceived like an irreversible line. Along that line marches progress, each step throughout history taking us closer to truth as we leave behind an archaic past.[3] This mountaintop view of knowledge, where the "rise in reason" leads us to the pinnacle of "rationality" making the past "obsolete," is deeply gendered. The past, devoid of reason, becomes irrational, chaotic, and disorderly (female) in contrast to the present, which is rational, reasoned, and orderly (male). Limiting history to a restricted and universal view of temporality as linear has not only been central to gendering knowledge, but has resulted in an "ahistorical" view of curriculum. In other words, as Karl Popper (1958) has so poignantly argued, without multiple and conflicting theories of what constitutes history there is no history but only a predetermined end. Hearing the echo of Sappho's call that "someone will remember us in the future" this book is a response.

Bringing history, and specifically curriculum history, into existence is the engendering this book undertakes. Engendering curriculum is an invitation to engage with history across time and space. Putting history back in time, enfolding it, brings it to life. History is not the past. It is not dead. It breathes and gives life. Thus conceived, history is a site of memory, or re-membering. Memory, as understood by Jane Addams is critical to agency and "social reorganization." What is remembered is implicitly understood as political, knowledge is power. Memory is thus not mere nostalgia or sentimental reminiscence, but an interpretative, political, and creative engagement that asks us to question: What does it mean to be human? How do we know? Who can be a knower? What is knowledge? That curriculum history has been central to shaping knowledge and gender is the memory work I undertake.

I draw on Foucault's notion of "effective history" to invert the relationship that "traditional history" (as Cursive and Monumental) has to its dependence on metaphysics. Knowledge, even under the banner of history, does not depend on "rediscovery," and it empathically excludes the "rediscovery of ourselves." History becomes "effective" to the degree that it introduces discontinuity into our very being—as it divides our emotions, dramatizes our instincts, multiplies our body and sets it against itself. History is not outside the self; it is our bodies, energies, desires, fantasies, and everyday experiences. "Effective history" is directed against traditional notions of reality, identity, and truth and includes elements of parody, dissociation, and sacrifice. The first—parody—is directed against reality, and opposes the theme of history as reminiscence or representation. Parody is a satirical imitation, a travesty. To understand history as *parody* is to acknowledge that history can never be recognized. It is always an imitation. The second is dissociative, directed against identity, and opposes history given as continuity or representative of a tradition. To understand that history is *dissociative*, is to understand that history can never be represented as an absolute. It cannot be identified. The third is sacrificial, directed against truth, and opposes history as knowledge. To understand history as *sacrifice* is to understand that we must offer it up, relinquish, or forfeit it. Like Abraham, who was asked to sacrifice his son, we must trust that in letting go, our faith in history will be restored. By embracing parody, dissociation, and sacrifice my intent is not to create a new master narrative. However, I do seek, like Gwedolyn Midlo Hall (2005), to "escape from the linear, mechanistic, logical constructs that prevail in the historical profession and that have little or nothing to do with reality" (pp. 291–292). To assume that history represents the past, that there is a direct correspondence between history and knowledge, is to neglect the powerful role that memory, consciousness, imagination, and power play in the construction of history. Histories are constructs that defy simple binaries or absolute truths. The "truths" of history are born both from fact and fiction, time and space, memory and re-presentation.

Thus, an engendered history is one that is grounded in *re-membrance* and representation, *reflexivity* and linearity, and *responsibility* and truth. It is necessary to distinguish "reminiscence" from memory or remembering. Reminiscence is the narration or telling of the past (the precursor of "traditional history"). It situates the teller as the subject and the story of history as the object. Memory, on the other hand, is the process of re-membering. Re-membering is not only about what gets remembered, by whom, how, and when, but also about the very limits of representation and the resistance to remembering certain events (Simon, Rosenberg, & Eppert, 2000). Memory work thus becomes an interactive, dialogic process between past and present and future. *Mnemosyne* was the personification of memory in Greek mythology. Her daughter, Clio, one of the nine Muses, meaning "recount," is the muse of heroic poetry and history.[4] She is often represented with a parchment scroll or a set of tablets and is also known as the Proclaimer. "Recounting" was not intended to be a representation of reality. History was not read by the ancients as "sequences of events that were linked casually, but as manifestations of timeless realities that were expressed as repetitions and themes" (Davis, 2004: 29). Repeating, going back over and over again, in and through time, is not only what establishes connections but is central to resisting the logic of identification or representation as absolute reality. Memory as repetition, as recursion, as reflexivity is both the doing and undoing of representation; it is "impossibly double, both the stake and the shifting sand: order and potential disorder, reason and madness" (Salverson, 2000).

History as memory work disrupts linearity, progress, and truth by embracing the work of the historian as one of re-membering the complex process of becoming. This complexity, as Baker and Heyning (2004) suggest, demands that our historical interrogations of curriculum offer "insights into the 'conditions of possibility' for certain discourses to take hold, for questions to be posed as they are currently posed, and for ascertaining when/how things were formulated into being an 'educational problem' relative to other timespaces" (p. 29). In this book, I play with writing a history that is reflexive, generative, and that resists closure. From this perspective, curriculum history has less to do with "knowledge" and everything to do with the subject positions that it makes available. Those subject positions are inscribed in discourses, modes of thought, and structures of knowledge that appear as normal and obvious and provide what is thinkable and what is not. In taking up several discourses (imaging, embodying, decolonizing, unsettling, and experiencing) to examine as sites of identity construction, I seek to understand how gendered subject identities are taken up, resisted, appropriated, and contested. These discourses are not in the past but present as shadows and traces, moving throughout and within our memories. While curriculum is constituted of infinite discourses, I have chosen to focus on five discourses that weave in and through curriculum history that I believe have been pivotal to the construction of gendered identities. The image below represents a history with no beginning or end, that is continually circulating, that enfolds, overlaps, and is pulsing with energy. Like Clio it draws us in to recount, reconnect, and remember—to engage in the ongoing process of becoming.

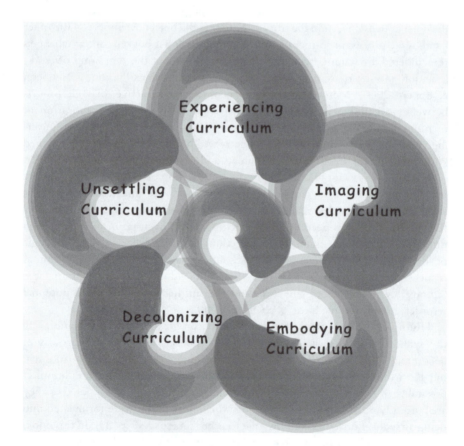

FIGURE 1 Engendering Curriculum History

Engendering curriculum history, I invoke the Muse Clio, to bring to life a sense of parody, disassociation, and sacrifice. The chapters in this book make an attempt to re-present curriculum history as a form of memory work, in which each chapter examines a way in which identity could be re-membered through particular discursive practices that "run" (*currere*, the Latin word from which "curriculum" is derived) through and in space and time. What makes identity as we know it possible? How have subject identities changed and shifted over time? While some sense of linearity, as we know it, exists, each chapter circles through time to fold the past into the present, and the present into the past. My responsibility as a curriculum theorist is to re-member and recount, to reconnect through seeking patterns and themes. This is the recursive or reflexive moment that is history.

The chapters that comprise this book are by no means a "complete" rewriting of curriculum history, nor was that my intention. I have chosen to enter "spaces" of history—particular moments—where cultural and social understandings of what constitutes "knowledge" have made profound shifts. These shifts, as I understood them originally, were deeply intertwined with parallel shifts in the ways sub-jectivity was gendered. While my original goal was to trace direct relationships between gender and knowledge the past did not comply in such a tidy manner. Gender is not a static or fixed concept, but is a constantly changing dynamic relation. As a concept, gender does not have an independent existence, but only exists in relation to a multiplicity of other discourses. The discourses that structure this work (imaging, embodying, decolonizing, unsettling, and experiencing) by no means exhaust the discursive spaces in which gender/knowledge intersect, but are moments that serve as sites for memory work for remembering the ways in which women theorists, philosophers, social critics, and activists have negotiated their identities as "knowers."

At the outset I could not have anticipated the profound and contradictory ways in which meanings were made across time and through space. I was continually challenged by the past to unpack my own taken for granted assumptions about what constitutes knowing and how we come to know. I was not prepared for the role that spirituality (in some cases religion), love, eros, the body, passion, notions of the sacred, imagination, as well as reason, logic, and notions of science would play in the complex, and sometimes paradoxical, ways in which meanings are made. Most astounding was the recursive nature of many stories that echoed in the present and called me to "suspend" time in order to listen and be present to the past. The chapters that follow are a "response" to the call from women across time. They provide alternative narratives to the traditional educational/curriculum narratives to which we are accustomed, however, they are by no means complete. Each chapter is structured to provide a brief review of what we might consider the "traditional" history of a particular time period, then provides an alternative reading, and finally comes back to make connections to contemporary scholarship. This cyclical format is intended to disrupt notions of linearity, progress, and tidy endings through some form of recursion. While these efforts may not completely succeed they are attempts to envision history from a more relational perspective. The chapters are as follows.

Chapter 1, Engendering Curriculum History, provides a feminist, post-structural theoretical framework for analyzing curriculum history. Taking gender as a central analytical category, this chapter grapples with the calls to enlarge the conversation between the history of education and curriculum theory (Goodson, 1997). And yet, in these poststructural times, when the hallmarks of Enlightenment notions of history—origins, progress, and linearity—are emerging as fictions, this has become an increasingly complex task. How do we write history when its death toll has been rung? Rather than abandon history as a "relic of humanist thought" (Scott, 1989: 35), I outline a feminist, poststructuralist reading of curriculum history which seeks to disrupt the search for origins or a unitary subject by conceiving of processes so interconnected that they cannot be disentangled. Rejecting a compensatory approach to rewriting history, which leaves dominant historical categories intact, I examine how the narrative structures of curricular histories are implicated in the construction of gendered subjects. My goal is to question the notion of the unitary subject without giving up the political work of recovering women's history.

In Chapter 2, Imaging Curriculum, I turn to creation stories as the site of the first engendering of curriculum. Most curriculum histories begin with the ancient world of the Greeks and Romans, thereby excluding the vast terrain of "pre-history." The field of curriculum has been dominated by a Christian teleological view that has seen pre-Christian history as merely a preparatory stage for "true" history. This chapter examines pre-Christian, Chinese, Judaic, Early Greek, and Gnostic epistemologies. While focusing on women or feminine images such as Nu Kwa, Deborah, Sappho, Theano, Phintys, and Mary Magdalene, the primary focus is on how knowing is understood in a world that is for the most part polytheistic, mytho-poetic, and pre-word. I argue that curriculum was understood not as "knowledge" but as images that represented a holistic, non–dualistic, and paradoxical understanding of the world.

In Chapter 3, Embodying Curriculum, the body as a site of knowing is examined to explore love, eros, and passion as central to knowing. The emergence of a worldview based in monotheism, duality, reason, and language was predicated on a mind/body, male/female dichotomy and a corollary epistemological shift which situated knowledge as within the individual and a product of reason. In response to this shift, which functioned to marginalize women as knowers, this chapter explores the "ways of knowing" of medieval women religious and mystics (Hildegard of Bingen, Julian of Norwich, Teresa of Avila, and Mechthild of Magdeburg). I consider embodied knowing as a way in which women (and sometimes male) religious embraced a holistic worldview that encompassed body, mind, and spirit. I explore the "body" as a site of knowing as a means through which medieval women religious posited alternative epistemologies that rejected gender dualisms and reinscribed gender with infinite possibilities.

From embodied knowledge, I turn in Chapter 4 to Decolonizing Curriculum. The emergence of scientific discourse in the 16th century maintained that what had once been a sign of divine inspiration, mystical experience, was now considered the work of the devil. Enlightenment discourses, embedded in rationality and reason (male) as the sites for knowing, necessitated the repression of the body (female) as a site of knowing. While colonization is traditionally understood as the conquest of the "other" by Europeans, this chapter suggests that colonization required a radical reconfiguration and mapping of subjectivity in which an understanding of the body as a discrete entity, with an interior space, was central to "Enlightenment" concepts of knowledge which made possible the binary constructs of reason/emotion, subject/object, male/female, self/other, public/private, and colonizer/colonized. Colonization is understood here as a discursive practice that functions not merely as a direct power relationship between colonizer and colonized, but as a complex ideology that has been critical to "educating" subjects and constructing notions of subjectivity, specifically gendered ones. I examine the writings of Christine de Pizan and Margaret Cavendish, among others, as examples of how they resisted their colonization as objects of knowledge and the strategies they embraced to claim and name their knowledge. My focus is on how gender becomes a primary trope through which bodies and minds are colonized. How women curriculum theorists take up subject identities in relation to these discourses is the topic of this chapter. I suggest that one response to women's colonization was to create "New Edens" in the "New World." My argument is that women colonists entered the North American scene as both colonized and colonizer and thus assumed a different position within these processes of signification. I examine the writings of Maria of the Incarnation, the Ursuline sisters, Anne Hutchinson, and the Sisters of the Holy Family to analyze the subject positions they take in relation to "colonization" and what this tells us about ways of knowing.

In Chapter 5, Unsettling Curriculum, I examine the ways in which women curriculum theorists negotiated the imposition of subject identities embedded in "republican motherhood" and the "cult of domesticity." These discourses emerged directly from "Enlightenment" political thought and culminated in classical liberal democracy. Central to these supposed "democratic" discourses was the basic premise that the destiny of the nation was dependent on gender-defined roles for women. Women's impact was to be indirect, it was to represent influence, not actual power, and it was to be exerted through others and for others. This subject position, it has been argued (Grumet, 1988), was not motivated by altruistic visions of democracy, but instead by the needs of an emerging industrial nation which required the repression of the individual to the state (also a gendered construction of private versus public). This repression of the private (read female) necessitated curricular ideologies such as "common school movement," "feminization of teaching," and eventually "progressivism" that required separation from, and continual repression of, the feminine.

The "unsettling" of this "pedagogy for patriarchy" is examined in this chapter. One curricular response to this repression was the social reform work of the settlement house movement. I posit these institutions and movements as curricular innovations which not only expanded the opportunities of education to a large segment of the population, but challenged the very assumptions of education as public, individual, and male. I argue that these innovations provided an alternative educational philosophy grounded in community, as opposed to the individual, as the site of learning. In particular, the scholarship of Anna Julia Cooper, Jane Addams, and Ida B. Wells will be examined as central to retheorizing curriculum at the turn of the century. Special attention is given to Jane Addams and her critique of liberal democracy and dominant discourses of education (including social efficiency and progressivism), and her counter-discourse of community, rather than individualism, as the primary epistemological site for theorizing the relationship between education and democracy.

Lastly, in Chapter 6, Experiencing Curriculum, I examine the gendered discourse of pragmatism as it was articulated by women curriculum theorists of the "progressive" era. Drawing on the work of Walkerdine (1990), who has compelled me to ask "What's progressive about the progressive movement for women?" I interrogate what desires are met by progressivism's illusive hold on 20th-century education. Progressivism situated teachers as "facilitators" of knowledge thereby reinforcing the gender plot in which women are not "knowers" in their own right, but merely carry out the ideas of others. This chapter examines the scholarship of women pragmatists, including Ella Flagg Young, Charlotte Hawkins Brown, Lucy Sprague Mitchell, Margaret Naumberg, Elsie Ripley Clapp, Nannie Helen Burroughs, Laura Zirbes, and Marietta Johnson. I argue that they engendered pragmatism by disrupting the concept of "experience" as universal by including gender, race, class, and region. This gendered notion of experience was the foundation for their understanding of democratic education. Contesting social reconstructionist views of democracy as indoctrination, they theorized that democratic education can never be imposed or taught but must be experienced. I examine the various experimental and community schools these women curriculum theorists developed and conclude by looking at both the possibilities and limitations of "experience" as a curricular construct.

The future is now and the project that I undertake is one of remembrance. This book is based on the premise that the current ahistorical nature of curriculum, in which the past is irrevalent, and in some cases a fiction, constitutes "dangerous knowledge" (Britzman, 1998). The primacy of a cosmology of science, rationality and logic, in which knowledge is neutral, absolute, and finite, functions to obscure the need for historical understandings. When we are bereft of history we can never be truly present. My hope is that this project will provide inspiration to educators that will enable them to re-member and engender new curriculum histories.

1

ENGENDERING CURRICULUM HISTORY

That history produces subjects rather than subjects producing history might seem a poststructural "fact."[1] Yet, how the discourses of curriculum history collude in producing normative assumptions of gendered, raced, and sexed subjects remains relatively unproblematized. The primary focus of this chapter is to examine the ways in which the discursive practices of curriculum history make particular subject identities thinkable. However, to interrogate the "subject" of history at the same time that the death toll of "history" and the "subject" has been rung is a seemingly contradictory position. It is this site of dis–ease, doing history while simultaneously being suspicious of it, which I embrace. What does it mean to do history if there is no longer a subject? What are the implications of history being in flux at the very moment that the histories of those traditionally marginalized are being articulated? As a woman curriculum theorist I ask, "Can I give up history before I even have one?" When history has functioned as a primary form of oppression, "Do I even want one?" What does it mean to do curriculum history at this particular juncture?

Rather than abandon history as a "relic of humanist thought" (Scott, 1989: 35), I seek a feminist poststructuralist reading of curriculum history that attempts to disrupt the search for origins and to decenter the unitary heroic subject, either male or female. I also want to challenge the myth of progress by conceiving of history as the confluence of processes so interconnected that it cannot be reduced to a unitary storyline (grand narrative). Rejecting a compensatory approach to re/writing history, which leaves dominant historical categories and periodization intact, I examine how the narrative structures of curriculum histories are implicated in the construction of gendered subjects. To problematize the notion of the subject, without giving up the political work of "recovering" women's history, is the feminist poststructuralist challenge, which I take up. I maintain that we must

[handwritten margin note: History should not have 1 grand story line]

become comfortable with a more complex, less tidy, nonlinear understanding of the history of curriculum theory, which disrupts the very categories that make "history" intelligible.[2]

History as Memory Work

> History as celebrated by memory is deciphering of the invisible, a geography of the supernatural . . . It brings about an evocation of the past . . .
>
> *(Jean-Pierre Vernant, 1983)*

> History is the memory of things said and done.
>
> *(Carl L. Becker, 1935)*

History has always provided me with a way to reshape the future through reimagining the past. As a young girl it was history, rather than literature, science, or art, that provided me with a way to understand who I was and more importantly who I was not. History held extraordinary power. As a young girl this was a profound insight. Having learned my history lessons well, I knew I was to be seen, not heard. This silencing was not the result of explicit sanctions. There was no need to cut my tongue out, to gag me, or to banish me from public places. Unlike the women in history books, this was not necessary. Astonishingly enough, I had already learned to silence myself—bite my tongue, hold my peace. This repression is the history that has no voice. My knowledge that women's experiencing of the world is invisible is a painful reminder that history, and in this case specifically curriculum history, is predicated on subjugation and erasure.

Consequently, I begin with the premise that to conduct history in these poststructural times is to recover from the "epistemic violence" (Spivak, 1988), which has been history. Put more simply, "history is what hurts, it is what refuses desire and sets inexorable limits to individual as well as collective praxis" (Jameson, 1981: 102). These limits are the consequence of the modernist obsession with objectivity and rationality that function to make "natural" the concepts of the subject as unitary; temporality as linear, continuous, and coherent; and progress as the inevitable consequence of history. By problematizing the very nature of knowledge as objective and corresponding to any reality, the deconstructionist turn has been central to problematizing modern forms of knowledge, like history, that seem natural but are in fact contingent on sociohistorical constructs of language and power (Baker, 2009a; Foucault, 1977; Polkinghorne, 1988; Young, 1990). This is not to suggest that there is no past. The past is real and there is evidence of it. However, evidence does not reveal the past, but instead it points to interpretations of the past. As Frank Ankersmit (1998) suggests:

> Evidence is not a magnifying glass through which we can study the past, but bears more resemblance to the brushstrokes used by the painter to achieve

a certain effect. Evidence does not send us back to the past, but gives rise to the question what an historian here and now can do with it. (p. 184)

Historians, as Hayden White (1978) maintains, do not "find" patterns of meaning in the past but "construct" meaning from and impose meanings on the mosaic of sources and evidences that are available from the past. As a curriculum theorist, my interest is in the narratives we have constructed in relation to who can be a knower and what can be known, and what this reveals about us as a culture, particularly in relation to gendered identity and subjectivities. I contend that the construction of history as linear, as inevitable progress, and as embedded in the individual is one possible telling—one which I maintain has functioned in complex ways.

According to Jane Flax (1990), modernist history's "appearance of unity presupposes and requires a prior act of violence" (p. 33).[3] The subject of the traditionalist history—unitary, male, heterosexual, White—is made possible through the deconstruction of its other.[4] History's appearance of unity, of coherence, of order is predicated not on any direct correspondence to a reality but on the suppression of contradictory stories, most often those of women, people of color, and the working class. History as we know it is not possible without this silencing. This suppression is the "epistemic violence" upon which the myth of a unified and fixed subject, which functions to "universalize" history and make it gender-less, is contingent (Smith, 1995). History as we know it limits contradiction, multiplicity, and difference. Remembering this suppression is the memory work that must be done.

"Righting" or "Writing" History

My dis-ease in "doing history" is the result of the tension between the need to write/right the histories of "women," "African-Americans," and other marginalized groups into curriculum theorizing while simultaneously deconstructing those categories of history that have made possible the violence of erasure and subjugation. Rather than see these views as incommensurate, I will try to avoid the binary simplicity of either/or arguments. I maintain that one sickness of contemporary theorizing is to continue to seek unitary theories despite our acknowledgment that knowledge is multiple, contradictory, and always in flux. To envision both of these standpoints as compatible and, in fact, necessary, I will briefly review their theoretical histories.

To write women back into history has been a primary aim of feminist scholarship. However, "doing history" which adds the stories of women, Blacks, and marginalized others, does little to disrupt history as usual. Merely adding the names of women would be to ignore Joan Kelly's (1984) salient reminder that "what we call compensatory history is not enough" (p. 2). Just to include women heroines would be to perpetuate the often silent and hidden operations of gender in shaping historical analysis. For example, although we include women—such as Margaret Haley or Ella Flagg Young or Ida B. Wells—in the story of progressivism, the very concept of periodization of the "progressive movement" as gendered and gendering remains unproblematized.[5] In essence, the classic formation of narrative history as suggested by Susan Paddle (1995)—a unified subject and a plot predicated on the unfolding of a tale with implicit motifs of progression, development, and growth—remains the same. As a consequence, history retains the illusion of a seamless narrative written by an omniscient, invisible narrator. In other words, history remains grounded in an epistemology based on objectivity, and the very categories of history that have functioned to make women invisible remain intact.

Ironically, then, this compensatory view of history can contribute to reinforcing the notion of objectivity by claiming to make "better" history or at least a more rigorous, complete history. Susan Friedman (1995) reminds us that "this search to discover the 'truth' of women's history that could shatter the 'myths' and 'lies' about women in the standard histories operates out of a positivist epistemology that assumes that the truth of history is objectively knowable" (p. 14). Consequently, this kind of compensatory or oppositional history has been deeply problematic for many feminists (Riley, 1989; Scott, 1987) because it constitutes "women" as an essentialized and fixed category. The diversity of women's experiences is not only ignored, but what becomes obscured is that "woman" itself is a social construction, a product of discourse. Events or selves, in order to exist, must be encoded as story elements. What compensatory history makes invisible is that there is no identity outside of narrative. Narrative, as Paul Ricoeur (1976) reminds us, imposes on events of the past a form that in themselves they do not really have. Because events and selves are reconstructions, original purity of experience can never be achieved.[6] For feminists concerned with writing women back into history, that is a profound theoretical as well as political concern.

History as Discourse or History as Anorexia?

To give up the concept of woman or even "women" because it is a fiction—a product of language or discourse—is potentially to delegitimize any concern for the "real" and "experience." Gayle Greene (1993) refers to this lack of referential as a kind of "professional/pedagogical anorexia" in which endless deferral functions as a form of self-erasure, "an analogue to our obsession with thinness, a way of assuring ourselves and others that we'll take up less space" (pp. 16–17). This "disappearing act" raises serious concerns regarding not only the ability to write women back into history but also about the ability to make any feminist knowledge claims.[7] The invisibility and silencing of women proceeds as usual. Thus, the deconstructive turn potentially allows the subject to "stand free of its own history . . . and the depoliticization of knowledge can proceed more or less at will" (Said, 1989: 222). To be free of history is to sever the memory of inscription. Thus, despite my discomfort with a positivist epistemology, I am reluctant to give up the notion of "real women." If we abandon a representational view of history, do we set ourselves up for erasure, do we in fact become complicit in the modernist dream of history as universal, objective, and, in essence, genderless?[8]

Of course, the binary of whether history is fact or fiction is part of the dis-ease (Margolis, 1993). History is always a fiction (White, 1978), but this does not make it less real. How the story is told—why and at what point the fictions are conceived (Adams, 1990; Portelli, 1991), the discrepancies between what is told and what is experienced—are themselves theoretical constructs (Pagano, 1990). To recover from history is in part dependent on reconceptualizing and remembering the suppression, the contradiction, the pain, the fiction that is history.

History is not the representation of reality, it never has been. For the early Greeks, memory was not a means to situate events within a temporal framework but to understand the whole process of becoming. History, as a function of time, loses the poetic, the imaginative, and the power to evoke. History as an evocation of memory becomes our relationship to, and experiencing of, the identities made possible or impossible through historical narrative. In other words, history is the evocation of what makes invisibility possible. The Popular Memory Group suggests that memory is a dimension of political practice. As Gramsci has argued, a sense of history must be one element in a strong popular socialist culture (Popular Memory Group, 1992). History is the means by which a social group acquires the knowledge of the larger context of its collective struggles and becomes capable of a wider transformative role in society. This "recovery of history" is not intended to function as a corrective, to make history right, but as a process through which a group may "consciously adopt, reject or modify" history (p. 214).

To remember our experiencing of ourselves as objects is to "witness" or "testify" to the trauma of silencing, distortion, and invisibility. To testify, according to Shoshana Felman (1992), is to "vow to tell, to promise and produce one's own speech as material evidence for truth" (p. 5). This, according to Felman, is not a statement of fact but a speech act. Drawing on the autobiographical life accounts given by Holocaust survivors, Felman suggests that testifying

> enabled them for the first time to believe that it is possible, indeed, against all odds and against their past experiences, to tell the story and be heard, to, in fact address the significance of their biography—to address, that is, the suffering, the truth, and the necessity of this impossible narration—to a hearing "you," and a listening community. (p. 41)

To make "something lasting out of remembrance" is the task of both the poet and historiographer as Hannah Arendt reminds us (1954: 45).[9] To remember, to conceive of history as memory work, is to confront the myths of what can and cannot have a history. How the narrative of curriculum history genders is the memory work that must be done.

Myth 1: The Line History Draws

Like a fairy tale, the story of curriculum history in the United States produces and reproduces a narrative as soothing as a bedtime story—the lone scholar in the wilderness (colonial school master) is confronted by the threat of industrialization and urbanization. This struggle between the old and the new is the site for rebellion and transformation. The narrative is a familiar one—an age of innocence, crisis, and enlightenment. Embedded within this plot is a deeply gendered tale. It is the quintessential hero's tale predicated on separation (lone schoolmaster), individuation (common school movement), and control (reforms—progressivism, technical rationalism, and professionalization, and conspicuously masculine discourses that focus on individuality and autonomy). It is a tale of repression and fear that has little to do with a "real" sequence of events and everything to do with how gender is produced through the narrative we call "history."

Narrative authority in Western culture is, according to Charlotte Linde (1993), predicated on the ability of the narrator to create a sense of continuity (cause and effect), coherence (connection of past and present), and individuation (sense of separate self). These narrative conventions are not constraints on history; rather, they create the possibility of narration (Martin, 1986). Thus, locating how continuity, coherence, and individuation are inscribed in history as "real" provides ruptures and possibilities for interrogating how history is central to the production of subject identities. In the case of the tale of schooling, what identities/subjects are made possible or impossible when curriculum history presents itself as an apparently unified, linear story of the one-room school house, common school movement, and progressivism? And, how might we disrupt the tidiness of curriculum history to allow for the complexity of gender and history?

Curriculum history usually begins with the tale of the emergence of public schooling.[10] Horace Mann and Henry Barnard are most often credited with this democratization of education.[11] To view this sequence of events—from the one room schoolhouse to the public common school—as a natural culmination of events or process of development is to make real what is the product of narrative. Made invisible is the reconstruction of gender necessitated by this shift of education from the private to the public realm. To construct education as public/male required reinscribing the home or schoolhouse as private/female. The emergence of the discourse of the "cult of domesticity" and its corollary, "teaching as women's true profession," suggested that women's role as educators, as knowers, was to be indirect, it was to represent influence, not actual power, and it was to be exerted through others and for others. Not only was the task of educating understood as the domain of men, but knowledge itself was gendered as public, as male. Separation from the private (family/female) to identify with the common (public/male) realm provides the mark of male gendered identity. This gendered analysis was hinted at by Bernard Bailyn (1960) when he suggested that in early America "the most important agency in the transfer of culture was not formal institutions of instruction or public instruments of communication, but the family" (p. 15). While he credits the Puritans with the shifting of the locus of cultural transmission to public schools, it is Madeleine Grumet (1988) who maintains, that the common school movement "colluded in support of a program of centralized education that exploited the status and integrity of the family to strip it of its authority and deliver its children to the state" (p. 39). The traditional tale of the common school movement as part of the democratization of America takes on more complex meanings when also understood as a gendered narrative.

The redefinition of gender, and thus, education, was also a consequence of social changes resulting from America's emergence as an industrial nation that required the repression of the individual (private) to the state (public). As Carl Kaestle (1983) suggests, the "pillars," or common schools, were founded as a means to encourage Americans' commitments to the public realm of "republican government, native Protestant culture, and capitalism" (p. x). While Kaestle maintains that the common schools functioned as a mode of social control in regard to class, to which there was resistance that is traditionally obscured in historical narratives, there is little attention to gender as critical to this revolutionary moment in which education is shifted from the private to the public. Central to the regulation of the individual, as Valerie Polakow (1993) has suggested, was the emergence of "pedagogy" and "pediatrics" as a means of fashioning identity. These arenas of social life, traditionally associated with the private realm and appropriated simultaneously with "democratizing" the nation suggest not historical progress or development but what Foucault has termed "episodes in a series of subjugations."

The irony of this is that the construction of "pedagogy" as grounded in women's natural nurturing capacities functioned in complex ways to both valorize and sabotage women (Grumet, 1988). Curriculum history most often portrays women curriculum theorists at this time—Catharine Beecher, Emma Willard, and others—as complicit in participating in the "pedagogy for patriarchy." Most curriculum histories present these women educators as the dutiful daughters who joined the fathers in the quest to expand democracy through public schooling. In fact, their supposed complicity contributes to essentializing emerging gender roles. This is particularly the case with Horace Mann and Catharine Beecher. Mann is commonly represented as the father of the "common school movement" and Beecher is credited with the feminization of teaching, and thus, a willing participant in the inscription of gender norms as unitary and fixed. However, when we acknowledge that there is nothing natural or fixed about these discourses, this opens spaces to explore how identities were being taken up, negotiated, and resisted.

To suggest that Beecher participated in this "pedagogy for patriarchy" is to deny legitimacy to Beecher's complex analysis of 19th-century gendered social relations and her vision of the role of women. Confident that women were better suited than men to facilitate human development, she argued that the duties of home, child rearing, and education should be placed in the hands of women. Appropriating the "cult of domesticity," Beecher was able to argue for women's roles becoming specifically gendered as female and public. To take up the discourse of the "cult of domesticity" as a site of knowing, as an epistemological site, not only interrupted this engendering but simultaneously functioned to secure a place for women in the public sphere as well as ensuring a rationale for the education of women. In effect, Beecher challenged the values that placed the public/political above the domestic sphere and the assumption that the domestic was not political (Martin, 1985). By embracing essentialist gender roles, she was able to advance women into the public sphere in spite of the dominance of patriarchal authority.[12]

By beginning curricular histories with Horace Mann and the "rise" of public education and the eventual "fall" through the feminization of teaching, the history of education becomes the story of public schooling. In constructing education as public, this plot excludes education in the home (parenting, domestic knowledge), education through aesthetics (art, quilting, play), and education through cooperative institutions such as women's study clubs, settlement houses, etc. Obscuring education in "other" spheres outside of the public, erases women's, African-Americans', and other marginalized groups' forms of knowing and being as a source for theorizing curriculum.

The neutrality implied in the natural progression of curriculum history from private to public also obscures the presence of large numbers of women teachers in the colonial and pre-industrial communities, thus "reinforcing women's invisibility in the more distant past" (Prentice & Theobald, 1991: 23). Prentice and Theobald (1991) suggest that a more appropriate redefinition of the period, in which women became the majority of teachers, is the masculinization of teaching. Like Grumet (1988), they maintain that the "feminization of teaching," ignores the ways that despite the increased numerical presence of women, teaching as well as education was increasingly controlled by men and ushering in "pedagogy for patriarchy."

Discourses like the "common school movement" and the "feminization of teaching" thus function not only as historical constructs but also as part of a narrative of coherence and continuity that genders knowledge and subjects. I would maintain that this focus on the feminization of teaching effectively obscured the ways that despite numerical dominance, what constituted knowledge and subjectivity was being deeply gendered as male. The very concept of the periodization of the "common school movement" and the "feminization of teaching" become incredible feats of fiction that function to ensure the maintenance of normative gender practices, and that for the male, necessitates separation from, and continual repression (i.e., individuation) of, the feminine. This repression continually manifests itself in the need to control through ongoing reforms embodied in "progressivism," technical-rationalism (with its focus on objectivity), and "professionalization" (with its focus on individuality and autonomy). This narrative of curricular history situates individuation, separation, and control as central to education and, as a consequence, history as we know it functions to gender understandings of knowledge. When the story of curriculum history begins with the emergence of public schooling, it not only obscures other ways of coming to know, but it predicates education on separation from the private. I wonder what desires and fears are thus contained in these curricular fictions? History performs incredible epistemological acts. Central to this is the myth of origins on which linearity, continuity, and coherence are predicated.

Myth 2: Origins: Disrupting the "Seminal" Plot and Other Ovarian Twists

Historical narrative works to suppress contradictions (multiple stories) through constructing the illusion of origins (the source of existence, derivation). Origins imply beginnings and endings. The history of curriculum, predicated on this search, guarantees a unitary tale that can be traced. And yet, this obsession with origins is essentially a patriarchal one. It is the story of control and suppression. Origins imply roots, certainly a phallic symbolism. Who is the father? Where did the seed originate? Whose is the seminal work? Who has carried on the work of the father?

The tracing of origins, and investment in family genealogies is, according to Sarah Westphal (1994), stored with meaning arising from the "history of the patriarchal family: the 'traffic in women,' the severance of the bride's ties of kinship and the loss of the mother's name, all to ensure the orderly transmission of property and title through the legitimate paternal line" (p. 155). To conceive of history as the tracing of origins—Mann/Common School Movement; Hall/Child Study Movement; Dewey/Progressivism; Tyler/Technical Rationalism—of establishing lineages, is to secure the exclusion, the invisibility, of women. How might we write this story without the search for origins that inevitably obscures women's and others' experiences? More importantly, how do we write in a fashion that acknowledges the continual production of gendered bodies through historical discourse?

The Traffic in Women: Dutiful Daughters and Spinster Sisters

The "traffic in women" is what makes curriculum history as we know it possible. Women, if they appear at all, are the "good daughters." They carry out the ideas of the father, thus securing his position as the originator. Catharine Beecher carries out the ideas of Horace Mann; Annie Julia Cooper of Frederick Douglass; Elizabeth Peabody of Froebel; Jane Addams, Ella Flagg Young, Mary Bethune McCleod of Dewey, and today the ideas of Foucault, Freire, and Derrida.[13] The dutiful daughter reproduces but is never generative in her own right. Women educators constructed as dutiful daughters ensure the orderly transmission of property (knowledge) and title through the paternal line. Daughters are never constructed as "seminal" thinkers; the severing of maternal kinship through their positioning as dutiful daughters, guarantees reproduction through the paternal. The separation from and erasure of the maternal is complete. Consequently, the identities made thinkable through this origin myth are limited to heterosexual, gendered discourses of the normative family plot.

Ironically, it is often the well-intentioned attempts to "include" women into the "story" of curriculum which further essentializes gender identities and perpetuates this family drama. David Tyack in *The One Best System* describes Ella Flagg Young as "one of Dewey's strongest advocates . . . a woman of great intelligence, and compassion, she taught teachers about Dewey's new education" (1974: 178). Young teaches about Dewey's ideas. Her work is derivative. Rarely is she portrayed as an intellectual or social critic in her own right.[14] Her body of scholarship has been largely ignored, as well has her intellectual contributions to pragmatism and commitment to feminism.[15] As the dutiful daughter she is the conduit through which others' ideas are trafficked.

The standard tale of Young's life (1845–1918) goes something like this. A dutiful teacher, she makes her way "up" the ladder from teacher to principal, studies with John Dewey at the University of Chicago, becomes the first female superintendent of a large urban school district and eventually the first woman president of the National Education Association (NEA). Her roles as the "first" female superintendent of a large urban school district and the "first" female president of the NEA are compensatory in the sense that they focus on accomplishments that are deemed important by traditional history, those that are male, public, individual, and thus defined as political. Young only becomes a "subject" of history because her life is fashioned to "fit in" with the male plot—the male career ladder, the story of the paternal, the story of fathers, of origins. In effect, the inclusion of this particular version of Young's story into history reifies essentialized notions of male/female identity. Although Young gets "included" in history, the gendered plot of the text remains the same.

Making gender boundaries appear natural through the reifying of the male plot obscures how the very tale of progressivism constructs gender. By focusing on the public and political, Young's subjectivity is coded as male (active/public) as well as unitary, making invisible not only her agency as a woman, but also her ongoing negotiation of gender discourses. This negotiation occurs within the complex intersections of two supposedly polar discourses—progressivism and social efficiency. Although conceiving of the purposes of education very differently, both progressivism and social efficiency were predicated on the assumption that women's influence on education should be indirect. In the case of "progressivism," women's agency was to be subjugated to the child, and in the case of "social efficiency," it was to be subjugated to the "expert" and "principal." By positioning Young as the "dutiful daughter" carrying out the ideas of Dewey, the contradictory and discontinuous ways in which Young negotiated, subverted, and appropriated these curricular discourses remains obscured.[16] To remember this negotiation and its erasure as a site for curriculum theorizing is the memory work that must be done.

Rethinking Origins: Discontinuities, Dispersions, and Difference

When the origin story functions to construct a unitary tale predicated on essences, the multiplicities of factors constitutive of an event, in this case the "progressive era," are rendered invisible. Foucault's "genealogical" method attacks the notion of founding subject and a continuous history. Poststructuralist thinkers have posited alternative metaphors—Deleuze and Guattari's notions of rhizomes rather than roots disrupt the phallic,[17] yet Derrida's notion of "dissemination" while striving for displacement and disruption remains embedded in a masculinist narrative (Flax, 1990: 39). Although "history" is reinvisioned outside the discourses of origins and linearity, each of these methodologies conceives of gender as a discourse or a technology of power. As Sarah Westphal (1994) maintains, to assume that gender is just another discourse is to neglect that we still don't know what gender is and to neglect the analytical power of gender in and of itself. How the discourses of progressivism and social efficiency shaped and were shaped by gender remains hidden when history relies on stories of origins that reinscribe and produce subjectivities that are unitary and fixed. Like Denise Riley (1989), I am concerned with understanding the conditions under which women "take up" identities of "woman" and how and why they do this. To engage in this particular kind of memory work is to remember that the discourses of "progressivism" and "social efficiency" have no essence or origin, nor are they either inherently libratory or oppressive, but they were and continue to be a site through which we can remember how we are gendered in complex and contradictory ways. I turn once again to Young's story to seek the discontinuities, dispersion, and play of dominations.

Young's work as an educator coincides with what Lynn Gordon (1990) has described as a period of female separatism, social activism, and belief in the special mission for educated women. As an active participant at Hull House, Young was engaged in the work of social reconstruction with other leading intellectuals and activists of the progressive era, including Jane Addams, John Dewey, and George Herbert Mead. Young, Dewey, Addams, and Mead worked together in a variety of projects aimed at social reform including women's rights, labor unions for women, the extension of suffrage, and higher education for women (Deegan, 1990).[18] Like other progressives, she believed that schools played a central role in social change. For Young, women's work as teachers was central to social reform because it functioned as a form of democratic practice. In order to be democratic, teachers needed full participation in decisions affecting their work. By focusing on the democratic practices embodied in teaching, Young argued for radical reforms which took seriously the experiences of women teachers as central to social reconstruction. As President of the NEA, she advocated not only increased teacher autonomy but "higher salaries, equal pay for equal work, women's suffrage, and advisory teachers' councils" (McManis, 1916: 156–157). Her work centered on developing participatory forms of leadership in which teachers (women) would have a central voice in the development of administrative and curricular policies.

At the same time, education historians (Kliebard, 1986; Ravitch, 1974; Tyack, 1974) have described this period as one of centralization and bureaucratization that emphasized increased efficiency, standardization, and reliance on experts that reduced the teacher to a mere "factory hand." Young's dissertation (completed in 1900 under Dewey at the University of Chicago) entitled "Isolation in the School" was an analysis and critique of the ideology of social efficiency. She claimed that the isolation of teachers resulting from centralization and bureaucratization functioned to disempower teachers (women), by removing their decision making power over curriculum and school policy, and placing it into the hands of supposed "experts" (male). When teachers were denied participation in decision making, Young warned that schools would develop a system comparable to a "great machine" (Reid, 1982: xxi).

These conflicting discourses/ideologies which signaled, on the one hand, a special mission for educated women through the discourse of teaching as women's true profession, and, on the other hand, the deskilling of teachers through increased control of education by experts, provide the context in which to understand Young's complex negotiation of conflicting gender ideologies. On the one hand, advocating teacher autonomy subverted the hierarchy of social efficiency. On the other hand, advocating teacher autonomy took up the discourse of professionalism, a subtext of social efficiency, as a means to argue for teacher independence. However, Young's focus on securing teachers' autonomy through decentralizing power and on securing teacher retention of curricular decision making were in direct contrast to the gender roles inscribed in *both* progressivism and social efficiency, which maintained that women teachers were to be facilitators of knowledge, not active agents in making knowledge claims.

By claiming women teachers' right to be active agents in decision making and central to shaping democracy through their work in schools, Young contested the control of education by experts (either progressives or those advocating social efficiency) through asserting that women's experiences as teachers was a site for generating knowledge. Claiming women's experience as an epistemological site threatened the normative gender ideologies embedded in both discourses, which required the subjugation of women's knowledge. The degree of Young's threat can be registered by the fact that in 1915 she became the subject of an Illinois state investigation in which her policies as school superintendent were decried as "Frenzied Feminine Finance" (Murphy, 1990: 82). According to Murphy, critics depicted Young as "virtually giving away the store to public school teachers out of her feminist sentimentality, her Catholic sympathies and her alleged near-senility" (p. 82). Young was accused by the Chicago school board of breeding rebellion and lack of respect for the school board authority. Although supported by Dewey, Mead, and Addams, Young stepped down as superintendent.

To brand Young as senile and feminist was to police the gender boundaries she was challenging through constructing her as a spinster. It is perhaps no coincidence that the image of the "spinster," often embodied in representations of teachers, emerged at the very moment when women teachers were contesting the gendered nature of the discourses of both social efficiency and progressivism. The spinster is represented as the sexless, manly, unmarried creature whose image embodies the consequences of women's refusal to comply with and be the subject of men's social and sexual power.[19] This sexually neutral social type, as Jill Conway (1971) suggests, is often identified with the professional expert or the scientist as compared to the woman sage who relied on women's special nature for knowledge. Young, drawing on her pragmatist tradition, did not claim that women's knowledge was the result of an essentialized feminine nature. She did, however, claim that women teachers' experiences, reflected upon (using the scientific method), could provide a site of knowledge and was in fact a way of coming to know. Claiming women's experiences as a site of knowledge, Young contested the discourse of social efficiency which claimed bureaucratization as the site of knowledge and the discourse of progressivism which claimed experience as gender-neutral and the providence of the child.

As the dutiful daughter, Young's understanding of and negotiations of gender are made invisible, as are the modes of subjugation that they elicited. Relying on a tale of origins effectively obscures the discontinuities and dispersions of gender central to shaping ideologies of progressivism and social efficiency, and ultimately a richer and more complex understanding of these ideologies. That these discourses are inconceivable without their investment in maintaining normative gender boundaries is the curriculum of control and separation that becomes hidden. The memory work that must be done is to remember that this erasure and subjugation proceeded under what has traditionally been termed as the "progressive" era. This myth of liberation embedded in the progressive era, and as experienced by women curriculum theorists, is what must be remembered.

Myth 3: Where's the Progress in the Progressive Era?: Disrupting the Family Plot

Modernist history is predicated on the premise that change is equivalent to progress. History is told as a sequence of singular and inevitable events in which humanity progresses from ignorance to enlightenment, barbarity to civilization, oppression to freedom. And yet, we have been reminded that the narrative of historical change is an enlightenment myth which obscures the succession of one mode of domination by another (Foucault, 1977). The notion that change is inherently progressive is, as Chet Bowers (1987) reminds us, deeply embedded in most educational thinking where "enlightenment foundations . . . contribute to thinking of liberal discourse as on the side of truth and progress, and only engaged in a power struggle for the purpose of liberation" (p. 80).[20]

Much of curriculum history is deeply invested in the myth of progress as liberation through struggle. Until recently (Baker, 2009b; Cormack & Green, 2009; Kliebard, 1992b; Winfield, 2007), curricular history was often described as a "problem of warring educational doctrines" or "warring extremes" or a "call to arms."[21] The notion of "progress" as deeply implicated in the discourses of subjectivity, modernity, the nation–state, and colonialism are entities whose borders are arbitrary. Bernadette Baker (2009b) pushes the boundaries of curriculum history by confronting the "polarities of a conflict/consensus template and its bedfellow, a struggle/submission framework" that must be deconstructed in order to open new possibilities for rethinking the past (p. 27). Likewise, Bonnie Smith (1995) suggests that history has traditionally been a "celebratory saga of male fantasies stressing combat and dominance" (p. 203). Liberation is contingent on a rebellion narrative of conflict, separation, and control. In the tale of progressivism, conflict first emerges in the competing factions of the humanist/child-study/social efficiency and social reconstructionist camps. The history of curriculum is told as a war between these competing theories. It is a conflict between W.T. Harris, G.S. Hall, F. Bobbitt, E.L. Thorndike, and L.F. Ward. This contest signifies not merely a dispute over the aim of education, but delineates the normative boundaries of what can be known, how we come to know, and who can be a knower. These boundaries constitute normative cultural identities that are inevitably classed, raced, and gendered. Women (Addams, Beecher, Peabody) and African-Americans (Du Bois, Bond, Cooper) who are curriculum theorists do not even enter into the conversation.

The focus on the struggle for the "right" curriculum reinforces the notion of progress, which ultimately situates the succession of progressivism, and its prodigal son, John Dewey, as the victor. Resisting social efficiency, he is the "rebel son."[22] The story continues as Dewey is followed by Tyler as the rebel son promoting technical rationalism, to be followed by neo-Marxists (Apple, Giroux) and so on. Ironically, the position of the father, as well as the dutiful daughter is guaranteed through the resistant son (Pinar, 1983). Women's culturally supposed complicity (and thus erasure) enables the signification of the "rebel son," whose rejection of the father supposedly guarantees progress and change.

Mirroring the Oedipal father/son plot, this focus on conflict reproduces the story of the male gender identity. Progress is the result of separation, individuation, and control. In the story of progressivism, this gender drama manifests itself through the ongoing struggle between a "conventional narrative" and a "liberation narrative." Whose knowledge is of most worth—the father (reproduction) or the son (resistance)? The irony is that the focus on "whose knowledge?" (traditionally a question asked by critical and neo-Marxist theorists), functions to suppress the knowledge of others. This Oedipal drama engenders a curricular master narrative bounded by the reproduction/resistance binary that results in situating individuation and repression of connection as central to the curricular plot (Pinar, 1983). When the history of progressivism is articulated as the struggle between social efficiency and social reconstruction, father and son, this story is gendered in ways that necessarily exclude the experiences of women curriculum theorists. Although these curricular discourses are presented as genderless, and thus natural, the power of gender and gender oppression to structure history is evident in the ongoing family plot of the father, "rebel son," and dutiful daughter.

What, then, makes it thinkable or possible to conceive of the progressive era as progressive? Why is progressivism naturally understood as an advancement over an authoritarian approach to education based on social control (Marshall, 1995)? And, have the critiques of progressivism as a form of social control based in class (Bernstein, 1975) and grounded in the project of bourgeois liberalism obscured the gendered nature of progressivism as an ideology implicated in the constructions of "motherhood" (Steedman, 1989) and "childhood" (Baker, 1998, 2001) that functioned in complex and contradictory ways? The fact that progressivism continues to function as a libratory discourse despite current postmodern/post-structural critiques of its ideological embeddedness in enlightenment notions of change (Walkerdine, 1990), progress (Bowers, 1987), and the unitary individual (Aronowitz & Giroux, 1985) suggests the hegemony of this discourse. In fact, current attempts to reinterpret Dewey as "a postmodernist before his time" (Rorty, 1991: 201) suggest the deep investment in maintaining the category and myths of progressivism. This investment continues to obscure the ways in which the ideologies of progressivism work simultaneously as libratory and oppressive by rendering invisible the ways in which the discourses of progressivism are implicated in regulating normative gendered and raced identities. That the history of curriculum theorizing is complicit in reproducing a male, Eurocentric, and heterosexual subject is the forbidden "fruit" hidden under the guise of libratory/emancipatory discourses. How might we imagine a history of curriculum theorizing not trapped within a narrative of struggle, which depends on unitary notions of gender to construct its subject? And, how can we rethink the context and periodization of the "progressive" era when it is "freed" from the gendered ideology of "struggle" based in the reproduction of the family plot?

Progress for Women?: Child-Centeredness as the Regulation of "Woman"

Change in the case of progressive ideology was not necessarily progress for women. Progressive ideology required that a teacher subjugate her experience to that of the child. If left to unfold naturally (through activity-oriented approaches that released students' interests), without any imposition, the child would develop into an independent, free thinking individual and thus democratic citizen. Of course, there is much debate over what progressives, especially Dewey, really meant by "child-centered" or "experience."[23] What is clear, though, is that teachers were not to impart or transmit knowledge, but were to draw it out of the children.

What is obscured in the tale of progressivism is that this ideology was dependent on the already gendered construction of teaching. However, the assumption that this type of pedagogy was suited to women because of their natural nurturing abilities is misleading. Dewey (1900) was quite clear that the realm traditionally associated with the female—the home—was not a site of knowledge. He suggested

> the occupations and relationships of the home environment are not specially selected for the growth of the child; the main object is something else, and what the child can get out of them is incidental. Hence the need of a school. In the school the life of the child becomes the all-controlling aim. (p. 36)

The "child-centered curriculum" was predicated on the removal of the child from the home, where learning was "incidental" to the school. In effect, the "child-centered" curriculum functioned to displace the private/domestic/female as a site for learning or knowledge. The role of the female teacher in the progressive classroom mirrored this displacement by situating women teachers as "facilitators" of knowledge rather than as creators of knowledge. The teacher's primary role was passive—she was to "help" the child release his or her inner self. Valerie Walkerdine (1990) has argued that the

> liberation of children that is conceived in progressive terms did not mean the liberation of women. In some ways, it actually served to keep women firmly entrenched as caregivers. Women teachers became caught, trapped inside a concept of nurturance which held them responsible for the freeing of each little individual, and therefore for the management of an idealist dream, and impossible fiction. (p. 19)

She questions here the concept of liberation as freedom from overt coercion. As Foucault (1980) suggests, liberation opens up new relationships of power, which have to be controlled by practices of liberty. In the case of "progressive" teachers, they were to allow individuals to unfold and grow according to their own needs by providing maternal nurturance.

For Walkerdine, the suppression and control of rebellion through maternal nurturance guarantees the rational subject precisely because children who were not coerced would not need to rebel, thus guaranteeing the status quo. Thus, "they ensure the production of individuals who are self-regulating through the power of rationality" (Walkerdine 1990: 32) and highlight what Foucault has described as the shift from overt sovereign power to invisible power through technologies and apparatuses of social regulation. The subject identities inscribed through "progressive" discourses essentially reproduced and regulated unitary gender norms through dichotomies such as public/private and reason/emotion (Kohli & Munro, 1995). What, I continue to ask, is so "progressive" about that?

The Repressive Myths of Social Reconstructionism

What is obscured in the tale of the "progressive era" as inevitably libratory is that this ideology worked in complex and contradictory ways. On the one hand, child-centeredness drew on and reinforced traditional gender norms of female nur-turance, making it an acceptable ideology from which women could operate in the public sphere. At the same time, this ideology erased women's agency by further essentializing women's supposed maternal submissiveness and passivity. How the discourse of "child-centeredness" functioned to regulate gender norms to keep women in their place is revealed in the primary "battle" of the progressive era between the child-centered and social reconstructionist factions.

Despite the currency of child-centeredness as an alternative to social control, Dewey (1928) and Counts (1932) worried that those advocating child-centered-ness lacked social and political direction. The reluctance on the part of those advocating a child-centered curriculum to use education as a form of political socialization was in part because they saw democracy and political indoctrination as antithetical (Pinar, Reynolds, Slattery, & Taubman, 1995). As Stanley (1992) suggests, "most of these child-centered educators, reacting against the formalism of the past, tended to oppose any form of imposition or indoctrination" (p. 7).[24] Ultimately, child-centered progressives (usually women—Margaret Naumburg, Marietta Johnson, Jane Addams, Patty Smith Hill, Lucy Gage, Lucy Sprague Mitchell, Caroline Pratt, Laura Zirbes, Mary McCloud Bethune, and Alice Miel) were reluctant, and in some cases ambivalent, daughters who resisted articulating a fixed unitary theory of social reform. Interpreted as a lack of political theorizing, commitment, and vision by Dewey, Counts, and others, the rejection of those advocating "child-centeredness" as serious theorists signifies the ongoing necessity to maintain gender boundaries and repression of the maternal.

However, despite the dominant perception that those engaged in child-centeredness were not concerned with social issues and lacked a political vision, the meanings these women attributed their work often tells a different story. For example, the work of Patty Smith Hill's Manhattenville project (an urban renewal program she directed in the 1930s in her retirement) situated itself as part of George Counts's call for social reconstruction by acknowledging that the teacher played a large part in the building of a new social order (Association of Early Childhood Education, 1972). Other examples of women who saw their work as political, despite the assumptions that those advocating child-centeredness were apolitical, were Lucy Sprague Mitchell (founder of Bank Street College, originally known as the Bureau of Educational Experiments) and Caroline Pratt (an avowed socialist who taught in the settlement homes in New York and worked for the Women's Trade Union League) who collaborated in establishing the Play School. According to Antler (1987), although the school drew on the progressive philosophy of Dewey, the mainspring of its pedagogy was political, and both Pratt and Mitchell preferred the term "experimental" to "progressive" because "progressive" was considered "too vauge, snooty, and restrictive" (p. 243). Ironically, these two women (as well as others) rejected progressivism because it wasn't political enough (especially its lack of gender analysis). That many of these women educators saw their work as political and central to social change has not only been obscured by gendered assumptions embedded in the term child-centeredness, but by the exclusion of gender as a central analytical concept in theorizing progressivism. Because women were, and continue to be, situated differently in social relations their theorizing about social relations, especially notions of change, agency, and power, have taken different forms from universal positions claimed by patriarchy.

The reluctance to embrace social reconstructionism was also in some cases a critique of the gender-neutral analysis of social reconstructionist theories. For example, Jane Addams rejected naming herself a socialist not because she was apolitical, but because she opposed the class struggle advocated by Marxist theory and its truncated analysis of women's status and values (Addams, 1902; Munro, 1995a). For Addams, class struggle was a form of militarism which ultimately functioned to undermine the building of community that was necessary to democracy. Drawn to the cooperative philosophies of Tolstoy and Kropotkin, Addams embraced the concepts of non-resistance and pacifism as central to defining and changing class exploitation. The reluctance of many women progressives to put forward a comprehensive theory of social change has rarely been explored as a form of resistance to the gendered nature of progressive ideologies.[25] By reducing the history of the progressive era to the struggle between the social reconstructionist and the child-centered factions, gender binaries are essentially reproduced and normalized. The subject identities made available are restricted to the family plot in which the struggle between the father and "rebel son" defines what counts as power, resistance, and change. What would a history of the "progressive" era look like, I wonder, that was not dependent on interpreting women progressives as the dutiful daughters, whose ideas were extensions of, misreadings, or derivations of the progressive fathers?

How the theories of women progressives were framed by and were a response to the andocentric bias of progressive ideology is the memory work that must be done. The theorizing of progressive women educators must take account of the restrictive and normative gender subjectivities inscribed in the discourses of progressivism. How might their theories be a specific response to the limited gendered roles and subject identities made available through progressive ideologies? How were their theories a response to the degendering (or gendering) of knowledge through the discourse of rationality and child-centeredness? How was the taking up of the discourse of "child-centeredness" by some women progressives in fact a form of resistance to the erasure of gender? In acknowledging that no discourse is "innocent," we must simultaneously ask what forms of domination women's theories and ideas perpetuated. That women educators actively negotiated the erasures and silences of gender implicit in progressive discourses, simultaneously appropriating and disrupting them, is the complexity I seek. To make visible these complexities, discontinuities, and contradictions would be to disrupt the father/son plot of reproduction and resistance by telling a messy, more complex story.

Progress as Reform as Castration Fear

To claim the progressive era as progressive is to obscure the ways in which this ideology deeply genders notions of teaching, curriculum, and education by excluding women's experiences. In fact, to claim the progressive era as progressive is to forget that in the 1930s (simultaneously to the critique of child-centeredness), gender ideologies like the spinster emerged to invoke and regulate gender. Geraldine Clifford (1989) maintains that despite the rhetoric of teaching as women's true profession, during the 1930s the "woman peril" in education led to concerns about the feminizing effects on boys due to the large number of female teachers. The influx of women into teaching, both numerically and in the form of the threat of the child-centered movement, necessitated control and reform. Consequently, supposed reform efforts like progressivism can in fact be read as fear of the feminine (castration fear) which necessitates separation, control, and repression. This regulation of gender continues in current reform movements through the discursive formation of teacher identities as either "professionals" (reproduction) or as "intellectuals/activists/cultural workers" (resistance) (Goodman, 1995; Munro, 1995b). The father/son plot remains the underlying structure of the narrative and continues to exclude women's agency, subjectivity, and knowledge that women have constructed. What desires, then, I wonder, are fulfilled by constructing a unitary tale of the progressive era as progressive? What continues to be rendered invisible by the telling of this myth? I would maintain that the telling of "progressive history" as the battle between "child-centeredness" and "social reconstructionism" has little to do with "actual" history and everything to do with policing dominant gender boundaries.

In Collusion with Conclusions

Despite the supposed postmodern turn, the narrative strategies of curriculum history remain deeply embedded in the myths of history as linear, as the search for origins, and as inevitably progressive (Popkewitz & Brennan, 1998). As a consequence, although history is *both* fact and fiction, story and myth, memory and representation, it continues to operate as if it were real. Of course, I remain concerned about reducing complex political questions to the simplistic question of whether history is fact or fiction. To frame the "problem of history" as the choosing between history as fact or fiction is to ignore the complexity of "narrative" as a way of knowing. To write in these postmodern times is to acknowledge the textual nature of curriculum history—its construction through narrative, its mythical nature.

Myth is considered by many the "sacred" narrative. Sacred in the sense that myth is worthy of our reverence, our respect. Myth's sacredness lies not only in its explanatory power but in its role in justifying institutions and rights. Myth tells us how something came to be as it is. The fashioning of curricular myths—the democratization of education through public schooling, the plot of curriculum history driven by the struggle between reproduction or resistance, the triumph and tragedy of progressivism, and the heroes and their dutiful daughters—are narrative sleights of hand deserving our respect.

Engendering curriculum history is to interrogate the ways in which narrative makes particular subject identities possible or impossible. What, I continue to ask, would a narrative of history look like that did not depend on linearity, coherence, or a unitary subject as the organizing tropes of history? The purpose of the memory work I undertake is to incite my imagination to envision history in less diseased ways—where plot has no beginning, middle, or end, but is recursive and discontinuous; where historical texts induce contradictions, rather than unitary story lines; and where paradoxes, rather than cause and effect, evoke action. It is the complex and contradictory ways in which curriculum history silences, distorts, and makes invisible that is the ongoing memory work that must be done.[26]

2

IMAGING CURRICULUM

To speak of the imaginal world is nothing less than to contemplate a metaphysics of Being where subject and object are born together in the same creative act of transcendental imagination.

(Christian Jambet, 1983)

One day, a king received the god Theuth, who invented numbers, geometry, written characters and so on. As Theuth claimed that the written characters would make the king's people wiser, the king replied "No," because "souls will become more forgetful once they have put their confidence in external marks instead of relying on themselves from within."

(Paul Ricoeur, 1976)

Yield and overcome, bend and be straightened; empty and be full.

(Lao Tzu, 600 BCE [1990])

Truth did not come into the world naked, but it came in types and images. The world will not receive truth in any other way.

(Gospel of Philip, 69)

It is difficult to imagine a time when humans did not depend on the written "word" to "know" the world. But, in fact, as recounted above in the story of the Egyptian King of Thebes, in the ancient world the written "word" was suspect. Plato, who originally presents this myth of the King of Thebes in *Phaedrus*, suggests that reliance on "external marks" is not reminiscence, but sheer rememoration. Writing brings not reality, but the "resemblence of it; not wisdom, but its appearance" (Ricoeur, 1976: 38). Reliance on exteriority generates *non-living* being—the word is "death." Wisdom in the ancient world relied on inner knowing (not external knowing as situated in the word, the law, or a God). Knowledge was not predicated on "representation or *mimesis*, meaning imitation (this is that)" (Trueit, 2006: 97). To be educated or wise did not depend on "representing" the world. Wisdom, not knowledge, was the heart of curriculum and as Garrison (1997) suggests, wisdom is beyond knowledge. Wisdom is "about those desirable imaginative possibilities that morally ought to be actualized even though they are not here now and may never have been before" (p. 81). Those imaginative possibilities emerged in an intersubjective, holistic, creative process that was not directed toward representing the world, but toward understanding the larger questions of meaning. Meaning-making was a communal act that was embodied, holistic and was not dependent on outside authority or law. It was an act of the imaginal. The imaginal (accessed through myth, symbols, ritual, divination, dance) was the space in which creative interpretation or *poiesis* (Trueit, 2006) was intended to address "matters of existence and questions of meaning" (Davis, 2004: 26). Wisdom, predicated on imagination, the poetic, the paradoxical, the mythic, and the symbolic represents a kind of knowing outside the limitations of language, reason, and the binaries of subject/object and male/ female.

This time period in history in which "image" instead of the "word" formed the basis for human understanding has been described as one in which awareness is diffuse or peripheral—what Berman (2000) has characterized as horizontal. Mary Douglas (1999) suggests that this horizontal worldview is not based on dialectical principles, "its arguments do not run on a linear, hierarchical model" (p. 16). It is based on correlative or analogical or aesthetic ordering. Douglas goes on to describe correlative thinking as involving "the association of image- or concept-clusters by meaningful disposition rather than physical causation" (p. 16). Human understanding during this time is not characterized by a search for definitive meaning: it simply accepts the world as it presents itself. One did not "deal" with alienation (the split between the world and the self, an ontological understanding that emerges much later and that some attribute to the invention of writing) as much as live with it and accept it as a generative site of imagination. It is a moment of suspended animation, a moment of pure "Is-ness" or "Being" that cannot be framed in terms of any formula or ideology.

Harry Broudy (1988) argues that historically and theologically the material of the imagination—the image—precedes "the word," i.e., concepts. Consequently, Broudy suggests that the cultivation of the intellect—the capacity to generate, analyze, and synthesize concepts—necessarily requires cultivation of the imagination. The ancient world (which I will define here as 100,000 BCE to approximately 600 CE) can be characterized as one that is "before the word." Although symbol systems and language emerge during this time (3100 BCE), *logos*, as the primary organizer of social relations, does not emerge until the end of this period (600 CE).[1] Because this period precedes the "word," it is a rich area for curriculum theorists to explore and gain a deeper understanding of the imaginal, a way of knowing that is not shaped by a binary way of seeing the world or in which there is a correspondence theory between "reality" and "knowledge." The shift from an oral to a written culture in which the locus of knowledge shifts to an external source (the written word, the law, or a covenant) marks a radical epistemological shift, one that is deeply gendered. This chapter will focus on this Paleolithic period that can be characterized as polytheistic, and nomadic, as well as trace the shift from an oral, horizontal, mytho–poetic culture to one that is written, vertical, and logo–analytical.

Rarely has this historical time period (pre–600 CE) been taken seriously in curriculum studies or educational philosophy. According to Alan Block (2004),

> the field of curriculum has been forever dominated by the discourses derived from Greek, Roman and Christian principles and by practices and methods that derive from those principles. These are the principles found in the works of Socrates, Plato, Aristotle, Augustine, Aquinas, and Descartes. (p. 10)

Curriculum histories usually begin with the ancient world of Greece and Rome. Socrates, Plato, and Aristotle and then Cicero and Virgil make up the foundation of curriculum and educational thinking. These philosophers are credited with approaches to education that have shaped Western liberal arts notions of education including the nature of the teacher–student relationship, the role of the disciplines, and pedagogy. Yet, I would argue that these philosophers provide only one image of what it means to be a knower, what can be known, and how we come to know. By beginning curriculum histories with the "Greeks," the vast terrain of "pre–history" and of ancient civilizations outside of Europe has been excluded from our understanding of curriculum. As Gerda Lerner (1986) suggests:

> As long as the Christian teleological view dominated historical thought, pre–Christian history was seen merely as a preparatory stage for the true history, which began with the birth of Christ and would end with the Second Coming. When Darwinian theory dominated historical thought, pre–history was seen as a "barbaric" stage in the evolutionary progress of humankind from the simpler to the more complex. (p. 15)

The assumptions that have dominated our interpretations of the past are clouded in myths that represent the past as primitive, simple, and mysterious—it is understood as "other" and often is associated with nature and Mother Goddesses, thus signifying this time period as gendered. The exclusion of this time period as a serious site for theorizing curriculum is made possible through the imposition of a narrative of progress as linear in which the past is "uncivilized" and the present signifies "civilization." This imposition has obscured a serious interrogation of "pre–literate" societies for their theories of knowing.

Thus we must suspend a sense of linearity, of permanence and duality as we engage with the "images" of the wisdom age. Curriculum as "image" transcends time and space and, like Serres (1982), encourages us to fold the present into the past and the past into the present. This journey begins in China with the ancient wisdom traditions exemplified by Nu Kwa, then to the Middle Eastern Jewish concepts of wisdom, then to the Grecian traditions including Sappho, Pythagoras, and the Sophists, and then finally to early Christian tradition, focusing on the Gospel of Mary and the Gnostics. To generalize across these vast historical epochs and cultures is dangerous, yet not to "image" curriculum outside a solely Western perspective is to limit us as well.

In Whose Image?: Before the Word

In the ancient worlds, "truth" or "knowledge" was based not in the "real" or material world. In polytheistic, pre-literate societies, knowledge was experienced outside of logical, rational modes of thought, what Mary Douglas (1999) has termed the mytho-poetic or, as I suggest, the imaginal. The imaginal was an inter-subjective realm in which "knowledge" was understood to inhere in the cosmos. The wonder and awe, the mystery, the unpredictability of nature exceeded all human capacity to explain it. The profound mysteries of the natural world and interconnectedness of all things made incomprehensible the notion of "repres-entation" as we know it today. The physical world was understood by most cultures as temporary and certainly not as separate from, or outside of, the human experience. Interdependence with the natural world made inconceivable the separation of humans from nature that in contemporary times is assumed by many to be natural. The impermanence of life (the continual cycle of life and death) and the sense of interdependence are manifest in a worldview in which the world was not an object or a paradigm, but dynamic and unpredictable (Berman, 2000; Ong, 1982). Thus, knowledge as we know it was unthinkable. Curriculum understood from this perspective is one that speaks to the unrepresentability of knowledge.

In the world of the imaginal, myth and symbol were central to understanding the world. Images encoded as myths and symbols, not knowledge, were the heart of curriculum. According to Karen Armstrong (1993),

> symbolic stories, cave paintings and carvings were an attempt to express their (ancient peoples) wonder and to link this pervasive mystery with their own lives . . . these dramatic and evocative stories of gods and goddesses helped people to articulate their sense of the powerful but unseen forces that surrounded them. (p. 5)

These myths, like the Sumerian tale of Gilgamesh, the Greek myths of Zeus, Persephone, or Demeter, or the creation stories of Nu Kwa or Adam and Eve, were not intended to be taken "literally," but were metaphorical attempts to describe a reality that was too complex and elusive to be described in any other way. Mary Aswell Doll (2000) suggests that we are not meant to read mythic images with our "mind but with our ear. Mind, in Sumerian, means ear and wisdom" (p. 139). This way of knowing was not concerned with description in explicit and direct terms—in other words, they did not seek literal explanations or representations for natural phenomena (reality was understood to be beyond human comprehension). Instead, they sought to link the pervasive mystery around them with their own lives. According to Davis (2004), "the point of myth or an allegory is not to label the world, but to weave a meaningful backdrop for a labeled world" (p. 34). Wisdom was understood as a process (through intuition, divination, ritual, myths, art, and dance) that sought connection, not separation, from the universe. Within these ancient civilizations, there was, according to Armstrong (1993), "no gulf between human beings and the gods. The natural world, men and women and the gods themselves all shared the same nature and derived from the same divine substance" (p. 9). Unlike today, this intersubjective, holistic worldview was not constituted through contemporary notions of self/other, male/female, or nature/man. Consequently, to engender curriculum history in the ancient world means to suspend current-day gender constructions. Imaginal ways of knowing suggest ways of being in the world that are not predicated on a binary worldview and instead imagine other ways of being in the world.

Our earliest knowledge of how humans came to know and understand themselves is through creation stories. "Stories are humankind's oldest way of talking about and taking in truths" (Edwards, 1991: 1). In effect, stories—myths, parables, fables, allegory, fairy tales, and folklore—"tell us how to be human, and their powers lie in the fact that metaphor, symbols, and other figurative tools can be used to address matters of meaning in ways that logic and reason cannot" (Davis, 2004: 27). Stories provide "images" of how human beings face the vast mysteries of the universe and are able to make sense of their world and imbue it with meaning. All creation stories cluster around four basic questions: Who creates life? In whose image are we made? Who brings evil into the world? Who mediates between humans and the supernatural? (Lerner, 1986: 146). The first creation stories told to address these questions were virtually universal in the dominance of the Mother Goddess (Lerner, 1986: 148).[2] In Egypt it is the goddess Nun, in Sumeria the goddess Nammu, in Greek mythology the goddess Gaia. According to Armstrong (1993), in the Paleolithic period "when agriculture was developing, the cult of the Mother Goddess expressed a sense that the fertility which was transforming human life was actually sacred" (p. 5). The earliest creation stories are predominately maternal in nature and provide a range of answers to the questions asked by human beings. Perhaps one of the oldest creation stories is that of the Chinese female deity Nu Kwa. Nu Kwa, the great Ocean–Snail–Snake–Dragon Woman, gave birth to all life and the patterns of the universe.[3] In the texts of the Chou period (about 1000 BCE) and the later Han period, it was written that Nu Kwa created all people, thus revealing her nature as the original parent or most ancient ancestress (Stone, 1979). She was also described as the one who established harmony, arranging the order of the seasons, and setting the stars and planets upon the proper paths. It is this complex and omnipotent view of the mother, not only as she who first gave birth to people, the creator of human life, but also as she who arranged the workings of the universe, the patterns of nature that reveals that the image of the most ancient ancestress was that of Nature herself. Thus, we cannot assume that the Mother Goddess is female (as we understand gender), in fact an understanding of this early period in history as matrilineal or as a time of original matriarchy as early feminists (Gimbutas, 1991) and Marxists (Engels, 1884) posited has been critiqued (Ruether, 2005). To suggest that prior to patriarchy there was a peaceful, blissful matriarchy in which there was equality between men and women is to impose current gender ideologies. Even less plausible is the concept of the goddess as a monotheistic focus of religion. Within the ancient world, subject identities were not unitary, humans understood themselves as connected to the cosmos, as intersubjective and part of the much larger cycle of life and death. Gender, understood as distinct, separate identities of male and female, would have been inconceivable. It is the interconnectedness of all living things that would have shaped understandings of the world. The focus was on harmony, balance, and meaning-making that sought to ground one in the experience of Being.[4]

A careful reading of the *Tao Te Ching* (the most fundamental book of Taoism), believed to have been written about 600 BCE by Lao Tzu (which means ancient teacher), is to some degree a mirror that reflects the ideas and beliefs that may once have been the theological and philosophical core of ancient goddess reverence in China. In the *Tao Te Ching*, the concept of the female divine is not external to, or separate, from earth and ourselves. Rather, the understanding of human nature as the maternal spirit essence is inherent in all that exists and occurs. The concept of the female divine is also found in the texts of India, concerning the goddess as Shakti or Devi, and in the texts of Egypt, concerning the goddess Maat. It is the gentle omnipotence of she who is the essence of the patterns of the universe, all that is implied when we speak of Mother Nature, that appears to be the core of wisdom and of the *Tao Te Ching*. This wisdom has at its core an understanding of the impermanence of all things, the interconnectedness of all life (intersubjectivity) and an acceptance of the dynamic and unpredictable nature of being. The image of the goddess or female divine suggests a curricular understanding that honors *being* in the world rather than a need to *control* the world or even to understand it.

The Great Mother remained "imaginatively important for centuries" (Ruether, 2005: 5). She was absorbed into later belief systems and usually was one of the most powerful gods. In ancient Sumeria she was called Inna, in Babylon Ishtar, in Canaan Anat, in Egypt Isis, and in Greece Aphrodite. The stories told are remarkably similar; they reflect a belief in a female life-giving force, a female deity who creates life. But she was also associated with death. She was praised and celebrated for her virginity as well as for her maternal qualities. The duality of the goddess represented the cycle of life observable in nature, night and day, life and death, light and darkness. Embracing duality (rather than privileging one over the other) suggests an epistemology of paradox in which there is a holistic view of creation. These oral traditions were central to passing on "meanings" (I refrain from using the term passing on knowledge, since I do not believe that this was what was intended) that helped each generation make sense of the world around them as well as guidelines or ethics for "Being" in the world. Although these stories are diverse and divergent, they share several things in common:

- There is darkness and light (good and evil/paradox).
- There is an endless circle of life and death (impermanence/nonlinearity).
- Reverence for nature (connection, not objectification).
- Humans are not separate from the divine (holisitic, horizontal view).
- Interconnectedness of all things (intersubjectivity).

Current scholarship in religious studies, anthropology, and history has contributed a great deal to enhancing our understandings of these early stories as legitimate history (Plaskow & Christ, 1989). As curriculum theorists, these stories have much to teach us about how to make sense from a mytho–poetic, paradoxical, nonlinear, holistic, and intersubjective way of experiencing the world. It was an epistemology that was grounded in unknowing, mystery, awe, being, harmony, balance, and connectedness. It was an epistemology that embraced paradox, contradiction and sought meaning-making, not representation. This state of *Being* prompts very different understandings of how we come to know and what can be known as opposed to an ontology of the "word" which begins to emerge as humans develop an existential awareness of having a self separate from the environment. About 35,000 years ago, artifacts suggest the emergence of a self-conscious awareness. This differentiation of heaven/earth, God/man, male/female, subject/object and its resultant epistemology was one which I maintain evolved slowly and ultimately codified itself by 600 CE. This period in history in which there is a shift from consciousness based in image, diffusion, paradox, and a cyclical sense of time as compared to one based in the word, verticality, abstraction, and linearity is, in part, the result of humans' understanding of their own agency (this is a result of their growing capacity to shape and control the natural world through fire, agriculture, and reproduction). This marks the beginning of the separation of humans from the natural world and the cosmos (the divine). The earth is seen as an object and creation is no longer understood as an organic process but as a concept and thus for the first time, being becomes abstract. The question of "In whose image?" shifts from one of pure awe and mystery to one which includes human consciousness. This separation is one that ultimately results in the concept of "otherness" (and self-conscious awareness) that makes it possible to imagine gender as a duality and for epistemology to be radically altered. This was however, not without struggle.

In Whose Image?: The Struggle

While the image of Mother Earth and the cosmos as reflecting an intersubjective, holistic worldview would eventually recede, the images of the Mother Goddess did not disappear. The fact that they prevailed and were re-imagined in other stories speaks to their power. The mythic memories of the creation story of Nu Kwa, for example, are recorded in early Chinese texts as the Era of Great Purity. In the Chuang Tzu, written in the third century BCE, the time of Great Purity is described as a time when all people lived in a state of innocence, being genuine and simple, spontaneous and direct in their conduct. They were in harmony with the seasons and with the ways of nature; animals and humans did no harm to one another. The Chinese texts then explain that this paradise was destroyed by mining minerals in the mountains, felling trees to build houses, hunting, fishing, and even by learning to make and control fire. The period of the obliteration of this perfect life, and the loss of touch with the patterns of nature was referred to as the Great Cosmic Struggle. Nature had been defied and this was said to be the original cause of discord and problems (Stone, 1979).

This creation story parallels other stories in terms of its narrative structure: a time of innocence and purity (harmony and connection), a fall from grace (disharmony and separation), and the resultant struggle for reconnection, to be one with the cosmos again. When the divine, nature, and humans are in harmony there is purity; it is good. In essence, there was no separation from the divine, no sense of otherness or difference. This separation can be said to symbolize the birth of consciousness, the emerging concept of separateness and individuation from nature and thus consequently the divine. What causes disharmony or lack of balance is humanity's estrangement from the divine through reliance on its own self-knowledge (symbolized in this story by fire and in the Christian tradition by the apple). Consequently, humans no longer see themselves as created in the image of the divine, but in their own *self-image*. In the Jewish and Christian traditions, the Genesis story has both the tree of life and the tree of knowledge which represent these two ways of being in the world. By choosing the tree of knowledge or in the Chinese narrative, fire, humans become conscious of their separateness from the divine/nature. This shift from the tree of life (a horizontal, intersubjective, paradoxical way of being in the world) over the course of several thousand years to the tree of knowledge (a vertical, dualistic, logical way of being in the world) is the Great Cosmic Struggle or the fall from the garden.

This separation between human/divine, male/female, soul/psyche, paradox/control, language/image becomes the first curriculum struggle over what counts as knowledge, who can be a knower and how knowledge is legitimated. Borne out in centuries of myths and stories, the central question of "In whose image?" shaped the curricular discourses of the earliest civilizations. What is knowledge is the heart of this struggle. Knowledge in the wisdom age was based on an episte-mology grounded in impermanence, intersubjectivity, paradox, and union/

connection with the cosmos. What would emerge as humans came to see themselves as separate from nature was an epistemology of separation and going "alone without the divine." Although somewhat reductionist, this shift has also been understood by Jungians as the primordial struggle between consciousness and unconsciousness, or by Julia Kristeva as symbolic of the relationship between the prelanguage and language state.[5]

Characterizing this struggle in such a dichotomized way obscures the profoundly diverse ways in which humans have struggled to understand and give meaning to their lives. It also privileges the binary human/divine as the primary image. Undoubtedly, the earliest human experiences of the life-giving power of women must have been profoundly mysterious. The awe this must have inspired clearly is reflected in the early creation stories. As the story of Nu Kwa suggests, the life-giving force was not solely conceptualized in the image of women (thus it was not gendered in the way we might think of gender today) but woman did represent the life-giving force of nature, of earth, of all the mysteries of life.[6] (In this sense women represent the psyche, the unconscious.) While the creation stories clearly derive some of their aspects from the worship of female fertility, it is nature, and its force and mystery that the goddess represents. As men learned of their role in the process of creation, there was an epistemological shift. I would maintain that this shift was not one that automatically or necessarily resulted in patriarchy, but a shift in which creation stories become more interdependent (both male and female), and then eventually emerged in some major religions as a monotheistic male, God.

The transition from polytheism to monotheism reflects major changes in society as well as a curricular shift. As society moved from a more nomadic/hunting gathering existence to one characterized by agriculture, militarism, and a strong kingship, religious beliefs shifted to mirror social organization. Thus, many gods were replaced with one strong God. The shift from polytheism to monotheism or from goddess to God required a shift in symbols, 1) from the vulva of the goddess to the seed of man; 2) from the tree of life to the tree of knowledge; and 3) from the celebration of the Sacred Marriage to the biblical convenants (Lerner, 1986). According to Ruether (2005), in Sacred Marriage a goddess espouses a king and establishes him on his throne. The goddesses represent the divine side of the sacred marriage whereas the kings represent humans. These goddesses are not docile wives but independent queens like Ishtar and Anat who are linked to storms and war. The symbolism of the Sacred Marriage reflected not only the alienation from the divine, but the desire to reconnect. It is essentially a metaphor for the reunion of the divine with humans. While male and female unite, the female image does not conform to later Western stereotypes of what is acceptable behavior. Thus, eventually the role of the Sacred Marriage in symbolizing re-union is replaced by the "covenant."

Prior to this shift to a male God who establishes a covenant with his people, there is a transition period in which the recognition of the necessary cooperation of the female and male principle in the process of creation seems to be firmly established, at least in Sumerian and Akkadian mythology (Lerner, 1986: 149). Later, creation stories include the element of the Mother Goddess associated with a male partner, brother, or son, who assists her in the fertility rites by mating with her. In myth and ritual, the male god is young and he may have to die in order for rebirth to take place (this is the Sacred Marriage necessary for the annual cycle of seasons to begin). And, while the creative act is performed by the goddess, the male god is frequently decisively involved in initiating the process of creation. In the Assyrian creation story, the wise Mami (also known as Nintu) fashions humans out of clay, but it is the male god Ea who opens the navel of the figures, thus completing the life-giving process.

In the fourth and third millennia BCE there is a shift in terms of the concept of creation, from being merely a mystic force of female fertility to being a conscious act of creation. This element of consciousness, expressed in "the idea," "the concept," "the name," of that which will be created, may be the reflection of an altered human consciousness. The time when these concepts first appear is the time when writing has been invented, and with it history. Record-keeping demonstrated the power of abstraction (Lerner, 1986: 151). The elaboration of various symbol systems altered people's perception of their relation to time and space. The common-sense observable facts of female fertility and conception shifted to a symbolic creativity that was expressed in "the name" and "the concept." As Lerner suggests, "it is not very far from that to the concept of the creative spirit," separate from human activity, as the center of the universe. It was this shift that was a precondition for monotheism.

Despite these shifts, the female divine figures were synthesized and reconfigured due to the power that they held for everyday people. One example is the Egyptian Isis who, like Nu Kwa, was the "throne woman" in the earliest period, where she embodied the sacred kingship and mysterious knowledge. Later, she became the prototype of the mother and faithful wife. She taught her brother-spouse, Osiris, the secrets of agriculture and restored his dismembered body to life. In the Hellenistic period, she was worshiped as the Magna Mater of western Asia and the Greco-Roman world. According to Lerner (1986), in the second millennium, "men and women stood in the same relation to the mysterious and awesome forces represented in the gods and goddesses" (p. 160). Gender distinctions were not yet used to explain the causes of evil, the problem of death, or the process of creation.

Generativity encompasses both creativity—the ability to create something out of nothing—and procreativity—the capacity to produce offspring. Religious explanations of generativity shifted from the Mother Goddess as the sole principle of universal fertility to the Mother Goddess assisted in her fertility by male gods or human kings; then to the concept of symbolic creativity as expressed first in "the name," then "the creative spirit." The shift from the all-powerful Mother Goddess to the all-powerful Storm-God, whose female consort represents a domesticated version of the fertility goddess is perhaps best represented in ancient Greece (to which we will turn shortly). However, this shift to one single male God also occurs in the Book of Genesis (Lerner, 1986: 180). Yahweh is not allied with any female goddess nor does he have familial ties. Yahweh represents symbolic creativity, an abstract notion of divinity that is totally separate from human action.

This shift from imaginal/intersubjective knowing to abstraction is described by Berman (2000) as a shift to a vertical rather than a horizontal way of making sense of the world. He terms this vertical organization the Sacred Authority Complex (SAC) and suggests that it coincides with the emergence of an agricultural, sedentary civilization. There is a lack of trust, and the fear of death has assumed a prominent place. The human being is not so much *in* the world, as he is having a worldview, and it tends to be vertical in nature (ziggurats and pyramids). The SAC establishes itself by 2000 BCE in the Judaic tradition with Abraham and then later Moses (as well as Miriam). It is characterized by ascent experiences which provided psychological security (Greek Mystery cults where ritual practices were used to obliterate consciousness, to submerge the ego into the One, the Absolute). The pain of ego-consciousness was offset by means of a mystical experience that merged the psyche with the rest of the creation—what Freud called the "oceanic experience" (Berman, 2000: 5). Many civilizations (predominately those of the West) have been preoccupied with transcendence and Salvationist properties. Religion becomes the transitional object between world and self. This formation has profound influences on curricular understandings that will emerge in a variety of ways in the Judaic, Greek, and early Christian and later Muslim religious traditions.

Monotheism is neither better nor worse than previous modes of answering "who creates life?" What it signifies is a shift to abstract thinking represented by the transformation of creativity into "a concept," "a name," God's breath creates. Creativity is no longer an intersubjective, relational process in which humans are profoundly engaged but creativity is relegated to an abstract God. The development of monotheism in the Book of Genesis reflects the development of abstract thought. Lerner (1986) has suggested that this "advance" occurred in a social setting and under circumstances that strengthened patriarchy. We will return to the Book of Genesis numerous times, since this is the critical text in Western culture that establishes the primary metaphors of knowledge. However, I would disagree with Lerner that patriarchy emerged as a monolithic entity as a result of the "text." The emergence of Christianity, and its evolution from the nexus of cultures in the Middle East, including Greek, Judaic, and Eastern thought, produced not a monolithic belief system but multiple interpretations. Let us turn to the Middle Eastern world to examine both Judaism and Christianity since they represent the first monotheistic belief systems.

The Image is the Word

Study, as is prayer, is the awareness that we live amidst daily miracles, and that there is more to the world than we will ever know.

(Alan Block, 2004)

The beginning of awe is wonder, and the beginning of wisdom is awe.

(Abraham Joshua Heschel, 1959)

The insistence on history is an insistence on the reality of the world, and so the action of God is a saving action, rather than one of dissolution. Religion, of Israel, is this relation with God. There is a relation with God in covenant, A God who created the world and who wants the world to be lived in— according to his intention.

(Raymond Gawronski, 1995)

Jewish mystical writing, called the Kabbalah, used the word "daath" for the insight that the truth is accompanied by great feeling.[7] Daath is the knowledge that comes from the union of conscious and unconscious minds, a kind of knowing that is a deeply erotic experience. Daath is the word used by Kabbalistic writers to refer to the union of God with his bride (the Sacred Marriage), the Sabbath. Shekina meaning Sabbath, is the name for the Feast of the Full Moon, which once celebrated the menstruation of the Great Goddess. Originally honored once a month, Her Holiness came to be observed every quarter moon (once a week). The Friday evening that began her honor was the night in which the husband of the home made love with his wife, recapitulating the union of the God and Goddess. The shift from the imaginal to the rational, however, lessened interest in the power of love between male and female deities (Sacred Marriage) and consequently, the Sabbath became more an observation of the minutiae of the law. From this point the Shekina, once goddess of Babylon, and then of the Jews went underground.[8]

During the period of warfare between the Israelite tribes and the Canaanites, which took place when the entire region was under Philistine dominance, there was a further consolidation of monotheism over polytheism. According to Lerner (1986), it was the prolonged ideological struggle with the Canaanites and the persistence of the fertility goddess Asherah, the Canaanite goddess, that must have hardened the emphasis on male cultic leadership and the corresponding religious beliefs in one male God. As recounted in the Jewish Bible:

> In the twentieth year Jeroboam, King of Israel, Asa, King of Judah, began his reign; he reigned for forty-one years in Jerusalem. His grandmother's name was Maacah, daughter of Abishalom. Asa pleased the Lord like his forefather David banishing the temple prostitutes from the land and removing the idols his father had made. He also deposed of his grandmother Maacah from her position as queen mother because she had made an outrageous object for Asherah, Asa cut down this object and burned it in the Kidron Valley.
>
> *(1 Kings, 16: 9–14)*

Maacah, in reverence of Asherah erected wooden poles (asherot), just as stone pillars (massebot) were erected in honor of the god Baal. Both were placed near the altar in a Canaanite shrine. From ancient settlements along the Tigris, Euphrates, and the Jordan, Semitic peoples often called upon the Holy Mother Asherah. She was the Holy Lady who walked the sea. She was the Mother of all Wisdom. She gave birth to the 70 deities in Heaven and in her sacred groves, she was known as she who builds, teaching people the art of carpentry, the knowledge of the bricks. At her temple in Jerusalem, women wove woolen bands of mourning that were wrapped around her tree, the tree upon which her son's lover had died (Stone, 1979). As Judaism consolidated a monotheistic belief that privileged a belief in an abstract/vertical notion of a creator, it was necessary to suppress a vision of the cosmos that was cyclical, intersubjective, and horizontal. Thomas Cahill (1998) maintains that the "Jews were the first people to break out of this circle, to find a new way of thinking and experiencing, a new way of understanding and feeling the world" (p. 5). However, this new way of understanding was predicated on suppressing other ways:

> These are the statutes and decrees which you must be careful to observe in the land which the Lord, the God of the fathers, has given you to occupy, as long as you live on its soil. Destroy without fail every place on the high mountains, on the hills, and under every leafy tree where the nations you are to dispossess worship their gods. Tear down their altars, smash their sacred pillars, destroy by fire their sacred poles, and shatter the idols of their gods, that you may stamp out the remembrance of them in any such place.
>
> *(Deuteronomy, 12: 1–3)*

The banishing of temple "prostitutes" (those engaged in the rituals of the Sacred Marriage), the destruction of sacred poles and the idols of gods are carried out as a means to obliterate from memory a different way of understanding the world.[9] Lerner clearly sees this as the consolidation of patriarchy. As we will see shortly, women also participated in the promotion of monotheism, making the claim of patriarchy as central to monotheism weak. From the perspective of consciousness, the unification with God, rather than the splintering of energies among various gods, signifies the beginnings of reconnection, the reintegration of the "true" self after the great struggle of separation. Clearly, there are many perspectives from which we might analyze this. However, my interest is in what this means for our understandings of curriculum. Knowledge was shifting from "images" encoded in stories, symbols, and myths to an abstract concept of creativity. According to Lerner, this new order under the all-powerful God proclaimed to Hebrews and to all who took the Bible as their moral and religious guide that women cannot speak to God.

Yet, there are several Jewish women prophets who proclaim Yaweh as the only God. The prophet Deborah is one of these:

> Gone was freedom beyond the walls
> Gone indeed from Israel

When I, Deborah rose,
　　When I rose, a mother in Israel
New gods were their choice;
　　Then the war was at their gates.
Not a shield could be seen, nor a lance
　　Among forty thousand in Israel!

(Judges, 5: 7–8)

Deborah, who lived around approximately 1300 BCE, is generally attributed with being a well-known warrior, a military commander, and judge who led an army into battle because her general would not go without her. Called by God, Deborah led a battle against the Canaanites that resulted in the Israelite tribes enjoying 40 years of relative peace. Deborah was also a prophetess, someone with whom God had a special relationship and whom he commissioned to speak in his name. She is above all a spiritual leader who unites the Jewish people and reminds them of their covenant with God, in spite of the "New Gods who were their choice." This covenant signifies a direct relationship with the divine that does not require rituals or sacrifices that reenact the cycle of life and death. It requires a belief in a creator who has made a pledge or contract that does not require material signs but asks for actions. This covenant symbolizes the shift to a vertical belief system that dramatically influences notions of curriculum and pedagogy. A covenant or SAC belief system is an epistemology based in abstraction, verticality, reason, and ultimately the "word" as compared to an imaginative, horizontal, intersubjective, and cyclical epistemology. One might conclude, like Lerner that this dualism is part of the establishment of patriarchy. Yet, many female Jewish prophets, including Miriam and Sarah, see the covenant as equally important. What engenders this shift is not so much the difference between monotheism and polytheism, or God versus goddess, or imagination versus reason, but the belief that one way of understanding the world necessitates the exclusion of other ways. This suppression is the mark of gender because it limits the subject identities made possible.

Over time, women's roles changed dramatically the further removed Judaism became from the notion of a female divine deity. By the time formal education was instituted in the Judaic tradition in the 2nd or 1st century BCE, it was limited to male students. Although women had been prophetesses and were spiritual leaders early on, as Judaism became more codified and patriarchal, women became less visible in shaping or participating in the public sphere. It was considered a religious duty to teach their sons the Torah, but this was not required for girls. And until the 4th century CE girls could attend public meetings for the reading of and discourse about scripture.

It was under the prophet Ezra that the canonization of Jewish teaching occurs. The revolutionary aspect of Jewish monotheism was its absolute faith in one, invisible, ineffable God, its rejection of ritual as proof of holiness, and its demand, instead, on adherence to and practice of ethical values (Lerner, 1986: 167). According to Cahill (1998), the relationship between the divine and humans is no longer unpredictable, paradoxical, and contingent on rituals, but one in which the divine is the initiator, "he begins the dialogue, and he will see it through" (p. 93). This is a face-to-face relationship with God. The great innovation of the synagogue was that it was a place for religious assembly and the reading of scripture, instead of a site of cultic practice monopolized by a sect of priests. This made the Jewish religion mobile, exportable, flexible, and communal (p. 167).

Judaism was radical not only because it established monotheism, but also because of its understanding of curriculum. "In the beginning God created the heavens and the earth." According to Block (2004), this statement, the first in the Hebrew Bible, is a supreme challenge to the entire classical tradition of Western metaphysics. By suggesting that matter is not eternal, that the world had a temporal origin, and that substance came into being through divine hands threatens the very foundations of Greek ontology. Unlike Greek thought, Hebrew thought holds that "the world could not be perceived through Reason because there were no natural laws that could be rationally explicated or logically deduced: the universe was not naturally formed: rather, the world was created" (Block, 2004: 13). Reason is a human construct, not the manifestation of the natural order. Greek thought is based on the assumption that meaning preceded the word. There is meaning and it must be found. In contrast, for Hebrews there is always another interpretation of text because "what is at stake is not final knowledge but daily practice" (p. 14). Deliberation is the very center of Talmudic discourse (Block, 2004).

Once "the word" was embraced, interpretation took the place of revelation. Wisdom for the Jews was a process and not a destination (Block, 2004: 20). The Platonic concept of the real—real concepts and real ideas—a belief that mind could grasp these concepts and ideas through reason—is opposed by Jewish practice which "seeks not the truth but a life that is true "(p. 20). (Socratic teaching is not at the heart of Jewish pedagogy.) Meaning is not in the text, but may be made with the text (likewise, meaning is not in God, but may be made with God). Rabbinic thought encourages multiplicity of meanings and offers not knowledge but ways to create knowledge. In contrast, Western philosophical tradition establishes a dualism between the intellectual and the spiritual whereas in the Talmud, these are intimately connected.

This understanding of education as deliberation and as an active process continues to resonate, as Block reminds us, in the work of the curriculum theorist Joseph Schwab (1971, 1977). Schwab's work reminds us of these ancient traditions whose influence continues to recur in contemporary thought without appreciation for their deep-rooted history. In these ancient Jewish traditions education is the *process* of seeking answers, not the answers themselves. In drawing on the Talmud, the emphasis is placed on dialogue, in the working through of thought. Talmudic pedagogy is one focused on thinking of questions, not finding *the* answers, but asking another question (Block, 2004: 13). Talmud is not concerned with the merely theoretical, but insists on the particular and on the intimacy between thought and action (p. 23). Whereas the Western view of knowledge rests on the assumption that knowledge is timeless and universal, for the Hebrews "only God—not truth—is eternal and omniscient" (p. 25). God exists beyond human knowledge; human reason will never comprehend God. Consequently, the focus in the Jewish tradition is on the practical or the deed, how might one best obey God's word. Thus, the Jewish focus on textual interpretation is hermeneutical.

Block (2004) suggests that in her book *Leviticus as Literature* (1999), Mary Douglas distinguishes between two types of thought—mytho-poetic reasoning and discursive logical reasoning. I would suggest that Jewish thought shifts from paradoxical thinking (hunter-gatherers/polytheistic) to mytho-poetic (agricultural/monotheistic) and that canonical Greek thinking can be described as discursive logical reasoning. These present three very different ways to think about curriculum, each of which represents a different way of being in the world.

Block claims that Jewish thought had to be excluded in order for the Greeks and early Christians to justify their worldview. This exclusion, he claims, altered forever pedagogical purpose and practice (p. 27). Christianity replaced the textual mediation of Jewish practice with the insistence of personal mediation (with Jesus as mediator). For Christianity, faith in Jesus as teacher substituted for the immediacy of textual authority and the primacy of interpretation. The text is made flesh through Jesus, and meaning is based on personal experience of Jesus.

In summary, Jewish thought resulted in the following. In essence, God is separate from humankind. The great "advance" in abstract thinking, monotheism, is represented by the symbolification of creativity into "a concept." The shift from wisdom to word (*logos*) situates knowing as external. "God" is seen as wholly other, as "out there" and the source of creativity. This separation shifts the agency of creativity to a male, monolithic God. Consequently, the understanding of wisdom or knowledge as linked to the cycle of life and death as a continuous process of re-generation is replaced by one in which the divine is separate from the realm of death. Death, rather than being embraced, is feared. It becomes part of the unholy from which God is separated and from which those who worship him must separate themselves in order to come into the presence of the holy (Ruether, 2005). This separation of life and death also marks the elimination of any female deity in the process of creation; all motherly qualities are taken over by the divine father. Yahweh is not allied with any female figure goddess nor does he have familial ties. In theory, this would be the end of the Sacred Marriage. However, it is appropriated in the relation between Israel as the bride or wife of God. According to Ruether, "the male elites had to imagine themselves collectively as female in relation to God. Hebrew females were then even more severely distanced from the places of power and communication with God" (p. 81). The world of wisdom is defined by relations between men, between human men and God, played out in the relations between fathers and sons, male teachers and students

(Ruether, 2005). Women as agents, as seekers of knowledge "cannot assert themselves into this world of male–male relations without fundamentally reconstructing its gender symbolism" (p. 97). Not only do women have no role in the creation of wisdom, but also, for women, to seek independent knowledge (the apple) is a sin.

Image as Reason: The Greeks

> The beginning of philosophy marks the "abrupt" end of the "dialogical act of prayer." A "knowledge that keeps itself to itself." The world of myth is the world in which God and man stand apart from each other; the world of philosophy leads both "to the limit of identity."
>
> *(Raymond Gawronski, 1995)*

While Jewish thought was consolidating a monotheistic, male God whose relationship with humans would always be beyond knowledge, the Greeks were also wrestling with the questions of who created, in whose image, and what this meant. The Delphic admonition "know thyself" originally meant nothing less than "Go inside yourself, let yourself be told by God that you are only a man" (Gawronski, 1995: 29). The Greeks accepted their place as mortals before the divine. The attempt to go it alone without God was considered by the Greeks a sin: "sin is simply the arrogance to want to manage without God." The etymology of the Greek word for sin—*hamartia*—is "to miss the mark" (Leloup, 2002: 50). For the ancient Greeks, man is essentially in need of God. Although most curriculum histories begin with the "Greeks," the philosophers who undoubtedly receive the most attention are Socrates, Plato, and Aristotle. By beginning with the Classical philosophers, the Greeks who preceded them are excluded. Western educational thought is attributed to the "Classical" philosophers of Socrates, Plato, and Aristotle, and their writings have formed the foundation for what is considered the basic ideas about education. These include:

• The idea of striving for an integrated intellectual, physical, and moral personal excellence.
• The belief that there are culturally essential, or core (basic) studies.
• The debate over the most desirable relationship between teacher and student.

The overriding influence that has shaped Western thought from Greek philosophy is Plato's belief that the universe is essentially rational. According to scholar Karen Armstrong (1993), "this was another myth or imaginary conception of reality" (p. 36). Taken for granted in the Western tradition as "truth" and the basis of all science and legitimate thought, rationality and logical thought have achieved the status of the "real" rather than being seen as a myth or image. One way to restore their position as myth is to place them in relation to the other myths or images that were circulating at the time. Greek society (I will focus on the period from 500 BCE to 500 CE) was an extremely diverse and complex society. This period in history marked Greece as a crossroads of Persian, Babylonian, Greek, Jewish, Eastern, Egyptian, Roman, and early Christian (or Jewish renewal) cultures.[10] The confluence of these diverse cultures resulted in a cacophony of voices and ideas that defy any single characterization of Greek society. Consequently, to limit our understandings of curriculum history to Socrates, Plato, and Aristotle is to exclude a vast diversity of thought in relation to curriculum theory.

This period was one of great pluralism in which poetry, myth, legend, philosophy, religion, sacrifice, and ritual from all over the world contributed to an astounding array of knowledge, speculation, and spirituality available to men and women of the ancient cities. This was prior to the major process of Christianization in the Roman world (Sawyer, 1996: 47). In terms of religious practice and belief, this was a time of adventure and experiment for both men and women. There was a proliferation of Greco-Roman cults such as Cybele and Attis, of Isis, and Mithras or Dionysus. All these cults invited initiates to explore and identify with ancient myths of sex and sexuality, of life and death. By contrast Judaism occupied a very different place in the ancient cities, offering a religious belief system based on a moral code and the interpretation of text, but without ritual as the central site for understanding. It also offered the protection of one God and creator of the universe.

What these religious belief systems shared was the increasing exclusion of women from roles as mediators or knowers of the divine. One of the main influences of the Hellenistic world on women's lives was an "intensification of the dichotomy between private and public worlds" (Sawyer, 1996: 35). In Greek society, women were restricted to the private. Two distinct influences encroached upon the position of women in the period of late antiquity: one were the long-standing traditions of the Hellenistic world, and the other was the evolving situation of Roman society. Most Romans were engaged in correct observance of rituals at important points in the year and in their lives and they strove to give the gods the honor due them. They were unworried by souls and afterlives, reckoned their moral behavior was up to them and not what others thought of them, and had no notion that they needed to be "saved" from anything, other than bad harvests, disease, and childlessness (p. 50). In this context, religion did not demand any complex belief system. Philosophy was a discipline that existed apart from the deities and their myths and rites. On the other hand, Christianity, as well as the cult of Mithras and Isis, began to fuse religion and philosophy. (Isis included a perspective that looked beyond the mundane existence and explored the notion of immortality with the resurrection of Osiris.)

This fusion of religion and philosophy is perhaps best exemplified by Pythagoras. The word for philosopher, first used by Pythagoras, means "lover of Sophia." Sophia, whose name means "wisdom," had been the goddess of pagan philosophers for centuries.[11] Although the Pythagorians are often depicted as "intellectuals," many were mystics and devotees of the goddess. Parmenides, attributed as the founder of Western logic, also wrote a visionary poem in which he descends into the underworld to be instructed by the goddess. We shall return to Pythagoras in a moment, but first let us turn to the first Greek woman philosopher, Sappho (*c*.630–*c*.572 BCE) of Lesbos. According to Smith and Smith (1994), formal schooling began in the Greek era around the time of Homer. Sappho, the earliest Greek educator about whom there is any information, was head of what would be equivalent to a women's finishing school. The island of Lesbos seems to have provided extraordinary social and intellectual opportunity for Greek women, and maintained provisions for unmarried women to be educated.[12] Sappho wrote during a time of political unrest throughout Greece, in which the Greek city states were moving from aristocratic to democratic rule. Sappho's society was for the most part sexually segregated. After marriage, a woman remained excluded from worldly pursuits, often meeting with her husband only long enough to guarantee her pregnancy and thereby her husband's *oikos* (Glenn, 1997: 24).

Women were educated from all parts of Ionia by way of an all-female fellowship that was an education celebrating female life-giving and life-sustaining sources (Glenn, 1997: 24). Like their male counterparts, the girls studied music and dancing, as well as physical fitness and development—all arts that supported the study of poetry, the only literature of the day. They also learned the rules of etiquette, good taste and sensitivity in the arts of love, bound garlands of flowers and did handiwork. Young girls of well-to-do families lived together under the supervision of well-educated, experienced women. They spent their days performing cult rituals in the service of the love goddess, Aphrodite. Meanwhile, the traditional male curriculum consisted of music, gymnastics, reading, writing, and poetry (especially Homer's *Iliad* and *Odyssey*). These epic poems were written in praise of *arête* (honor resulting from a personally heroic deed). It was against this backdrop where the aim of education was to produce well-rounded, courageous, warrior citizens that Sappho wrote her poetry.

Living outside of a male-dominated society, Sappho exercised her verbal prowess, using her poetry to celebrate women's education, women's alliances, and especially, women's public use of persuasive language (Glenn, 1997: 25). According to Glenn (1997), Sappho was the only woman in all antiquity whose literary production placed her on the same level as the greatest male poet, Homer. She wrote nine books of lyric poems, nearly two hundred of which remain in fragments, only one poem surviving in its entirety. Plato invokes Sappho as the tenth Muse; and Aristotle honors her as a wise woman. Her writing, specifically her poetry, reflects an epistemological stance in which she defines women in terms of themselves rather than in relationship to men. At a time when the experiences of men were increasingly being valorized through epic poems of heroism, like the *Iliad* and the *Odyssey*, Sappho's poetry is a poignant testimony to the daily lived experiences of women.

The speaking subject of Sappho's poems was a woman, a woman "claiming the right to talk, the right to use her own voice" (Glenn, 1997: 26). She moves the lyric (poetry) from an expression of masculine heroism, political dominance, and male individuality to the ardor and nobility of the feminine soul, thereby contributing to literary rhetoric (poetics) and disrupting the continuum of male-dominated poetics (p. 27). Fragments of her poetry reveal her expertise in and resistance to all the traditional, male approved forms and subjects: epithalamia (bridal chamber songs), epiphany (prayer or invocation), and priamel (epigrammic catalog). Her poems celebrate the desires, rituals, and stages in a woman's life, as well as affirm female beauty and the pleasures residing in day-to-day living. In the Kristevan sense, then, Sappho's writings reflect a woman's sense of both cyclical and linear time.

Sappho's female subjects are mostly defined by and limited to their physical being and states of emotion. They were not immortalized, as were the subjects of male poetry, for glory achieved by doing. Sappho's philosophy was a subjective one, one that honored the mystic cults and the role of the erotic in achieving spiritual awareness. According to Garrison (1997), the ancient Greeks made the aim of education eros, or passionate desire. Passion and love, not reason and logic, are what fuel humans' desire for good. Sappho's poetry has love and desire as central to women's experience, and it is this cultivation of passion that results in the experiencing of the good and divine. For Sappho, both men and women had a role to play in achieving divine knowledge. Perhaps anticipating the shift in Greek society in which men would begin to take on a more public and solitary role in achieving enlightenment, Sappho provides a window into the lived experiences of women whose knowledge was still deemed as essential. The erasure of this aspect of the feminine divine was completed in 1073 CE when authorities in Rome and Constantinople burned all known poems of Sappho and her male contemporary, Alcaeus.[13]

The epistemological standpoint that wisdom is the result of divine union between male/female, God/human, consciousness/psyche was central to early Greek philosophers, especially Pythagoras. Pythagoras, to whom is attributed the term philosopher, which means lover of Sophia or wisdom. Although no contemporary accounts of the Pythagoreans exist, subsequent reports and the Pythagorean writings indicate that their academic goals became the template of Greek education that was to inform Plato's Academy, Aristotle's Lyceum, and Epicurus' school.

Two centuries before Plato, Pythagoras laid down the principle of equal opportunity for the sexes, a principle that, according to Glenn (1997), "he practiced as well as preached" (p. 30). The mainstay of Pythagorean philosophy was harmonia, the body of inflexible cosmic rules that informed sculpture, architecture, poetry, music, rhetoric, religion, morality, and human life. Pythagoreans viewed the cosmos or universe as orderly and harmonious in that everything bears a particular mathematical relationship to everything else. When things are in proper relationship to each other there is harmony and order (Waithe, 1987). Pythagoras' program of moral reform aimed to eliminate discontent among citizens and to produce instead a state of harmonia, or union of hearts and minds.

The fragments, whole letters, and complete essays of female-authored

Pythagorean writings concern themselves with "personal ethics," the ways women should and could preserve "personal and familial relationships" (Glenn, 1997: 31). Pythagoras' wife, Theano, explained the practical application of harmonia to the home and everyday life. She used letter writing as a form of moral education for women. According to Theano, women, being naturally temperate, bore the responsibility for using moderation and for respecting the natural laws of hierarchy (male over female) within the family and marriage, which were thought to be the microcosm of the state. To that end, every Pythagorean demonstrated an obligation to preserve, promote, and protect the harmony of domestic and public social relations (p. 31). Pythagorean women understood and accepted their measure of domestic power and acted on their responsibility for creating the conditions under which harmony, order, law, and justice could exist in the state and in the home (p. 32).

Phintys of Sparta, who wrote *On the Moderation of Women*, continues the argument that, although the social responsibilities of men and women are different, men and women remain equal and that the normative principle of harmonia provides for satisfaction within the context of those specific social responsibilities, both public and private. According to Phintys, women are equal to men in terms of courage, justice, and reflection; but men used these virtues for waging war and governing, while women managed the private sphere of home and family. She wrote (Waithe, 1987):

> Now, perhaps many think it is not fitting for a woman to philosophize, just as it is not fitting for her to ride horses or speak in public . . . But, I say that courage and justice and wisdom are common to both. Excellences of the body are appropriate for both a man and a woman, likewise those of the soul. And just as it is beneficial for the body of each to be healthy, so too, is it beneficial for the soul to be healthy. The excellences of the body are health, strength, keenness of perception and beauty. (p. 27)

Another Pythagorean work that focuses on the social and moral status of women in society is *On the Harmony of Women*, written, many scholars think, by Perictione, mother of Plato. Cole and Coultrap-McQuin (1992) maintain that this work is much more utilitarian than Phintys' work, and, therefore, perhaps more accessible to her lay readers. Perictione writes of ways for women best to achieve harmony within their circumscribed worlds, not within an idealized world. Reminiscent of the "Cult of Domesticity" that emerged in the mid-19th century, this worldview is not grounded in an epistemology of equality but rather one of difference. And yet, I would argue that this is not the *différance* of modern French philosophers. This epistemology is grounded in a fundamental belief that wisdom is the result of union or wholeness, balance. Essential for wisdom is a maintaining of opposites, a duality that results neither in the submersion of one or the other nor in equality. The union of opposites creates something new—wisdom. It is this imaginal space that was the site of knowing in which Sappho, Phintys, and Perictione were philosophizing.

In contrast, for Plato, wisdom was not a matter of union but of transcendence of the soul over the body. Plato held that wisdom was beyond human comprehension, so the journey to enlightenment that he describes differs significantly from his predecessors and from the early Christian thinkers who would be influenced by and draw on his thought. Plato argued that the true lover of wisdom cultivates the soul and is not concerned with the pleasures of the body (King, 2003: 41). Enlightenment is predicated on separation not connection. Plato based these views on a distinction between what is eternal, immutable, uncreated, and known only through the mind (the immaterial world) and what is finite, mutable, created, and subject to sense perception (the material world). Plato considered the material world to be only an inferior copy of the higher Divine Realm (in other words, man was not made in God's image) and that beliefs about it were not reliable. Thus, there are two worlds: the divine and the material. For Sappho, and other women philosophers, true knowledge was achieved through union and embracing the paradox of opposites. This required imagination, love, and eros. For Plato, it was the separation of the divine and the material through the use of reason that was critical to ascertaining true knowledge.

Plato subscribed to the view that human nature "sins," or misses the mark, when humans do not understand that their true nature is not material but spiritual. The source of understanding this knowledge is where early Christians (some Gnostics) and Platonists differ. For Plato, this knowledge is discerned through the exercise of reason (the elevation of the soul over the body); for non-canonical Christians (Gnostics), this knowledge comes through inner knowledge; for Jews it comes through the Word and interpretation; and for orthodox Christians, it comes through the belief in the death and resurrection of Jesus Christ as the way to salvation (or union with the divine). In Western thought, Plato and his belief in Reason have come to dominate our epistemology, excluding Judaic notions of pedagogy, or those based on paradox, as well as those pedagogies of Sappho that claimed experience as the site for understanding eros and harmony as central to divine knowledge.

Yet, not all Greeks held that knowledge was the result of unification with God. The Sophists avoided speculation about the cosmos and concentrated on human beings, their knowledge, and the practical skills necessary for solving human problems. Once again it is the multiplicity of ideas and cultures that circulated during this time that resulted in diffuse and often contradictory belief systems. Sophists had a humanist philosophy that propounded individual responsibility as well as political and social ones. The fruit of their philosophy was activated conscience and rhetorical maturity. The gods were no longer responsible for earthly actions; individuals were responsible for their own actions and were collectively responsible for the actions of the state. Sophists, since truth for them was relative, held that the main aim of education was to teach the art of practical politics (Block, 2004). Rather than rely on absolutes (notions of the divine), the Sophists desired to solve individual and social problems through drawing on experience. The Sophists held that education ought to enhance political power and was, therefore, intimately tied to the art of persuasion. They answered the question of "In whose image?" by relying on their own human experience. For most philosophers, this question continued to occupy a great deal of thought—specifically, the question of whether both men and women were created in God's image. And for most ancients, the relationship of the body to the soul remained critical. Were both the body and soul created in God's image? For Plato, only the soul was considered to be made in God's image; the body was material and thus derived from elsewhere. For Sappho, the body, desire, and eros were made in God's image and thus were central to understanding the divine. Likewise, the soul, as we have seen, was not understood as a unitary entity. The soul, in fact, not the mind, was understood to be the site of reason. The question of "In whose image?" was to remain at the heart of philosophical and religious debates for the next four centuries. What would emerge in the responses to this question was the central role of gender.

The Image Made Flesh: Early Christianity

> Christianity has been the most dominant religious, social, political and cultural influence on women's lives in the history of western civilization . . . Christianity's understanding of the nature and role of men and women has been the single most influential ingredient in the construction of gender roles and behaviour in western society and its dominions.
>
> *(Deborah Sawyer, 1996)*

The intersection of Greek, Jewish, and Near Eastern thought which collided during early Christianity resulted in a proliferation of thought regarding how humans could reach "homoiosis theoi," or unification with God. While the God of the Greek philosophers is very different from the God of the Jews, they both strove for an understanding of "union." For the Greeks, God was barely aware of the world he had created, whereas the Jewish God was passionately involved in human affairs. The Greeks believed that "reason," and thus their own efforts, would bring union with the divine, while the Jews sought union through revelation and interpretation of the word. Educated pagans looked to philosophy, not religion, for enlightenment (Armstrong, 1993). The Jewish philosopher, Philo, was one philosopher who tried to reconcile his love of Greek philosophy with his Jewish God. While Philo was trying to reconcile his image of God as accessible, with the Greek notions of an impenetrable God, a young Jew, named Jesus, was beginning his career in Palestine that would again present another image of the divine.[14] There was not a belief that Jesus was divine while he was living, and not until well into the 4th century. According to Armstrong (1993), "the development of Christian belief in the Incarnation was a gradual, complex process. Jesus himself certainly never literally claimed to be God" (p. 81). What he did claim was that the whole of the law could be summed up in the ethical obligation to "do unto others as you would have them do unto you." Charity and love, that is actions, not reason or the interpretation of law, would bring union with the divine. God was not a cruel and punishing God, but one that embodied love. For many followers of the time, Jesus led the ideal life, the life that God wants us to lead. He was a model. When people saw Jesus in action "they had a living, breathing image of what God was like" (p. 82). Wisdom came not through reason or the law but through surrender and openness to God. This "faith" in God was available to all—women, the poor, the Gentiles. This radical notion of equality, which suggested that men and women, Jew and Gentile could experience the divine was in sharp contrast to the emerging gender roles that relegated matters of the divine to men.

While Jesus's message was simple and attractive to many (especially women), the consolidation of Christianity with its belief in the incarnation of Christ, his divinity, and virgin birth was complex and took centuries. In a moment I will turn to the Gnostics as one example of the various interpretations of Jesus's life and meaning. By the 4th century CE numerous interpretations were repressed or con-solidated or adapted to create one Christian doctrine. This doctrine (the Nicene Creed) maintains that knowledge/wisdom is the result of believing in Jesus Christ as divine, as a personal savior, and that through meditation on Christ on the cross (death) one can come to understand the love of God. Emulating Christ, as personal savior, as embodied in his love for humanity, is the way to salvation or union with the divine. For the Jews, knowledge was the result of the word, for the Greeks it was reason and for Christians it was the personal experience of Christ. What is "sinful" in all three is "going it alone," thinking independently. Like the story of Adam and Eve, the fall from grace occurs when Eve chose the tree of knowledge rather than rely on an outside, external authority (God). While the myths are different (Persephone for the Greeks, or Adam and Eve for Jews and Christians) the message is the same "do not trust yourself." Knowledge is outside the self, in God, the word, reason, or in the person of Christ. Eisler (1988) maintains that in its strictest sense monotheism resulted in both authoritarianism and male domi-nance that were made possible by this shift in knowledge from an intersubjective, paradoxical worldview in which there was not separation between humans and the divine, or male and female, to one in which knowledge was independent of humans, where authority was placed outside of the inner self. Trusting one's own ability to discern, to imagine, to know became the "sin." This shift in ways of knowing was a radical transformation that not only contributed to the solidification of gender roles, but was central to establishing contemporary and dominant views of knowledge that are linked to control.

While this is the partial legacy of this time period there were of course ruptures, resistances, and paradoxes. The greatest legacy that eventually emerged is that there is only one way of knowing—reason. While it was not until the modern period that the final "death of God" occurred, the seeds had been laid for the time in which reason and reason alone would be heralded as the new God. What is critical is not so much that "reason" prevailed, but that we now have a worldview that assumes this to be the only truth. Reason no longer is an image or a symbol or metaphor, it is understood as truth as absolute. It was this fear of the "law" that Gnostics were so passionate about. I turn to them now as one last example or image of knowing in the ancient world.

Inner Knowing as Image

The death of the teacher Jesus did not result in a cohesive, consolidated Christianity. Rather, for the next 300 years there were numerous and contending schools of Christian thought. The discovery of the Gnostic Gospels in 1945 near the Egyptian town Nag Hammadi provides an alternative tradition to the orthodox Christian interpretation of the words of Jesus. These gospels are quite diverse. What they have in common, however, is the belief that salvation (wisdom) is the result of inner knowing. According to Elaine Pagels (2003), what the Gnostic Gospels, in particular the Gospel of Thomas, encourage Christians to do is "not so much to believe in Jesus, as to seek to know God through one's own, divinely given capacity, since all are created in the image of God" (p. 34). Although there are numerous Gnostic Gospels, I will focus on the Gospel of Mary due to the recent radical revision of much of what, until now, had been accepted interpretations of the early Church and women's participation in it. Biblical scholars, historians and theologians have contributed to the restoration of Mary of Magdalene as chief female disciple, apostle to the apostles, and first witness of the resurrection (Haskins, 1993).[15] Yet, the implications of her Gospel, and Gnosticism in general, have not been examined in relation to curriculum theorizing as modes of knowing.

Early Christianity, or as some understood it at the time, Jewish renewal, provided a contrast to both Platonic, Judaic, Sapphoist, and Greek Mystic thought. Yet, early Christian thought was not monolithic and it was not until the 4th century CE under Constantine at the Council of Nicea that Christian theology was unified and canonized. The image for Jewish thought was the word, for Platonic thought it was reason, for Sappho it was experience, for orthodox Christianity the teacher Jesus, and for Gnostics it was inner knowing. Gnosis signaled the turn from Socratic sobriety and Platonic epistemology back toward myth (Gawonski, 1995: 24). For orthodox Jews and Christians, the relationship of self and other (God) is one of separation. They insist that a chasm separates humanity from its creator: God is wholly other. Consequently, knowledge or wisdom cannot come directly from God, but for the Jews comes through the word, and for orthodox Christians, through the teacher Jesus. According to Pagels (1979), the Gnostics contradict this: self-knowledge is knowledge of God; the self and the divine are identical. What distinguishes gnostic thought (and, to some degree, Sappho's thought) and its epistemology is the lack of the subject/object dichotomy. This "lack" is an epistemology that is not predicated on separation of male/female (gender), divine/human, or heaven/earth as the starting point of wisdom.

Gnostics, from the Greek word *gnosis*, usually translates as "knowledge"(Leloup, 2002: xix). While those who claim to know nothing about ultimate reality are called agnostic (literally, not knowing), the person who does claim to know such things is called gnostic (knowing). But gnosis is not primarily rational knowledge. The Greek language distinguishes between scientific or reflective knowledge (he knows mathematics) and knowledge through observation or experience (he knows me), which is gnosis. As the Gnostics use the term, we could translate it as "insight," for gnosis involves an intuitive process of knowing oneself. And to know oneself, they claimed, is to know human nature and human destiny. Yet to know oneself, at the deepest level, is simultaneously to know God; this is the secret of gnosis (Pagels, 1979: xx).

The Gnostic Gospels, of which the most well known are the Gospel of Thomas and the Gospel of Mary, comprise part of the early Christian writings or apostolic writings that did not become part of the official doctrine of the Catholic Church and were, in fact, suppressed writings. This accounts for the fact that their discovery has prompted a radical rethinking of early Christian thought and theology. Although Gnosticism had a wide reach in the early centuries after Christ's death, I will focus below on the Gospel of Mary. In part, this is to include women as early philosophers and theologians. Educational philosophy texts often include Jesus or St. Augustine, yet they have not included Mary Magdalene or other early Christian women thinkers.

Gnosticism was one interpretation of early Christianity that differed from mainstream Christianity primarily due to the significance mainstream Christians placed on the death and resurrection of Jesus and the meaning of salvation. The literal resurrection of Jesus, was not as important to the Gnostics as was the life of Jesus as teacher and mediator of divine revelation (King, 2003). According to Pagels (1979), the Gnostics insisted that the resurrection was not "a unique event in the past: instead it symbolized how Christ's presence could be experienced in the present. What mattered was not literal seeing, but spiritual vision" (p. 11). According to Leloup (2002),

> The resurrection can be seen neither with the eyes of the flesh, nor with the eyes of the soul (psyche). This vision is no hallucination, nor is it any sort of fantasy linked to sensory, psychic or mental stimulation. Rather it is a vision of the nous—a dimension often forgotten in our anthropologies. In the ancient world, the nous was seen as the "finest point of the soul" or as some might say today the "angel of the soul." It gives us access to that intermediate realm between the purely sensory and the purely spiritual, which Henry Corbin so eloquently names as the *imaginal*. (p. 14)

For the Gnostics, the focus was on spiritual knowledge. This knowledge was an inner knowing that was mediated by *nous* or mind. *Nous* was understood as the dimension that mediated the in-between space of soul and spirit, body and mind, self and other, God and human. This dimension was an imaginal space in which "homoiosis theoi" or unification with God, could be envisioned. While neo-platonism also strove for unification, the mistrust of the body and its perceptions situated the site of enlightenment strictly within reason and rationality. The early Neoplatonists considered life on earth inferior to a life free from the body and its surroundings in the material world. The job of the soul is to free man from his earthly desires and get in touch with the intelligible world (heaven) and transcend life on earth. The focus of the Gnostics on mediating between body and soul, in contrast with the Neoplatonists, situates knowing as an intersubjective process of the imaginal.

Inner Knowing

> Become contented and agreeable in the presence of that other image of nature.
>
> *(Gospel of Mary, 3: 1)*

It is this focus on spiritual or imaginary vision that distinguished gnostic episte-mology from that of Platonic, Judaic, and other early Christian thought. According to the Gospel of Mary, Mary Magdalene, seeing the Lord in a vision, asked him, "How does he who sees the vision see it? [Through] the soul, [or] through the spirit?" He answered that the visionary perceives through the mind (Pagels, 1979: 11). Gnostic writers do not dismiss visions as hallucinations or fantasies; rather, they respect such experiences as events "through which spiritual intuition discloses insight into the nature of reality" (p. 12).

According to Jean-Yves Leloup (2002), the Gospel of Mary is witness to an altogether different mode of understanding that the masculine mind typically overlooks: "a domain of prophetic or visionary knowledge that, though certainly not exclusive to women, definitely partakes of the feminine principle, and is some-times known as the angelic or Eastern dimension of human knowledge" (p. 13). In the Gospel of Mary, Mary asks her teacher whether one receives a vision by the soul or the spirit. Jesus replies:

> a person does not see with the soul or with the spirit, rather with the mind which exists between these two. It is clear that Jesus the teacher is describing the tripartite composition of the true inner self; it is made of soul, mind and spirit. The mind conveys the vision, functioning as a mediator between the spirit and the soul.
>
> *(King, 2003: 64)*

Following Corbin (1990), we could say that in the Gospel of Mary we are freed from the dilemma of thought versus extension (Descartes), as well as from a cosmology and epistemology limited to either empirical observation or intellectual understanding. Between these two lies a "vast intermediate realm of image and representation that is just as ontologically real as the worlds of sense and intellect" (Corbin, 1990: 14).

What is real is the spiritual, not the material. Here Gnosticism was, perhaps, influenced by Eastern thought. The material world is not real. According to Leloup (2002),

> A living deity who wants to communicate thus necessitates an intermediate realm between God and human, between the visible and invisible . . . it is in this intermediary realm that Mary has her meeting with the resurrected Christ. . . . as with the ancient prophets, God activates the necessary vision-ary, imaginal forms in her, so as to bring her to the Divine. (p. 15)

Here we go beyond any metaphysical opposition of subject vs. object. We are in the presence of the metaphysics of openness—a place of meeting, confrontation, and merging of subject and object known in their interdependence. Reality is neither objective nor subjective; it is an "inclusive third state where the two imaginally become one" (Leloup, 2002: 16). This reveals a field that has been little explored by contemporary philosophies, which still oscillate between the meta-physics of Being (Heidegger) and of Otherness (Levinas). The Gospel of Mary prompts us to be engaged with a philosophy of openness, or the in-between realm, a third space in which the physical and metaphysical are interrelated.

Gnostic thought has several implications for curriculum theorizing. Gnostic thought is a process oriented belief system. It is understood that God, or Good, or knowledge is beyond comprehension; it is a mystery. An understanding that absolute knowledge (metaphysical) does not exist shifts the focus of knowledge from the metaphysical to the everyday, practical knowing embodied within the individual. As Autio (2009) explains, Gnostics rejected the idea that there was a consistent divine plan for the world. This rejection of a predetermined cosmology reflected their belief in the human ability to discern understanding and knowledge from within rather than to seek the existential authorization from outside authorities. Knowledge can be found within the individual. However, for the Gnostics, the individual was not merely an empty vessel waiting to be "enlightened" or filled with spirit. Understand-ing or knowledge was a process of inner knowing that was based on continual dialogue. Autio goes so far as to suggest that it is in René Descartes' (1596–1650) theory of knowledge that "the Gnostic initiative of a self-assured, human-centered and individualistic tones of existence came to full fruition" (p. 78). The Gnostic belief in the capacity of the individual to discern through "inner knowing" is clearly shared by Descartes. However, I would maintain that the process of discernment engaged by Descartes (one grounded in pure reason) was not reflected by many Gnostics. Particularly in the Gospel of Mary, the process of inner knowing is one characterized by ongoing dialogue in which the physical and metaphysical necessitates a third space, a space in which knowing is always in flux, in process.

This contradictory/paradoxical or in-between space in which humans strive for self-knowledge while knowing that they will never know is what characterizes the Gnosticism of Mary as a form of spiritual knowing.[16] I call it spiritual or imaginal knowing. At the heart of this epistemology is the ability to embrace paradox and contradiction. Unlike the Platonists and later Descartes, knowledge is not grounded in reason that seeks to uncover laws and universals. Paradoxical knowledge, because it is both/and, is the tension that creates spaces for imaginal vision and thought. Knowing is not the product of rationality, law, or science, it is what emerges in the process of negotiating the in-between spaces that are created in dialogue between the self/other, human/divine, male/female, conscious/unconscious, and earth/heaven.

According to Karen King (2003), "throughout the journey of the soul toward comprehension, dialogue is key" (p. 31). Dialogue is the primary form of instruction because it insists on active participation. For the Gospel of Mary, this active participation was the dialogue between the teacher (Jesus) and the student. The model for this dialogue is the ancient ideal of a pedagogical relationship in which the "teacher's words and acts comprise a model to which the disciple ought to conform" (p. 31). Unlike Judaic tradition where dialogue occurs between the text and the student, early Christian thought was deeply suspicious of writing if it was detached from the intimate relationship between teacher and student. For early Christians, especially Gnostics, Jesus (the word made flesh) and not scripture was the truest revelation of God. In the Gospel of Mary, communion with God was the consequence of a dialogical relationship with the teacher. The message of the dialogue, according to King, is that "relationship is fundamental to salvation, both between the teacher and the student and that formed among the disciples in community of faith and their mission" (p. 32). Rather than accept an external authority, students are to engage in the process of ongoing relationships. It is being present to the *relationship and relations* (the heart of the student/teacher encounter) that creates spaces for discovery and ultimately freedom.

Spiritual or inner knowledge comes from dialogic relationship, not from the word. This distrust of writing is closely linked to Gnostics' distrust of the law or any external authority that would inhibit inner spiritual knowledge. According to the Gospel of Mary, 4: 9–10, Jesus said, "Do not lay down any rule beyond what I have determined for you, nor promulgate law like the lawgiver, or else you might be dominated by it" (King, 2003: 52). Spiritual knowing cannot be achieved through external regulation. Consequently, the concept of sin takes on a different meaning in the Gnostic gospels. In the Gospel of Mary it is recounted that Peter asks Jesus "What is the sin of the world?" Jesus answers:

There is no sin.
It is you who make sin exist,
When you act according to the habits

Of your corrupted nature;
This is where sin lies.

(King, 2003: 13)

Sin is the condition of human estrangement from God/the divine. When humans are not connected to their divine natures, that is understood as sin. Sin is the result of attachment to the material world. To be separate is sinful. As I have stated, the original Greek meaning of the word sin was to "miss the mark." For the Gnostics, it was understood that following the desires of the material world instead of nurturing the spiritual self is the sin. Original sin occurred in the Garden of Eden, where Adam and Eve chose to eat of the tree of knowledge (not the tree of life) and thus came to know their separateness from God. Symbolically, this signifies human consciousness. This separation, according to the Gnostics, does not signify "evil" but is part of the human journey in which we engage in a continual process of separation (death) and connection (life).

For the Gnostics, then, sin has little or nothing to do with Eve. In fact, for the Gnostics, God is both male and female (Gospel of Thomas) or beyond gender. The theological basis for Gnostic thought "lies in understanding that the body is not the true self; the true self is spiritual and nongendered, even as the divine is nonmaterial and nongendered" (King, 2003: 62). Consequently, in order to achieve spiritual knowing one must abandon the distinctions of the flesh, including sex and gender.

For non-orthodox Christians, human beings' true nature (or self) is not material, but spiritual. However, the total erasure of the body has been problematic for many, including orthodox Christians as well as feminists whose concern is that the lived experiences of the body become negated. Orthodox Christianity, according to Pagels (1979), "implicitly affirms bodily experience as a central fact of human life" (p. 101). Bodily experience—eating, drinking, sexual experiences, or the experiences of torture and suffering—are all part of one's religious experience. In particular, the martyrs, the thousands of early Christians who were brutally killed, identified their bodily suffering with Christ's bodily suffering on the cross. Their bodies did experience insufferable pain and that experience was a religious one.

In the orthodox Christian view, the whole person, body and soul, should turn to God. The Platonic split between the body and soul results in a devaluation of the mortal body in favor of the immortal soul. This privileging of the soul functions to delegitimate the human experience. Especially when the body is that associated with women, the privileging of the soul over the body becomes a way to erase women's experiences. For Plato, the form of man was clearly imagined as a male image; women were deviations from the ideal male norm, in effect because we have bodies that are central to shaping our experiences. (Christ is born by a human body, signifiying the importance of the body, as well as female body. In fact, theologically, Mary did not need a man.) This distinction in thought between Platonic/non-orthodox Christian and early Christian thought will be taken up again in greater detail in the next chapter which addresses the concept of embodied knowing as central to women religious in the Middle Ages.

As feminists have suggested, the body is also central to social and political action. Women's experiences of rape, sexual harassment, and objectification are real experiences that can be delegitimated when the body is not taken seriously. And although Gnostic thought might lead one to conclude that its focus on inner knowing and imagination might obscure bodily, material as well as political action, King (2003) is adamant that the Gospel of Mary is not aimed at nihilism, "but at cultivating an uncompromising, utopian vision of spiritual perfection and peace rooted in the divine Good, beyond the constraints of time and matter and false morality. Social criticism and spiritual development were irrevocably linked together in this vision" (p. 78). One might see it as an escapist ideology due to its focus on interior spiritual development, yet the mythic framework of the Gospel of Mary allows the spiritual, the psychological, the social, the political, and the cosmic to be integrated under one guiding principle; resistance to unjust and illegitimate powers (p. 79). Yet, for orthodox Christians, the focus on God as creator and on humanity as created precluded that humans could find God within themselves. Instead humans needed to be "enlightened by divine revelation—by means of the Scriptures and the faith proclaimed in the church" (Pagel, 1979: 122). This difference between Gnostics' focus on inner knowing and orthodox Christians focus on Jesus as mediator of knowledge because he was divine has had profound implications for Western epistemology. As Platonic and orthodox Christian thought became codified, the split between public and private, soul and body, and divine and human became more solidified. While Neoplatonic thought and Gnostic thought differed on the exact role of the soul, what they shared was the understanding that knowledge of the divine was not capable of being expressed and defined clearly and logically. According to Armstrong (1993), "religious insights had an inner resonance that could only be apprehended by each individual in his own time during what Plato had called *theoria*, contemplation" (p. 114). All knowledge of the divine (wisdom) required a third space, a third eye, an imaginal space or as Gregory of Nysaa expressed it a vision "pure of any concept." Ultimately, Gnostics claim that God can never be understood intellectually. It was this belief that eventually divided the church. Eastern Christianity was to remain much more grounded in mystical traditions that sought to prevent God from becoming too rational. In Western Christianity, theoria or theory no longer implies contemplation, but instead means a rational hypothesis that must be logically demonstrated. This differentiation was to profoundly shape Western epistemology.

This split in the early Christian Church resulted in the West constructing its own dogma. Central to the solidification of the early Western Christian Church was the focus on establishing Christ's absolute divinity since this allowed the Church to consolidate absolute power due to the abstract (disembodied) nature of the divine. This divine nature of Christ, his absolute separateness from humans, in which man is understood as evil, required salvation. This redemption was the role of the Church, as the bride of Christ. In this vision of Western Christianity, the individual as knower and inner knowing are dangerous and ultimately heretical (or hysteric, female). While the early Church had been quite positive for women, by the 3rd century, orthodox Christianity had solidified the following beliefs: 1) despite Jesus's message of spiritual equality women were seen as spiritually inferior to men; 2) the Gospels were reduced to the four canonical scriptures (Matthew, Mark, Luke, and John) excluding those written by the Gnostics and women; 3) the Gnostic belief that knowledge of God was directly accessible through experience was replaced by the belief that access to the deity necessitated the intervention of a religious hierarchy (in other words, authority was external); and 4) evil, associated with woman and the body, was seen as central to the creation story. Ultimately woman signified by the body was understood as unholy, unclean, and sinful and this legitimated patriarchal power and authority.

From the perspective of curriculum theory, the poetic wisdom of the ancients and the Gnostics was lost (Fleener, 2005). Knowledge, which had been understood as process, interaction, paradox, and imaginal was now understood as transmission. This resulted in "experience" and inner knowing and imaginal knowing being excluded as sites of knowing. In 529 CE, the ancient school of philosophy in Athens was closed by the emperor Justinian and Western Europe closed itself off from the intellectual traditions of the East. As a result of this separation, orthodox Christianity solidified its canonical beliefs and developed a patriarchal and hierarchical organization (Fiorenza, 1983). As a consequence, not only have early Christian (100–600 CE) women theorists and writers like Mary Magdalene, Thecla, Perpetua, Macrina, Paula, and Egeria been forgotten, but their *image* of Christianity as egalitarian, of women as knowers, and personal experience as central to knowing has been excluded from understandings of curriculum theory (Oden, 1994; Trousdale, 2007). By 600 CE it was commonly understood that "man" was created in God's image, woman was a derivation. Yet, beginning in the 6th century both men and women religious sought to recuperate the body and experience as a site of knowing as well as returning to an understanding of the divine as both male and female or outside of gender. Thus in the next chapter, I turn to the concept of "embodied" knowing.

Reflections

Technical, methodological, material and scientific images have for some time dominated, constraining our thoughts about education, aimed at overcoming or solving life's difficulty and ambiguity, rather than giving voice to them and entering into them in faith. Honored in this, is the letter of the law, instead of the spirit of the Word.

(Molly Quinn, 2001)

Imaginal knowing is not something of the past. As Molly Quinn suggests, the images on which we base our understandings of knowledge have just radically changed. The notion of paradox, the rejection of dualisms, the focus on imagination, intuition, and inner knowing have been dismissed in exchange for faith in external marks of knowledge: the word, the text, the law. This binary is one that is deeply gendered. The imaginal world characterized by unknowing, paradox, mystery, intersubjectivity, being, and awe is one that is not "controlled" and not controllable. Education as we know it is consumed with control and its corollary—method (Doll, 2005). Imaginal knowing prompts us to reconsider the limits of control, to re-imagine the very purpose of knowledge.

Recently, the work of Maxine Greene, Dwayne Huebner, and Ted Aoki speak to the imagination and inner knowing as central to wisdom and a sense of awe that is necessary for learning. The sense of spirit and process with its focus on the evolution of the soul is also central to the work of Bateson, Wittgenstein, Hegel, Nietzsche, and Heidegger. Imaging, as a way of knowing, cannot be relegated to the past. To create images is central to the human experience—it is what makes us human. We continue to ask "In whose image?" and "For what purpose?" Curriculum understood as image is a never-ending dialogue.

3

EMBODYING CURRICULUM

As if an instant I learn what I know . . .

(Hildegard of Bingen, 1098–1179)

Love makes me wander outside myself.
Where shall I find something of Love
According to my heart's delight,
So that I may sweeten my pain?
Although I attend her school,
She will not agree with me in anything.
In a moment this becomes all too clear to me
Alas! I speak from heart's distress;
My misfortune is too great,
And for me, to do without Love is a death,
Since I cannot have fruition of her.

(Hadewijch of Antwerp, 13th century)

The important thing is not to think much but to love much; and so do that which best stirs you to love.

(Teresa of Avila, 1515–1582)

Let a woman learn in silence with all submissiveness. I permit no woman to teach or to have authority over men; she is to keep silent. For Adam was formed first, then Eve; and Adam was not deceived, but the woman was deceived and became a transgressor.

(St. Paul, I Tim. 2: 11–14)

The 12th to 15th centuries saw an unprecedented number of female mystics (Bynum, 1992). Against Paul's dictate that women should not speak, teach, or have authority, women religious transgressed gender norms. Although mysticism was not a new phenomenon, the concentration of female mystics within this time period is significant. And yet, while female mystics outnumbered male mystics, we are undoubtedly more familiar with St. Augustine of Hippo, St. Bernard of Clairvoux, St. Francis of Assisi, St. Thomas Aquinas, or Meister Eckhart than with Hildegard of Bingen, Julian of Norwich, Mechthild of Magdeburg, Hadewijch of Antwerp, or Teresa of Avila. Both men and women religious claimed the body as a site of knowing during the medieval period. Yet, whereas men religious focused on the liberation of the soul from the body, women experienced the body not as a container from which to free the soul, but as limitless possibility.

Medieval society was one dominated by the Roman Catholic Church. Beginning with St. Augustine of Hippo (354–430 CE), whose *Confessions* was the first spiritual autobiography, the question of "how can the human soul, united as it is with a body subject to time, change, and mortality, make contact with its divine spiritual source" became a critical question faced by theologians in the medieval period (Colish, 1997: 29).[1] Christian theology had followed, for the most part, a Neoplatonic metaphysical view of the divine. Only through reason could union be achieved. The body was a problem to overcome. As early as St. Paul and later St. Augustine, as well as St. Thomas Aquinas (1225–1274 CE), the inferior, defective, and physical imperfection of women was based on her "biologically determined preference for sensation over reason" (Glenn, 1997). Women were seen as incapable of reason.[2] Reduced to the body, medieval women were to remain silent. This historical devaluation of women's experience has resulted in women mystics not being taken seriously as thinkers and philosophers who theorized about who can be a knower, what can be known, and how we come to know. Consequently, this chapter takes seriously women mystics as philosophers who experienced mysticism as a way through which they could authorize themselves as knowers and establish embodiment as a way of knowing.

While the early Christian Church had held a view of inclusion of women rather than exclusion, the medieval Church was based on a gender hierarchy. Women had participated in monastic life from the 4th to the 12th centuries and emerged in the 13th century as leaders in a resurgence of institutional piety, although they had always been excluded from philosophical debate and from leadership roles. The emphasis in the late medieval period on Christ's humanity (rather than his divinity) resulted in a link between female spirituality and the body of Christ.[3] Like women, Christ nurtured, fed, and comforted as well as suffered. The focus on Christ's human suffering, culminating in the crucifixion, and the life-saving bread and blood of his body, were a profound reminder of the bodily nature of the divine. "Given that medieval thought associated masculinity with mind and spirit and femininity with the body, women with all their inferiority and subordination, could be felt to have a special connection with Jesus in his Passion, and through their bodies they could hope to have special access to the sacredness associated with his body" (Spearing, 2002: xi). As Carolyn Bynum (1992) has suggested, "bodiliness provides access to the sacred" (p. 186). This focus on Christ's humanity paralleled the emergence of Mary, mother of Jesus, as a site of worship. Mary also signified bodily, procreative powers, because her body was the vehicle for redemption. Mary became exalted as the Holy Mother, and in some cases as Wisdom or Sophia. These shifts created a space in which both women and men religious could revision the body as a site of knowing. Still, the ways in which women religious could recuperate the body as a site of knowing were significantly different from those of men. While both men and women religious engaged in disciplining the body through fasting and prayer as a way in which to transcend the physical to apprehend the divine, women's bodily manipulations were not circumscribed by repressing the body, but also sought pleasure and rapture as means to express desire and union with the divine (Bynum, 1992). It is the complex ways in which the body became the site for a discourse of knowing that this chapter explores.

Myth, Mysticism, and Mystery

According to Karen Armstrong (1993), there is a linguistic connection between the three words "myth," "mysticism," and "mystery." They are each derived from the Greek verb *musteion*: to close the eyes or the mouth. The experience of darkness and silence is central to knowledge. It is perhaps no coincidence then that women turned to mysticism. Mystical experience was the direct knowledge of God through inspiration, divine revelation, and intuition.[4] Knowing was not solely an "idea," resulting from abstract, linear, objective thought; it was an experience, an unmediated experience of God. In rejecting rationality as the sole means of knowing, mysticism opened spaces for other ways of knowing and being. For women mystics, it was the direct experience of God through and in the body that created a space in which they could legitimate and validate their lived experience. In other words, a disturbance of, in and through the body was the site through which knowing took place. Their knowledge came through bodily experiences, including illness, visions, and disturbances such as stigmata, mystical lactation, pregnancies, and catatonic trances. The significance of this epistemological shift to the body is apparent in light of the traditional association of the body as female, in opposition to mind as male, and in light of mainstream religious beliefs that the body, in particular the female body, was the site of sin. To resignify the body as a site of knowing is to claim women as knowers. By taking up the body as a site of knowing, women religious contested dominant expectations of who could be a knower as well as what could be known. This chapter focuses on medieval women religious and their experiences of the body as a site of knowing. I will pay particular attention to Hildegard of Bingen, Mechthild of Magdeburg, Julian of Norwich, and Teresa of Avila, all of whom received their visions in tandem with bodily experiences. Through their visions, these mystics legitimated themselves as knowers and were able to make knowledge claims that contested normative gender roles.

Situating Mysticism

Mysticism has a long tradition both within Christianity and other world religions. Within Western Christian tradition, the mystic is seen as having direct access to God. Historically, especially within the medieval period, being a mystic conferred considerable authority on an individual. What was defined as mystical experience and who was considered a mystic was, then, of considerable import since a person who claimed direct knowledge of God was in a position to challenge any form of authority which he or she saw as incompatible with the divine will. In the Middle Ages, the experiencing of mystical visions was not an unusual form of knowing. Women mystics' claims as knowers were legitimated not only because of their direct access to God, but because God in his divine wisdom spoke to them in profound bodily ways. It is perhaps inconceivable for us to imagine as legitimate Hadewijch of Antwerp's vision of her bodily union with Christ as real, much less as a site for theorizing how we come to know. Though this is what she did in her "School of Love" poems in which she puts love before reason as the source of coming to know the divine. Our skepticism toward mystics is certainly understandable. Our perception of the universe as "controlled, atomistic and one-dimensional is in stark contrast to the chaotic, holistic and multi-dimensional reality" within which men and women of the Middle Ages lived (Flinders, 1993: 84). As inheritors of the enlightenment project, the Western cultural heritage is grounded in a Kantian notion of knowledge which maintains that "human knowledge can never extend to knowledge of things as they are in themselves, the best we can hope for is accurate knowledge of things as they appear to us. Knowledge of God, must therefore remain forever beyond human capability" (Jantzen, 1995: 7). According to Gerda Lerner (1993), mysticism, a tradition preceding Christianity, allowed for another mode of cognition. Lerner writes,

> mysticism asserted that transcendent knowledge came not as a product of rational thought, but as a result of a way of life, of individual inspiration and sudden revelatory insight. Mystics saw human beings, the world, the universe in a state of relatedness, open to understanding by intuitive and immediate perception. (p. 124)

God was accessible not through reason, but through unconditional love and concentrated dedication manifested through sincere prayers and religious devotion. Central to mystical experience was the profound, unexplainable way in which God shared his knowledge through mind (reason), body (physical), and soul (spiritual). Thus, the study of medieval mystics throws into relief our taken-for-granted assumptions about how we come to know and who can be a knower. In other words, it becomes apparent that there is nothing "natural" about our current epistemological beliefs that locate reason as the "soul" means of knowing.

However, as more and more women began to claim visionary gifts, the more suspect this form of knowing became. Ultimately it was considered hysteria and heretical. What had been a way through which women could claim themselves as knowers was, by the 15th and 16th centuries, considered taboo. It is perhaps no coincidence that by the late Middle Ages, universities, with their emphasis on rationality were challenging knowledge claims based on mystical experience. By the 15th century female mystics, previously revered for their wisdom, were burned at the state as heretics (one exception was Marguerite Porete who was burned in 1310 for insisting on teaching her ideas in public). While mystical visions had at the time been considered "natural" or normal female behavior, they were considered the work of the devil in the 15th century. In the early 20th century, the vision of these mystics (more likely defined as hysterics) were interpreted as the result of psychological imbalances. Modern philosophers' preoccupation with the psychological states of consciousness of mystics is, according to Grace Jantzen (1995), a serious distortion of what the mystics themselves desired. The epistemological shifts women mystics were forging (the body as a site of knowing) reflect how ways of knowing and who counts as a knower are continually gendered and culturally and historically situated. Consequently, female mystical experience provides a window into the ways in which women have struggled to authorize themselves as knowers.

Despite the eventual suppression of mysticism, women mystics of the 12th to 15th centuries found the authority to speak, write, teach, and influence people. And they were not merely content to claim their experience as valid. They challenged deeply entrenched Church doctrines that contested normative gender roles by actually reinscribing gender in more complex and destabilizing ways. As Lerner (1993: 88) suggests, this took a variety of forms: 1) the development of a female God, language, and symbolism; 2) the re-conceptualization of the divine as both male and female; 3) women's direct intervention in redemption and salvation; and 4) a deliberate and often scholarly feminist Bible criticism. While these challenges suggest an oppositional ideology, it is especially the contradictory ways in which these reconceptualizations simultaneously functioned as subversion and as a form of accommodation that is of interest to me. In exploring these in-between spaces, a deeper understanding of the complex intersections of gender, the body, and ways of knowing can be illuminated.

Handmaidens or Heretics: Religious Life in the Middle Ages

From our current perspective, the choice to give one's life to the Church is hardly considered as a radical or liberatory act and even less a feminist act. However, in the early Middle Ages when a young woman of Christian parents would have been expected to marry and produce children, the decision to embrace perpetual virginity could have been an act of resistance to cultural norms for women. In choosing religious life, a woman would not be bound in obedience to a husband, and she would not be repeatedly pregnant and giving birth. We must also remember that being a nun was a site of privilege. Monastic life was primarily for the nobility since the Church required a dowry just as if it were a marriage arrangement. For women, who could not own property, being unmarried or a widow, often left them with few alternatives except the convent. The Church required funds to house, clothe, and feed those who entered its institutions. The poor might enter but they would retain their status as serfs or servant, never as equals with those of the nobility.

In the early Middle Ages, formal learning could be acquired only through tutors or in religious institutions. For a woman with intellectual interests, the convent provided access to books, literacy, leadership opportunities, and a "room of her own." Jantzen (1995) suggests "the extent to which such women were asserting their freedom in a Christian alternative to oppressive cultural patterns should not be underestimated" (p. 58). However, despite the liberatory potential of the Church for women, this alternative must always be seen as existing within a deeply patriarchal institution. The Church circumscribed women's lives in different ways. Essentially, women were considered inferior. Women were considered to have a weaker mind and intellect, to be more subject to emotions and sexual temptations and to be the cause of evil. While they could be baptized, receive penance and communion, attend mass and be buried, they could not participate in the public sacramental life of the Church, hear confession, or grant absolution and they could not preach, teach, or give the sacraments. *The Ancrene Riwle* (Salu, 1955), which laid out the rules to be followed by anchoresses, is quite clear in its reminder that St. Paul forbade women to preach: "I suffer not women to teach." Women who felt themselves called to teach or write had to find a way to legitimate this forbidden act. However, within these conscriptions, women were able to push the boundaries of gender norms and expectations. It is within this context that visions provided a source of authority for women.

In the 7th century more women entered monastic life than ever before, primarily due to the conversion to Christianity of Anglo-Saxons and Franks. In Britain, Hilda of Whitby (614–680 CE) founded several convents, but is best known for becoming the abbess of Whitby, a double monastery (both men and women) famous for its learning. Education was strongly valued since Hilda believed that in order to live by scripture one had to know scripture (Bauer, 1996). Hilda hosted the Synod of Whitby in 664 CE which brought together the Celtic and Roman branches of the Church of her time. Throughout the Middle Ages, royal and noble women founded and endowed convents, in which the daughters of nobility and some of the poor received an education in religion, Latin, reading, writing, simple arithmetic, and chants. Girls also received domestic training and instruction in needlework. Nunneries might specialize in fine embroidery or in the transcription and illuminating of manuscripts.

The 10th and 11th centuries were marked by the birth of religious communities (Cluny in France, St. Francis and St. Clare in Italy) that sought reform to the institutionalized Church. Several famous canonical abbeys were founded in Saxony which developed a tradition of female scholarship, resulting in literary figures like Hrosvitha of Gandersheim (930–990 CE) known as the "German Sappho." Familiar with classical and religious texts, Hrosvitha composed in Latin legends of the saints, epics, poetry, and plays. "Her legends of exemplary saints and her plays counter the images of weak corruptible women that she found in the secular and religious literature" (Anderson & Zinsser, 1988: 186). Writing against the dominant narratives of women as submissive, her storylines provide women with ways in which not only to achieve power but also salvation. These storylines include the power of virginity, salvation through martyrdom, and drawing on women's history. Her focus on women's agency, and women as the central characters that move the plot forward as they claim their bodies as their own (especially against rape which is central to her stories), highlights how within this historical context, virginity functioned as a form of resistance.

As the medieval period "progressed," changes occurred. The large double monasteries with powerful abbesses ceased to exist and the restrictions on women within the Church increased. During this period, women religious sought other means through which to assert themselves and their understanding of the world. Mysticism became one of those ways. Although mystical experience cannot be generalized, especially since the women mystics I will discuss cover different countries and time periods, there are several common elements. First, they all worked within the confines of the Catholic Church while being critics of it. Their agency was directed to shaping the Church as an embodiment of the life of Christ. This meant that they felt called to critique Church corruption and decadence, gender inequality, and the hierarchical nature of the Church. Second, despite having ideas of their own, they consistently claimed that they were unlearned or unlettered. Had they claimed themselves as the source of their ideas, they would not have been taken seriously or worse would have been accused of heresy. In claiming that their knowledge came from God, through mystical experience, they deferred their own agency, thus complying with dominant gender norms, which ironically allowed them to have authority because it came from God. Thus their strategy of deferring their agency allowed them ultimately to subvert gender norms by critiquing 1) the male dominated hierarchy of the Church that descended through God, the king, and to husband; 2) the handmaid role of the Virgin Mary in relation to the father and son; and 3) the notion of a tripartite God (the Trinity) that included no female component. Lastly, they shared a holistic notion of spirituality that claimed that body, mind, and spirit were each essential to experiencing the divine. Their vision of women as knowers, as the divine as beyond gender, and as personal experience (particularly bodily knowing) as central to knowing took up many of the themes of the early Christian women discussed in the previous chapter. While taking up similar themes, the vastly different historical, political, and cultural contexts resulted in very different rhetorical strategies, ones that drew on the body to radically shift taken-for-granted epistemological foundations.

Hildegard of Bingen: Sybil of the Rhine

Situated on the Rhine River, the current-day Abbey of St. Hildegard is in the midst of vineyards on the sloping hills that rise to form the Rhine Valley of Central Germany. The abbey rises like a phoenix from the gently rolling hills and is a testament to the stature of the nun who was considered one of the most learned women of the 12th century. According to Lerner (1993), Hildegard "exemplifies the breakthrough of a female genius who managed to create an entirely new role for herself and other women without, ostensibly, violating the patriarchal confines within which she functioned" (p. 52). Not only did she build a strong female religious leadership, but she also left an original body of writing (which ranged from scientific to musical to theological) which was influential for several centuries. She was a pioneer in combining spirituality, moral authority, and public activism to create what was to become a new civic role for women.

Born in 1098, in Bermersheim in the Rhineland between Mainz and Trier, the tenth child of a noble family, she quickly distinguished herself as a gifted and unusual girl who was highly strung, keenly intelligent, plagued by recurrent illness, and uncannily able to foretell coming events. She recalled later in her life that she began to receive visions at the age of three, which she described as a "brightness so great that her soul trembled." Her precarious health and visionary gifts, two phenomena which it seems were linked, most likely resulted in her parents' decision to dedicate her as a tithe to God. She arrived at the flourishing Disibodenberg Abbey, a Benedictine monastery, in 1106, at age eight, where she came under the tutelage of the highborn anchoress, Jutta of Sponheim. The cloister was at the time 400 years old, although it had emerged as a double monastery only since the arrival of Jutta. Under her supervision, Hildegard learned reading and writing, liturgy and singing. Her further education was entrusted to the monk Volmar of St. Disibod, who would become her lifelong friend, confidant, and secretary. In the enclosed, self-sufficient world of Disibodenberg, Hildegard was for a time isolated from the distractions of a tumultuous world in which papal schisms, Church corruption, and constant warfare were the norm of the day. During this time, Hildegard was able to devote herself to her studies and intellectual pursuits.

Her writing reflects that she must have been well educated in literature, biblical exegesis, philosophy, astrology, natural sciences, and music. She was well acquainted with the Latin Bible and stated that she heard the divine voice of God speaking in Latin. She was an avid reader who was familiar enough with Boethius' *Consolation of Philosophy* to quote from it freely; her mystical works show a Neoplatonic influence and her knowledge of the Scriptures was exhaustive, and their influence pervades her writing. In addition, she gained knowledge of plants and their medicinal purposes. Yet, as her fame grew, she felt compelled to act on her belief that it was the responsibility of the Church to act as a regenerator of society and that the cure for social ills was a more active faith. For Hildegard, a more active faith meant becoming a critic of the Church and voicing her opinion to the leaders of the time regarding corruption and bad governance. She warned Pope Anastasius that he was neglecting justice and threatened the Holy Roman Emperor, Frederick Barbarossa, who fell out with Hildegard regarding the papal schism. Confirmed by the Church in 1148 to have the gift of prophecy, Hildegard was widely read and sought out by leaders for advice. Her influence with leaders of the day made her extraordinary, but it was her holistic, integrated vision of the cosmos, nature, and humankind as central to creation that was groundbreaking in theological terms.

On the whole, the 12th century experienced a renaissance of spirituality, a flowering of optimism, confidence in the individual, and emphasis on life. A spirit of inquiry and intellectual growth and renewed confidence in Christian ideas was accompanied by a new respect for the intensity of personal religious experience to be found in monastic life. In this environment, in which monastic life was dedicated to coming to know the divine, Hildegard established a community in which mind (dedication to learning), body (the regulation of which was also the domain of the Church), and soul (prayer and mediation) were each cultivated.

As the cloister at Disibodenberg became renowned, the number of female obulates grew. When Jutta died in 1136, Hildegard, then 38, was the unanimous choice of the nuns to become the abbess. It is little wonder that this atmosphere was conducive to Hildegard developing her own thought and paying increased attention to her visions. In 1141, at age 42, she experienced a vision of blinding light that was accompanied by the divine call to "tell and write" what she heard in her visions. She recalled:

> When I was 42 years and seven months old, a burning light of tremendous brightness coming from heaven poured into my entire mind, like a flame that does not burn but enkindles. It is inflamed my entire heart and breast, like the sun that warms an object with its rays. All at once I was able to taste of the understanding of books—the psalter, the Evangelists and the books of the Old and New testaments.
>
> *(Newman, 1987: 7)*

Her visions were based on her spiritual awareness and were founded on what she called the "umbra viventis lucis," the reflection of the living light (Newman, 1987). In a letter to Guibert of Gembloux, written at age 77, she describes her vision in this way:

> In this vision my soul, as God would have it, rises up high into the vault of heaven and into the changing sky and spreads itself out among different

peoples, although they are far away from me in distant lands and places. And because I see them this way in my soul, I observe them in accord with the shifting clouds and other created things, I do not hear them with my outward ears, nor do I perceive them by the thoughts of my own heart or by a combination of my five senses, but in my soul alone, while my outward eyes are open. So I have never fallen prey to ecstasy in the visions, but I see them wide awake, day and night. And, I am constantly fettered by sickness, and often in the grip of pain so intense that it threatens to kill me, but God has sustained me until now. (p. 6)

Hildegard's mode of vision is most unusual in that she sees in the soul, with an inner eye, while still retaining and exercising the powers of normal perception. While remaining lucid throughout her visions, she experiences images presented as figures and signs that are accompanied by a divine voice that explains to her the allegorical meaning of the images she beholds. Thus, Hildegard explains that "I see, hear and know and as if in an instant, I learn what I know" (Lerner, 1993: 54). Hildegard asserts that not only images, but also their meaning, were revealed to her by God. In this way, she authorizes herself to be the interpreter of her visions.

This authorization was not without struggle. Hildegard had the overwhelming burden of proving her ability and right to think in opposition to the dominant gender expectations she was expected to fulfill. Although her authority is grounded in her mystical revelation and direct relationship with God, she still needed to reconcile it with her gender. She did this by embracing two seemingly contradictory strategies in which she both maintained and subverted gender norms. First, she never claimed that women and men were equal or that women have any special gifts. In fact, she claimed the opposite. Hildegard asserted that women are naturally more frail; consequently, her knowledge must be the work of the divine. Never does she suggest that, as a woman and a Christian, she had any right to teach or prophesy in the Church. Instead, she claimed that God had chosen a poor, frail, untutored women like herself to reveal his mysteries only because those to whom he had first entrusted them—the wise, learned, and masculine clergy—had failed to obey. Thus, Hildegard consistently referred to herself as an ignorant woman. No doubt this modesty formula heightened her claims of divine inspiration, but it also reinforced gender norms making her less of a threat. Simultaneously, her visions contained strong female figures which accentuated the feminine aspects of the divine. In reinscribing the divine with female attributes, it is clear that feminine virtues, and thus women, are to be valued. It was these seemingly opposing strategies that Hildegard used to reconcile the struggle between her own understanding of self and others' expectation of women's roles.

This inner tension, according to Dronke (1984), manifested itself physically in ever-recurring migraines and related ailments. According to Lerner (1993) the ongoing gender conflicts resulted in Hildegard's "life-long history of ill health and the nearly fatal illnesses that preceded various turning points in her life" (p. 57). Illness was especially prevalent when she resisted her inner voice. Hildegard speaks of "aerial torments that pervaded her body, drying up the veins with their blood, the flesh with its humoral juice (liver), the marrow with the bones. An aerial fire was burning in her womb. She lay motionless on a coarse cloth on the ground, and all gathered round her, convinced she was about to die" (Dronke, 1984: 159). Her illness was the outward sign of her inner revelations. Illness or bodily torments were also most prevalent when Hildegard did not attend to the visions. This was most marked when, in 1148, she received a heavenly command to move her nuns from the monastery at Disibodenberg and establish an independent convent at Rupertsberg near Bingen. The abbot refused her request at which time Hildegard became ill, a clear sign of God's displeasure that his command was not being carried out. In 1150 the move took place and the Rupertsberg convent was established which included some 50 women.

It was in this new home that Hildegard's creativity came into full play, and she began her work as writer, musician, artist, and scientist in earnest. Her view of her community of women was confident, proud, joyful; they were a splendid company, worthy to honor God on the special holy days with their beauty (wearing white and tiaras) rather than their penitence; they were not so morally fragile that the wearing of lovely garments as an expression of love for their Creator would tempt them to vanity (Beer, 1992: 24). The establishment of the Rupertsberg convent and the papal seal of approval, which were given to her writings in 1147 by Eugenius III, both helped to reduce her inner tensions and much of the self-doubt she might have had. Although she continued to refer to herself as "paupercula feminea forma"—a poor little figure of a woman—Hildegard now clearly saw herself as a mouthpiece of God. Throughout her life, illness plagued her when she attempted to do things that traditionally were forbidden to women. (This was the case when she was called to undertake a preaching journey and at any time her beliefs conflicted with those of the Church officials.)

In the next 25 years Hildegard wrote a trilogy based on her visions and prophecies about the role of humankind in the divine plan from creation to redemption. She also wrote two scientific studies on nature and medicine (one was a medical encyclopedia and the second was a handbook of physical and mental diseases and their remedies, with extensive material on sexuality). She also composed 77 liturgical songs as well as the first known morality play, *Ordo*. She left two books on a secret language she invented, a book of exegesis of the Psalms, and two biographies, honoring St. Rupert and St. Disibode. Her collected letters reveal an astonishing correspondence with notable political and religious leaders of the day including Henry II of England and Eleanor of Aquitaine, Bernard of Clairvaux, Popes Eugenius III, Anastasius IV, Adrian IV, and Alexander III, Emperors Konrad III and Frederick Barbarossa, and the Archbishops of Mainz, Trier, and Salzburg. According to Lerner (1993), Hildegard "dispensed advice, answered theological and moral questions, challenged political decisions and recommended action, always speaking in the inspired voice of 'God's little trumpet'" (p. 55).

The range and depth of the trilogy encompassed medicine, natural sciences, cosmology, theology, ethics, mystical revelations, and poetry. *Scivias*, or *Know the Ways of the Lord*, her most famous book, was completed in 1151. It consists of three sections, each made up of a series of visions—first she describes the vision and then she presents an exegesis delivered, she says, by a "voice from heaven." In essence this is a book of instruction on how best to live so that one may enter the city of God. *Scivias* was the first volume of her visionary trilogy. The second volume, the *Book of Life's Merits*, was completed in 1163 and the third volume, *On the Activity of God*, occupied her between 1163 and 1173. In *Scivias* her emphasis is doctrinal; in the *Book of Life's Merits*, ethical; and in the *Activity of God* it is scientific. According to Barbara Newman (1987), the "trilogy bears one unmistakable impress—it is a world instinct with order, mystery and flaming love" (p. 15). Although a complete analysis of her theological perspective is beyond the scope of this work, I would like to focus on three tenets of Hildegard's religious interpretations which challenge traditional gender norms: 1) her belief in the positive power of women; 2) her holistic view of the universe; and 3) the conceptualization of the divine as both female and male.

Redeeming Eve and the Body

For medieval Christians, the story of Paradise Lost was the site for all meditation on man and woman. One of Hildegard's earliest visions was the creation, marriage, and banishment of Adam and Eve. For Hildegard, Adam and Eve occupy a central place in the saga of cosmic history: their adventures provide a sequel to the fall of Lucifer and a prologue to the incarnation, for, in Hildegard's eyes, these events were three acts of one drama (Beer, 1992: 89). Unlike her contemporaries, according to Frances Beer (1992), Hildegard showed virtually no interest in the psychology of Eve and Adam, and scarcely considered the question of their guilt. Her approach was ontological, cosmic, and mythical, where the prevailing exegetical trends were psychological and moral (p. 107).

According to Beer, the "classical idea of women as defective male was augmented by the Middle Ages' view of her as moral cripple: if Eve had not disobeyed, we would still be in the Garden of Eden" (p. 21). Eve was the cause of the downfall and consequently all her daughters were more prone to vice. Hildegard's views for the most part, reflected the prevailing Christian tradition— "women are weaker, different in their physical and psychic structure from men and therefore destined to be subordinate to man" (Lerner, 1993: 60). She upheld the dominant belief that because man was transformed from clay into flesh he was stronger; woman was made directly from flesh, and therefore was weaker. Hildegard's acquiescence with this dominant ideology might lead one to conclude that Hildegard was in agreement with the conventional view of corruptible Eve as cause of the fall.[5] However, Eve's weakness stands in direct contrast to the strong female figures—Synagogue, Ecclesia, and Sapentia—which dominate Hildegard's visions. And, in fact, there is no indication in her writing that powerful women are dangerous or that they serve merely a supporting role for men. How are we to make sense of Hildegard's seemingly contradictory views of women and, in particular, her understanding of Eve?

First, her views must be placed in the larger context of her belief of the creation as an image of its Creator. Whatever is made by God must by definition be good, and to despise any aspect of the creation is in effect to despise its Maker. According to Beer (1992), "to see any aspect of the creation as inherently corrupt is to give too much power to the forces of evil, and suggests that the ultimate triumph of good may actually be in questions" (p. 40). For Hildegard, God created Adam before Eve not because he is morally, intellectually, or ontologically superior, but because his work precedes hers in the act of generation. He is like the summer, which fructifies the earth, and she is like the winter, which stores and ripens its produce. To chastise Eve for succumbing to bodily temptation, or to see her bodily temptation as evil, is to reject the Creator's ideal plan. The body of flesh which is given to temptation is not inherently evil. According to Hildegard, the desire of the body can tempt the soul away from its correct directions, but the soul can also, as Hildegard maintains:

> take possession of the whole body in which it exists, in order to achieve its own work by means of that body. . . . That body has been formed by God. (p. 40)

The soul, through reason, perceives the correct course of action, but it is integrally bound with the body; like the elements, and the rest of created things, they must stand in correct relation to one another. And, as the soul and the body need one another, so do man and woman. For Hildegard,

> God gave the first man a helper in the form of woman, who was man's mirror image . . . man and woman are in this way so involved with each other that one of them is the work of the other. . . . Neither of them could live without the other. . . . Man is an indication of the godhead while woman is the indication of the humanity of God's Son. (p. 41)

If she is the mirror, it is his form that she reflects. He looks at her and recognizes his own image and likeness, and he also sees in her the mother of his children. The mirror suggests woman as both the complement of man and the primordial mother. In this regard, Hildegard addresses a question central to medieval anthropology, and one that was still contested in her time: whether Eve, no less than Adam, had been created in God's image and likeness. If Adam sees his own image in Eve, then both must have been created in God's image.

Hildegard's recounting of the fall in *Scivias* takes into account that the devil chose to tempt Eve because she was weaker than Adam, and that Adam loved Eve so passionately that he would do whatever she told him. In addition, the devil was particularly envious of Eve, since she would give birth to the race that is destined to replace the fallen angels in heaven. Eve was responsible for the fall, since she, more than any other creature could lead Adam to disobedience. However, for Hildegard, the fact that women are weaker is seen as something positive. She explains that because women are weaker, it is logical that Eve should have fallen first to temptation. And this is a good thing, for if Adam had fallen first, his sin would have been stronger and salvation would not have been possible. Because Eve transgressed, the sin could more easily be undone since she was weaker. Hildegard emphasizes Eve's redemptive role in salvation rather than her role in causing the fall. In retelling the story of the fall, Hildegard removes blame from Eve and all other women. Eve neither seduces nor persuades Adam; she simply follows God's will and plan. And even though Eve's punishment for sin is pain in childbirth, it is nonetheless God-given and therefore must be sacred. Instead, the fall becomes almost preordained by the bodily weakness built into Eve by the Creator. It is through her physicality that salvation is possible. The body is not evil, but the site of redemption. This recuperation of the body as the site of salvation signifies not only Hildegard's rejection of the body/woman as evil, but disrupts the very notion of "evil" as central to the creation story.

Hildegard rejects a dualistic view of Eve as either lustful temptress or pristine angel. According to Beer (1992),

> Hildegard's refusal to accept the polarization of man and woman, and of "good" and "bad" women, ties in with her recognition that none of us on this earth can be either absolutely virtuous or utterly vicious; the tendency toward sinfulness is an essential quality of our humanity, and so is the capacity for repentance.
>
> It also reflects a rejection of the simplistic notion that the flesh is automatically more "susceptible" to sin; sins of the spirit are equally pernicious. (p. 42)

Body and soul are interdependent and both are necessary. In this way, Hildegard can reinvision her own gender identity. By redeeming Eve as having a positive role in creation she redeems all women. More importantly, the fall is interpreted by Hildegard as the precursor to salvation and thus as central to God's plan. Eve's succumbing to temptation is her first act in the process of salvation. Rather than the body being seen as the site of evil, Hildegard reinterprets the biblical story of creation to suggest that the body is central to humanity's deliverance from evil. While Eve, with Adam, sets the stage for salvation, it is the body of Mary (mother of Jesus) that will deliver salvation. This notion of the body as the womb for "light" (symbolically, Jesus) signifies an epistemology of embodiment in which humans are active participants in the cosmos/divine through and in the body. As Hildegard's own experience suggests when we are not in harmony or whole, the body's equilibrium is disrupted and illness occurs. When we are in harmony, it is as if "in an instant I know." Unlike Augustine, redemption for Hildegard was not predicated on "transcending" the soul, but on the union of body, soul, and mind. Hildegard's ability to contest the binary of gender is what allows her to envision strong female figures as well as a more holistic, less hierarchical epistemology. Hildegard's cosmology begins with the very notion of "creation" and God's vision of the "Church." As in the case of the story of Adam and Eve, she reinterprets traditional views in ways that transgress gender and embody creation and the Church in both female and male images.

Creation: Embodying Wisdom

Scivias, or *Know the Ways of the Lord*, was a work based on 26 of Hildegard's visions. These visions presented Hildegard with the story of creation. Like other medieval scholars, Hildegard's creation story draws on three female figures who reoccur throughout her visions: Sophia (Wisdom), Sapientia (representing the Church), and Scientia Dei (knowledge of God).[6] According to Newman (1987), the "flourishing cult and iconography of the Virgin gave an ever-increasing place to sapiential themes, reintegrating the feminine Sophia into Christian symbols in yet another form" (p. 44). In Hildegard's vision of creation, the link between God and creation "and the means of God's creation of the world, is Wisdom, also called Love (Caritas)" (Ruether, 2005: 166). Sapientia has to do with the ultimate mystery of creation, the bond between the Creator and creature. Hildegard's visions suggest that creation was a consequence of the relationship between God and Wisdom. She draws on Proverbs to describe wisdom:

> The Lord brought me forth as the first of his works, before his deeds of old;
> I was appointed from eternity, from the beginning, before the world began.
> When there were no oceans, I was given birth.
>
> *(Proverbs: 22–24)*

Sapientia stands on a platform supported by seven pillars, which is the traditional way of representing the House of Wisdom. She is both terrible and kind to mankind, revealing herself only fully to God. She is often referred to as the Bride of God. It is the union of God and Wisdom that results in divine ideas being "bodied forth in creatures, the world soul" (Newman, 1987: 45). Humans are the embodiment of the divine, not just a reflection as in Platonic thought. While Hildegard clearly draws on Platonic thought to suggest that human creatures are capable of access of the divine, the reason and virtue necessary for this union is shared by all human beings since we are all "bodies" of the divine union. In this regard she subverts the elevation of "rationality" as a property only of men.

Drawing on Hebrew scripture, Hildegard reclaims the figure of Wisdom which had been masculinized by the early Church when it identified Wisdom as Christ. For Hildegard, Wisdom is the energy or "greening power" (*veriditas*) that gives life to all things. Wisdom, or love, is the soul of the cosmos as well as the matter that founds all bodily material. Wisdom connects the divine and the material. The relation of Adam and Eve itself images this bond and the intended union of soul and body. According to Ruether (2005), while Adam images God, Eve images the humanity of God's son. She represents the body of the coming God—man (p. 171). Sophia is the "mother Church" who gives birth. The Church as mother represents not so much a literal gender translation, but the Church as both male and female and a creative, life-giving force.

Hildegard's cosmology reflects an understanding of the divine as a life-giving, light-giving, and a creative force (which does suggest both birth and death). Eve, prefigures Mary (as the mother of Christ), as part of the divine vision of the birth of Christ. Hildegard's interpretation (as she felt instructed by God) of creation, focuses on the mystery of the incarnation, envisioned as the center and final cause of creation, predestined by God. Newman (1987) maintains that "because this mystery was accomplished by means of a woman, it is evoked in visions that also highlight the feminine dimension (Sophia, Sapientia) of divine reality" (p. 45). Thus, creation (generative, life-giving energies which I would associate with wisdom) requires both male and female, which in this case symbolically represent love and wisdom. Wisdom, Sapientia, is the Bride of God. The Old Testament declares that the Lord of all has loved Sophia and describes her as playing before God at all times, playing in the sphere of the earth. Hildegard characterizes this play as a festival dance: God and his partner join in an eternal cosmic play. This focus on play disrupts the Platonic view that was commonplace in regard to the empirical world as a mere shadow or reflection of the true life possessed by creatures in the mind of God. Knowledge was just not reflecting back, but an active, creative dance and play between wisdom and love, female and male, man and God. This cosmic play is perceived in her last vision as the endless circulation of the energy of love. It is the incarnation, not the passion or the resurrection that is the focus of Hildegard's cosmology. It is not an historical event, but an event beyond time and history that symbolizes the role of the feminine divine in creation. For Hildegard, both male and female are central to creation. She transgresses bodily gender roles and instead sees male and female as different energies that circulate. Her epistemology is one that resembles a larger medieval worldview in which knowledge was sought through seeking correspondences.

Hildegard seeks a way to avoid dualisms and oppositions, and instead sees the world as a set of relationships or correspondences. In the *Book of Divine Works* she presents a system of metaphorical correspondence between the elemental layers of the universe and various parts of the body; she aims to establish correspondences between the geography of the earth and the soul, the weather and the humors, the literal and the allegorical, the physical and spiritual, the human and the divine, all with the view of glorifying God and his works. Her holistic integration of cosmos, nature, and humankind, which fuses the physical, spiritual, and rational, and the mystical aspects of existence, reflects her attempts to fuse male and female elements. Her theology rejects hierarchy in favor of wholeness, roundedness, and integration. Her illumination of the Cosmic Egg shows the oneness of the universe, the triumph of good over evil and the majesty and mystery of the Creator. Creation is the result of wisdom and love, play and dance, female and male. This vision most certainly contributed to her profound creativity as a writer, musician, healer, poet, ecologist, and artist.

Yet, Hildegard was the last of the great abbesses, and her holistic cosmology, while it took root, did not surface again until the late 20th century.[7] While Hildegard's intellectual achievements were revered in her lifetime, the power and privileges that nuns had were slowly lost to the male, ordained clergy. Her cosmological worldview was not one taken up by future mystics, although there are similarities. By the 13th century the cultural motifs shifted to ones that reflected a well-established feudal society based in the medieval court. While monasteries remained centers of learning and religious life, new forms of religious life emerged. Women, in particular, sought alternatives to monasteries whose control had increasingly come under those of male clerics. The number of women religious increased and with it a rich flowering of thought that continued to transgress the boundaries of gender norms. This was nowhere more apparent than in the poetry of Mechthild of Magdeburg, who was a member of the Beguines, a new informal women's community that emerged in the heart of Saxony. Like Hildegard, Mechthild had been a young girl (age 12) when she began to have visions. In 1250 (also around 40 years old) Mechthild heard the words spoken by Christ telling her that she was to be the witness to the light of the divinity. These words became her book *The Flowing Light of the Godhead.*

Mechthild of Magdeberg: Erotic Knowing and the Body of Love

> I seek thee with all my might
> Had I the power of a giant
> Thou wert quickly lost
> If I came upon Thy footprints.
> Ah! Love! Run not so far ahead
> But rest a little lovingly
> That I may catch thee up.
>
> Lord, now am I a naked soul
> And thou a God most Glorious!
> Our two-fold intercourse is Love Eternal
> Which can never die.
> (*Mechthild of Magdeburg, 1210–1297,* The Flowing Light of the Godhead)

The love poems written by Mechthild of Magdeburg to God are passionate, erotic and all about the mystical union of the bridegroom (male) with the soul (female). While Hildegard's theological focus is on the feminine aspect of wisdom and wisdom's role in creation, Mechthild's focus is on love, and the unique reciprocity of her relationship with God. According to Carol Flinders (1993), "When Mechthild writes of the soul's romance with God, she is not allegorist: in the depths of her being, she has found a lover who is fully, deliciously responsive" (p. 44). God tells Mechthild "Thou art my resting-place, my love, my secret peace, my deepest longing, my highest honour. Thou art a delight of my Godhead, a comfort to my manhood, a cooling stream for my ardour" (*The Flowing Light of the Godhead*, 2.23). Like Hildegard, the relationship between God and man is not hierarchical but one that is dialogic. While Hildegard seeks balance, Mechthild seeks union. It is through the experience of intense, intimate love that one comes to participate in the flow, life, and light of the Trinity. For Mechthild union with God is about desire, longing, and love.

The metaphors that Mechthild draws upon—bridegroom, love, marriage—reflect two major movements of the 12th and 13th centuries—courtly love and bridal mysticism. The rhetoric of courtly love emerged in feudal society as a language through which the rights and responsibilities of the various sectors of the society (king, lord, knight, lady, peasant) were articulated. Because this motif was the dominant discourse, it is understandable that Mechthild would draw upon it as a means to express her theology and philosophy. Yet, while she appropriates it, she also subverts it. Courtly love expresses earthly, material relationships whose expression culminates in physical union. For Mechthild, it is spiritual relationships that are signified in her style of the minnesingers of medieval court life. Her writing makes extensive use of the imagery, metaphors, and motifs of the culture of the medieval court: God and Christ are pictured variously as emperor, king, knight, and lord. The soul journeys to the imperial court of God, the heavenly palace, where Christ appears as a nobleman, gives her courtly garments, and speaks to her in courtly language. According to Johnette Putnam (1996), "in the mystical dance of union originating in Neo-Platonism and transplanted to Christian mysticism by Pseudo-Dionysians, Christ as a noble youth joins with her and the virtues in the contemporary courtly custom of the spring dance" (p. 219). While drawing on these dominant metaphors, Mechthild also reinscribes them with a worldview and epistemology that seeks not union for the sake of union, but union as a means to transgress social boundaries and barriers that impede love as a condition for learning what it means to be human.

For Mechthild, unlike Hildegard, the focus on divine union was on the bridal relation of the soul to Christ (Hildegard had focused on the bridal relationship of Wisdom to God). This more personalized vision was in part a reflection of a larger movement to a more individualized relationship with God. Bernard of Clairvaux's bridal mysticism became the primary reference for understanding the bridal relationship of humans to God. The metaphor that Bernard uses, according to

Putnam (1996), is that of sexual union between the bridegroom (God) and bride (the soul). Ruether (2005) maintains that "central to Bernard's understanding of psychology is the need to integrate love and knowledge. Without love, knowledge is dry and mere external theory. But love without knowledge is heat without light. Only when knowledge and love are united and mutually transformed is there true knowledge, a real possession of and participation in the thing known" (p. 178).[8] And yet, while Bernard embraces the soul as female, this is more a figure of speech than a valuing of the feminine as a distinct aspect of the soul.

Mechthild drew not only on bridal mysticism but fused it with the tradition of courtly love. This created a new genre of mystical love that Newman (1987) has called *mystique courteoise*. This genre resisted a dualistic notion of love and knowledge, and created a more vivid erotic language, more violent paradoxes of love and a gender fluidity that was absent in Bernard's work. For Mechthild, the "creation of the soul by God the Trinity was the primal work of God's love at the beginning of Creation" (Ruether, 2005: 180). Although the soul is separated from God by the transgressions of Adam and Eve, there is a hunger to be reunited. God desires the soul or bride and the bride desires her lover. In the manner of courtly love, Mechthild's writing depicts God bending his knee to Lady Soul and God "surrenders himself to her power" (p. 181). The soul in mystical union with God "begins to taste his sweetness . . . and the power of the Holy Trinity flows through soul and body" like mother's milk (Flinders, 1993). The source of God's love is the Holy Trinity, and those mysterious headwaters are as central a symbol for Mechthild as the divine "flood of love" that represents God. God is never an abstraction, but always a living, moving reality. The images of flow and liquid pervade her writing and speak to her view of a connective version of spirituality that contrasted with the hierarchical organization of the "official" Catholic Church. Knowledge of the divine is dynamic, reciprocal, moving, and over-flowing. Mechthild writes: "Great is the overflow of Divine Love which is never still but ever ceaselessly and tirelessly pours forth, so that our little vessel is filled to the brim and overflows" (p. 69). This is an active dynamic relationship with the divine that disrupts boundaries of body and soul, God and man, male and female. And while Mechthild ultimately bids her body farewell, "Ah! Beloved prison in which I have been bound, I thank thee for all in which thou hast followed me," the body has been a sojourner and thus deserves reverence (p. 71).

Although a Beguine who had lived the life of an avowed in Magdeburg for most of her life, the last years of Mechthild's life were spent at the Benedictine convent at Helfta in Saxony. At age 63, her powerful erotic writing had become suspect of being heretical. She retired to the protection of the convent where she wrote the last and final book of the *The Flowing Light*. Helfta was emerging as a vibrant center of learning for the daughters of young noble families, where novices were instructed in the seven liberal arts and theology. The Abbess Gertrude of Hackeborn, as well as another sister, Mechthild of Hackeborn, along with Mechthild of Magdeburg were considered to be divinely inspired. Their books were attributed with being the most passionate books of the day reflecting "impassioned fervor, intense realism and an almost boundless imagination" (Dieker, 1996: 232). Helfta became a center of mysticism in Germany. While Mechthild's book was translated into High German in 1344–1345, it was not published as a manuscript until 1869. This is perhaps explained by the fact that by the close of the 14th century monastic life as the center of learning (for either males or females) was being challenged. Study or scholarship slowly shifted from the monastic centers to exclusively male enclaves of the Episcopal schools of bishops in their cathedral chapters (Anderson & Zinsser, 1988). These eventually evolved into the universities such as Paris, Poitiers, and Oxford, where curricula became fixed and the opportunity to study limited. A prerequisite to study became ordination, and by the 13th century this sacrament and the priesthood had been officially closed to women. While women could devote themselves to a religious life, they had to be closely restricted and guarded. Women were not to teach boys, they were not to have contact with men except their confessors, they could not leave the convent or have outside contact. All of this because her body might contaminate or tempt; women had to be kept separate and subordinate. The flowering of women's religious thought whose emphasis was on a holistic, compassionate, loving God who surpassed all knowledge was suppressed. And yet, women continued to transgress by finding new forms of religious life and expression. If women were to be enclosed, then appropriating this enclosure became one avenue for women religious to contest the increasing control of their bodies and bodies of knowledge.

Julian of Norwich

Julian of Norwich (1342–1413?) was a profound and radical thinker. I have only begun to appreciate the complexity of her work. Her book, the *Divine Revelation of Love* written in 1373 (the first book written by a woman in English), refuses any linear or quick reading. Meanings are not in her text, but in the experience of reading; of circling through the words, of never finding a final resting place, and of being reminded that understanding requires patience. Scholars have focused on her theological innovations in relation to the concepts of sin, love, the Trinity, and prayer. She is perhaps best known for her thorough theology of God as mother. Like Hildegard, Julian is engaged in reconceptualizing gender in ways that allow women to take up a subject position in relation to the divine and thus become knowers. Julian does so through her bodily experience, as a site of knowing. Her appropriation of the body functions both to reproduce and disrupt the female subject. Julian's negotiation of gender is a powerful reminder that who can be a knower and how we come to know is always inscribed in gender relations.

Little is known about Julian. What factual evidence there is of her life is piecemeal and circumstantial. Her book gives us little personal information. In fact, she makes herself invisible in her text, both figuratively and literally. She decenters her very subjectivity by claiming that:

> Everything that I say about me I mean to apply to all my fellow Christians, for I am taught that this is what our Lord intends in this spiritual revelation. And therefore I pray you all for God's sake, and I counsel you for your own profit, that you disregard the wretch to whom it was shown.
>
> *(Wolters, 1966: 74)*

Her own narrative is one of fragments and erasure. Her own invisibility is a form of identity politics that resists fixed meaning claims of what constitutes a subject. What we do know is that Julian chose to become an anchoress sometime after her 31st year as a consequence of a succession of visions she experienced. Although we do not know if Julian had been associated with a monastery, she was part of a growing resurgence of women choosing to take up a religious life in the late Middle Ages.[9] Six categories of religious women existed in medieval East Anglia. They can be divided into two larger groups: those who lived in community and those who chose a solitary vocation. Women who chose to live communally had three choices to become: 1) a nun-living in a monastery; 2) a hospital sister, who took vows but tended to the sick and poor; or 3) a member of an informal religious community in which women took self-imposed vows (and were not recognized by the Church). These informal communities were unique to East Anglia. No other example of this type of female religious community has been found in other parts of medieval England.[10] Once again, it is important to note that although sisters lived under the dominance of the institutional Church, they enjoyed a certain independence. They managed their busy households and complicated finances without male supervision and interference, as well as decided the nature of their activities with local lay communities.

For women choosing a solitary vocation, like Julian, two primary options existed—that of an anchoress, derived from the Greek verb to retire, or a vowess. Vowesses were widowed women who vowed to lead a chaste life, usually in their own homes. An anchoress, like Julian, took vows, but was further removed from society by being walled in—literally buried alive—in small cells attached to a church. The anchoress was regularly referred to as dead to the world, shut up as with Christ in his tomb. This tradition of leading a solitary life has its roots in the desert fathers of the 4th century, who withdrew from city life. Medieval society placed a high value on these solitary ascetics for the severity of their lifestyles and for the prayers they sang for the benefit of all. The sacrifice of possessions and contact with human society was meant to focus their devotion to God. Although they were sought out as healers and counselors, once they were enclosed in their cell they never went into the outside world again. Anchoresses lived lives of solitary contemplations undertaken for the good of the souls of their fellow Christians (Clay, 1914).[11] After Julian there was a flowering of anchorites.[12] More anchorites and hermits are known to have lived in Norwich than in any other English town. By 1546, as a result of the dissolution of the Catholic Church, all anchorages had disappeared.

What prompted Julian to become an anchoress is unclear. Why she chose a solitary life rather than a monastic life can only be a matter of speculation. The turbulent world around Julian might have contributed to her wanting an escape, or perhaps find a place from which to make sense of the chaos engulfing her. In 1349, seven years after Julian's birth, the Black Death appeared in Norwich. In 1381, East Anglia was again disrupted by agrarian, peasant uprisings. Unrest with social conditions also extended to vigorous attacks on the church by the Lollards, led by John Wycliffe, an Oxford scholar and preacher who condemned clerical and religious corruption and abuse.[13] Believing that the Church should expose people to religion, not exclude them from it, the Lollards translated the whole Bible into English. Making the word of Christ more readily accessible to the common person was reflective of a growing critique that charged that the Church has lost its true mission of spreading the word of God. The increasing persecution of the Lollards was based at least in part on the fact that they translated the Bible in English and allowed women to participate in the ministry and to preach. The Bishop of Norwich, Henry Depenser, had authorized the death penalty for convicted Lollards.

From her cell, Julian would most likely have heard the cries of those burned in Lollard's pit—a clear reminder of the consequences for women who transgressed gender norms. That she wrote at all is astounding, as it was considered an heretical act. It perhaps also helps to explain why her manuscript was not in circulation during her lifetime and why the first published copy did not appear until 1670. It seems that Julian was quite aware of the risk of writing in English and thus kept the manuscript concealed. It is within this context that we can appreciate the truly radical nature of Julian's thinking.

I turn now to Julian's experience. Julian's revelations are in many ways a record of the complex ways in which one woman negotiated her own sense of authority within severely prescribed gender norms. A primary way in which Julian does this is through claiming the body (symbolic of female/irrational/emotion) as a site of knowing. The appropriation of the female body functions both as accommodation (because in claiming "the" body she reifies the very category of female) and as subversion (because that traditionally associated with the female, the body, is claimed and reconfigured as a site of knowing). It is in this in-between space that her desire to represent the female body as a site of knowing is inscribed.

Julian's Visions

In her youth Julian had prayed for three things:

1   For an understanding of the passion of Christ.
2   For a physical illness so severe that she herself and everyone around her would think that she was dying.
3   For three wounds: true contrition, loving compassion, and the longing of the will of God.

In her 31st year, Julian became violently ill. When her physical suffering ceased, a succession of 16 visions began, the first 15 lasting from early morning until mid-afternoon, the last seen late that night. They varied in their matter and manner. She writes: "All this blessed teaching of our Lord God was shewed to me in three ways: that is to say, by bodily sight, and by words formed in my understanding, and by spiritual sight." Teachings are thus conveyed through bodily, intellectual, and spiritual means.

Throughout her 16 visions, there is a fine counterpoint between Julian's suffering of illness and the suffering of Jesus on the cross. She is not an active participant in the visions; however, she carries on an animated conversation with Christ on the cross, asking him questions, probing for clarification and as Grace Jantzen (1995) describes it, "expects good answers from him" (p. 167). Julian also understood that these answers were not for her sole gratification. The visions were not given to her, but for all her fellow Christians. This was made clear in the first vision:

> In all this I was greatly moved in love towards my fellow Christians, that they might all see and know the same as I saw, for I wished it to be a comfort to them, for this vision was shown for all men.
>
> *(Wolters, 1966: 74)*

Julian's understanding is that her visions were for teaching others. Consequently, shortly after her unexpected recovery from illness, at which point she became an anchoress, she wrote down her visions (first in a short text) and then in a second text that would become her book *Divine Revelations of Love*. I turn now to her self-representations through and in the body as a site of knowing.

Inscribing Embodiment or Behaving Bodily

According to Elizabeth Spearing (2002), medieval piety saw a variety of developments. As far as women were concerned, one of these was that bodiliness provided access to the sacred. This emerged, in part, according to Spearing (2002) as a result of a "general shift in emphasis towards Christ's humanity, God inhabiting a suffering human body, culminating in the mutilation of that body in the Passion and Cruxification" (p. xi). Christ's pain, and the blood and water that flowed from his wounds, were the means by which it was possible for human beings to be saved. Given that medieval thought associated masculinity with mind and spirit, and femininity with the body, women for all their inferiority and subordination, could be felt to have a special connection with Jesus in his Passion. Through their bodies they could hope to have special access to the sacredness associated with his body.

Julian's life-changing spiritual experience, her knowing, began as illness, that is, as a disturbance in the body. Her "knowings" evolved from the body in pain, through the body on the cross, to the ecstatic and risen body. On one level, her narrative fits neatly within the orthodox religious discourses of identity and faith

(Gilmore, 1994). Yet, as Leigh Gilmore maintains "this discourse is interrupted through her resistance to the representation and interpretation of female gendered bodies and identities as unfailingly secondary" (p. 134). The nature of women's bodily experiences, and more importantly what they mean, signals a contested terrain over who controls the knowledge of how we come to know. What is paramount to remember is the irony that the appropriation of the body both reinforces women's powerlessness and turns it into a powerful force.

Julian asks for bodily knowledge of Christ's suffering through her own bodily experience. She writes:

> In this illness I wanted to undergo all those spiritual and physical sufferings I should have were I really dying, and to know, moreover, the terror and assaults of the demons—everything, except death itself.
>
> *(Wolters, 1966: 63)*

Julian becomes ill and it is during this time that she receives her 16 visions. She recalls:

> When I was half way through my thirty-first year God sent me an illness which postrated me for three days and nights. On the fourth night I received the last rites of the Holy Church and it was thought that I could not survive till day. After this I lingered two more days and nights, and on the third night I was quite convinced that I was passing away—as indeed were those about me.
>
> *(Wolters, 1966: 64)*

Julian was administered her last rites by the parish priest and a cross was set before her eyes. She writes:

> My sight began to fail, and the rooms became dark about me, as if it were night, except for the image of the cross which somehow was lighted up; but how was beyond my comprehension . . . then the rest of my body began to die, and I could hardly feel a thing. Suddenly all my pain was taken away, and I was as fit and well as I have ever been.
>
> *(Wolters, 1966: 65)*

She continued:

> Then it came suddenly to mind that I should ask for the second wound of our Lord's gracious gift, that I might in my own body fully experience and understand his blessed passion. I wanted his pain to be my pain: a true compassion producing longing for God.
>
> *(Wolters, 1966: 99)*

For Julian, this hunger for Christ and longing for union with him, reflects the desire for a body capable of representing the experiences of women. In this case, Julian's mystical self-representation insists upon the simultaneous presence of Christ's body in the mystic's and the mystic's body in Christ's. According to Gilmore (1994), the body of Christ offers something other than the absence of "male or female." In its anatomical maleness and its semiotic femaleness (feeds us with body and blood), the desire of and for both female and the male effectively undercuts the phallic mode of desiring (p. 140). Like Christ, her body is capable of miraculous transformation. It is a body that can resist the logic of gender and map a contradictory discourse of gender hierarchy into religious discourse.

Her bodily changes, that she "could hardly feel a thing" are the result of her meditations on and vision of Christ as he undergoes the profound changes he underwent in the Passion and Resurrection (rebirth). It is at this point at the outset of her illness that she receives her first vision: Christ's (female) bodily experiences on the cross. These are graphic and poignant descriptions of his bodily sufferings.

> Because of the pull of the nails and the weight of that blessed body it was a long time suffering. For I could see that the great, hard, hurtful nails in those dear and tender hands and feet caused the wounds to gape wide and the body to sag forwards under its own weight, and because of the time that it hung there. His head was scarred and torn, and the crown was sticking to it, congealed with blood, his dear hair and his withered flesh was entangled with the thorns, and they with it.
>
> *(Wolters, 1966: 89)*

According to Jantzen (1995), no male medieval writer, not even Francis of Assisi, ever focused so lovingly or in such detail on the physical body of Jesus on the cross. Julian revises the experience of being acted on by illness (the natural state of women), of being a prisoner of the body that suffers (Eve in childbirth); passivity turns into passion as her wounded body is conflated with Christ's. This union becomes the center of her autobiographical reflections in which she represents herself as an active agent in relation to the divine.

Clearly, Julian claimed the body as a site of knowing. However, this signification operates in complex ways. According to Caroline Bynum (1992), behavior in which bodiliness provided access to the sacred seems to have increased dramatically in frequency in the 12th century and to have been more characteristic of women than men. For medieval mystics, the body is a recurrent theme. Late medieval piety emphasized the body as the locus of the sacred. Both male and female saints regularly engaged in what we would call torture—jumping into ovens or icy ponds, driving nails or knives into their flesh, whipping or hanging themselves as a means to pantomime the crucifixion. The discipline of the body is seen as synonymous with and essential to the discipline of the mind and full devotion to Christ. Taming the body is necessary to resist temptations of all kinds. Both men and women manipulated their bodies through flagellation and other forms of self-inflicted suffering as well as illness.[14] To attribute this behavior solely to hatred of the body (or a form of self-regulation) is to neglect that the mystics emphasized the body as a theater of tremendous potential for self-representation. If we reduce their desire to control the body to machismo or self-regulation (both psycho-analytic and Foucauldian readings) we misread as passivity their passionate activity.

Because preachers, confessors, and spiritual directors assumed the person to be a psychosomatic unity, they not only read unusual bodily events as an expression of the soul, but also expected the body itself to offer a means of access to the divine. This was concurrent with medieval theological thinking in which the Platonic and Augustine notions that the person is a soul, making use of the body was being modified. The concept of the person as body *and* soul undergirded most scholastic discussions; thus persons were seen as their bodies (relics, pieces of dead people, were seen as the loci of the sacred). Because they associated the female with the flesh, they expected somatic expressions to characterize women's spirituality.[15] However, despite these bodily expectations, woman was inferior to man, and women clearly internalized the negative value placed on them by the culture in which they lived. Moreover, for all its expressiveness, the body was inferior to the soul. The locus of fertility and mystical encounter, it was also the locus of tempta-tion and decomposition (Bynum, 1992: 236). Whereas soul (male) was immortal, the body rose only after decay and as result of Christ's grace.

Simultaneously, the clergy encouraged somatic female behavior since it brought them under the supervision of spiritual directors and was a way for men to learn the will of God (Bynum, 1992: 195). Thus, although bodily experiences legiti-mated women as knowers, the nature of what counted as legitimate bodily experiences was defined by male clerics. It is within this politics of control that women mystics' rewriting of the body as irreducibly plural in its capacity to signify different levels of experience occurs. The spiritualities of male and female religious were different and this difference had to do with the body. For Julian, this difference had to do with "her resistance to the representation and interpretation of female gendered bodies and identities as unfailingly secondary" (Gilmore, 1994: 134). Cheryl Glenn (1997) maintains that Julian "unsexes the maleness of God, of Jesus, of Christianity, with a feminine and masculine Christology through which women and men could be liberated and redeemed—as women and men" (p. 100). This knowledge and Julian's theology are the results of her embodied knowing.

Thus, for Julian, her bodily illness which resulted in her revelations and union with Christ became a site of transformation in which gender is not only *transgressed* but *reconceived*. The body, that which signifies female, was not just a site within which revelations occurred. It was not a container or holder of experience, for this would ultimately render the body as passive. For women mystics like Julian, knowledge was generated from within the body. These psychosomatic manipulations included: stigmata, mystical lactations and pregnancies, catatonic trances, ecstatic nosebleeds, miraculous anorexia, eating and drinking pus, visions of bleeding hosts, and illness or recurrent pain. It is within this context that the extraordinary bodily qualities of women's piety between 1200 and 1500 must be understood. As Bynum (1992) suggests: "The body, and in particular the female body, seems to have begun to *behave* in new ways at a particular moment in the European past" (p. 195). I turn to Julian's symbolic association of women with blood (menstruation/childbirth) as a specific embodied site in which she recuperates female experience, disrupts it and thus creates her own unique understanding of knowing.

Blood

Julian's first revelation is the crowning of Christ: "At once I saw the red blood trickling down from under the garland, hot, fresh and plentiful . . ." (Wolters, 1966: 66). In medieval conceptions blood was the basic body fluid and female blood was the fundamental support of human life.[16] Medical theory held that the shedding of blood purged or cleansed those who shed it. Bleeding was held to be necessary, so much so that physiologists sometimes spoke of males as "menstrating" (hemorrhoidal bleeding) and recommended bleeding with leeches if they did not do so. Thus, Christ's bleeding on the cross was associated with female bleeding and feeding. This similarity was however, according to Gilmore (1994), not interpreted by women as "lack, but as a symbol of their power" (p. 141).

For women mystics, the blood and wounding of Christ and the menstrual blood and blood of childbirth associated with women's sexuality linked his blood and their blood and signified their union. This longing for union (longing is an ongoing theme throughout Julian's narrative) is not reducible to the desire of the phallus, but "persists as desire for the whole body of Christ and especially for a body capable of representing the experiences of women" (p. 141).

This is significant, for although the shedding of blood was seen as necessary, blood itself was seen to be impure, unclean—hence the association with pollution. Julian's revelation of the bleeding alternatively signals cleansing and healing:

> though God through his compassionate love has made an abundant supply of water for our use and comfort, he wishes us to use quite simply his blessed blood to wash ourselves clean of sin. For there is no comparable fluid that he would so like to give us. Of all it is at once the most copious and most costly/(because it is divine), and, because of his great love, it is the most suitable and gladdening we could want.
>
> *(Wolters, 1966: 82)*

Julian's fourth revelation is "God prefers that we should be washed from our sin in his own blood rather than in water; his blood is most precious" (Wolters, 1966: 82). His blood is Julian's blood and thus women's bodily experiences are reinscribed as precious. As a consequence both male and female experience is validated. The female body is inscribed—or is it?

On the one hand, this reading is comforting and, as a woman, soothes the wounds of a culture that has a love/hate relationship with women's bodies. It is a seductive reading. Elevating the body over the soul as the primary site of knowing is a powerful epistemological standpoint within a culture that, as Petroff (1994) describes, needs to control and purify the female body—a "grotesque" as opposed to a "classical" body, to borrow Bakhtin's terminology (p. 205). And yet, I am unsettled by this textualized "good" body since it implies that women's experiences can indeed be consolidated through the female body. Thus, it potentially functions to make the female body "natural" and persists in maintaining gender identity as either male or female as inevitable.

And yet, there is nothing "naturally" oppressive or liberatory about the discourse of the body.[17] What appeared to me initially as a subversion of gender, Julian's recuperation of the female body, functions on another level to keep binary concepts of gender intact, which then reproduces the body as natural, as opposed to a social construction. Judith Butler (1990) maintains that positing a strong or autonomous female subject leaves intact gender bipolarities and institutional structures that support given gender positions. More importantly, it retains notions of power as a source of liberation. Thus, I am back to a heroine's reading of history which reinforces duality and essentializes gender.

Another possible reading resists my desire for closure, for a tidy rereading of the female body. A second reading of Julian's use of the body is done within the context of Julian's experience in which knowledge of Christ was shown to her in three ways. At the end of the first revelation in which she is in union with Christ's bodily pain during the crucifixion she states: "All this was shown me in three ways, in actual visions (physical), in imaginative experience (mind) and in spiritual sight (soul)" (Wolters, 1966: 76). The body does not become a mere conduit for experience, but bodily experience is spiritual experience and imaginative experience. Julian writes:

> For just as the body is clothed in its garments, and the flesh in its skin, and the bones in their flesh, and the heart in its body, so too are we, soul and body, clothed from head to foot in the goodness of God.
>
> *(Wolters, 1966: 70)*

Thus, in reading gender, the body is textualized not as either male or female, but as both male and female. In this way, mystical self-representation resists the duality and finality of gender (Gilmore, 1994: 133). Julian is not privileging the body but on some level suggesting an integrated theory of body, soul, and mind as an epistemological framework. To say that God—that which she has signified as female—is three entities in one is to insist that no single conceptualization can encompass the divine (Flinders, 1993: 95).

What was ultimately shown to Julian through these mediums was that souls and bodies are clothed in the goodness, the love, of God. Jantzen (1995) maintains that "Julian's teaching concerning spiritual progress has everything to do with receiving and trusting the faithful love of God and nothing to do with standard themes of distrust of the body and especially sexuality" (p. 140). Julian reconceived the female body from the site of evil and temptation to one in which she has absolute conviction that the body is a site of goodness and the love of God. The body embodies goodness, and thus, control and repression of the female body (the normative Christian reading) are absent in Julian's text. Julian is not privileging the body, but on some level is suggesting an integrated theory of body, soul, and mind as an epistemological framework. This epistemology is in stark contrast to a Platonic or traditional Christian (or even Buddhist) understanding of the body in which the body must be transcended in order to achieve union with the divine (Hendry, 2007).

For women mystics, bodily experiences, like the union with Christ, in Julian's case through their mutual bleeding, is such a profound and sensual experience that it goes beyond the senses and words for describing them. I quote Julian, "His suffering and self-abnegation so far surpasses anything we might experience that we shall never wholly understand it" (Wolters, 1966: 105). This is in contrast to male mystics (Eckhart or Walter Hilton) who write of being at a core or ground or inner point of understanding (Bynum, 1992: 192). Julian claims her bodily experience as a site of knowing and simultaneously suggests that we can never know. Her resistance to fixed meaning claims, that knowing cannot be put into words, functions to destabilize and keep in flux any unitary reading of gender and thus how we come to know. Julian exchanges normative secular practices of femininity for a lifelong attention to an eroticized body discourse that moves beyond gender. This positioning allows her to reread herself as a subject, and a subject who knows. In this way Julian's narrative pushes us to continually ask, "What makes it possible for us to think of the body as natural" who defines the limits and possibilities of our knowing and how is the body implicated in this inscription? Julian not only claims the female body as one site for knowing, but also that in becoming one with the body we can embody love.

Love

> Wouldst thou written thy Lord's meaning in this thing? Learn it well: love was his meaning. Who shewed it thee? Love. What shewed he thee? Love. Wherefor shewed it he? For love.
>
> *(Clifton Wolters, 1966)*

According to Colish (1997), Julian's most distinctive contribution to Christian mysticism is her understanding of the affective bond between the mystic and God in terms of maternal love. Julian was by no means the first to articulate Jesus or God as mother. The idea of God as mother can be found in the Bible and in the monastic writings of Augustine and Bernard of Clairvoux, as well as among other female mystics. Hildegard of Bingen writes, "God showed me his grace, again as . . . when a mother offers her weeping child mild . . .", Hadewijch speaks of the soul being nursed with motherly care; Bridget explains that "this bird represents God, who brings forth every soul like a mother" (Spearing, 2002: xii). This emphasis on God as mother coincided with a general shift in the Middle Ages toward an emphasis on Christ's humanity, God inhabiting a suffering human body, culminating in the mutilation of that body in the Passion and Crucifixion (Spearing, 2002). Christ's bodily experiences of bleeding, feeding us with his blood and body, were likened to those of what a mother does for her child. The maternal love of the Virgin as the universal mother of all Christians also contributed to an image of God as mother. Julian chose motherhood to describe God's love because she regarded it as the purest, most selfless, and most moving form of human love.

Julian has been attributed with the most developed concept of the reconceptualization of Christ as female through her theology of God as mother. However, a close reading of her text suggests that she is not simply substituting female for male. In fact, Julian subverts the gender dichotomy that this metaphor reinforces. She writes: "And so I saw that God rejoices that he is our father, and God rejoices that he is our mother, and God rejoices that he is our true husband, and our soul his beloved wife" (Wolters, 1966: 99).

Julian spoke of creation as a maternal act because God, in taking on humanity in the Incarnation, gives himself to us as a mother gives herself to the fetus she bears (Bynum, 1992: 206). God made himself totally vulnerable by embodying himself as human in the life of Jesus through Mary.

Historically contextualized, the notion of Christ as female was quite accepted within medieval theological doctrine. Both male and female mystics called Jesus "mother" in his Eucharistic feeding of Christians with liquid that exuded from his breast and in his bleeding on the cross which gave birth to the hope of eternal life. Jesus took on female characteristics through the Eucharist of nourishing with his body and blood. Both male and female mystics saw Christ as female. Male mystics (Bernard of Clairvaux, Francis of Assisi, Richard Rolle) whose religiosity was most experiential and visionary, often described themselves in feminine images and learned their pious practices from women. Yet, taking up the notion of Christ as female took on different meanings for men and women religious. For monks and Church officials, this signification might have been an expression of a desire to "project a more loving, less authoritarian image of leadership" (Lerner, 1993: 89). This signification is not insignificant since it occurs just at the time when the Church was under severe criticism and attack for its elitism. This symbolism of Christ as female also coincided simultaneously, not with an increase in women's power in the Church, but with the curtailment of women's power.

This image of God as mother is quite congruent with dominant medieval conceptions of gender as more fluid. Julian's appropriation of God as female is perhaps more complex. If we look at the quote above, Julian resists a unitary reading of God as female. God is both male and female. What Julian does is to reconceptualize the son of God as both male and female, thus disrupting the very notion of gender as binary. Julian writes:

> And thus in our Creation God almighty is our kindly father, and God who is all wisdom is our kindly Mother, with the love and the goodness of the Holy Ghost—all of Whom are one God and one Lord . . . Thus in our Father God we have our being, and in our mother of mercy we have our reforming and our restoration, in Whom all parts are united and all made into perfect end, and by the yielding and giving grace of the Holy Ghost we are fulfilled . . . for our nature is whole in each person of the Trinity which is one God.
>
> *(Lerner, 1993: 90)*

This disruption of gender as a binary functions on two levels. First, it disrupts traditional notions of women as evil and sinful. This functions for Julian as a form of rebellion to normative gender roles. Second, this disruption suggests that dualisms such as male/female deter us from more holistic, integrated, and inter-relational modes of being that form the basis for love and compassion. In fact, according to Thomas Long (1995), it is the union of binary opposites (like male/female, yin/yang, mind/body) that are required for knowledge or wisdom.

Julian's revelations are a profound reminder of the body as a contested terrain for knowing and the continuity of women's experience of the body as a site of regulation (Hendry, 2005). Julian's narrative provides a unique picture into one 14th-century woman's ongoing negotiation of gender, of a woman compelled to push at the male-defined ecclesiastical boundaries while simultaneously being subservient to them. Julian emerges from suffering and illness with a new "body of knowledge" that transcends all conceptual formulations. It is a transgendered epistemolgy in which the body, emotion, and love are radical disruptions of the binary concept of gender. Her disruption of the subject, of absolute truths, is an affirmation of that which makes us human—the ongoing ambiguity of searching for meaning while simultaneously knowing that what makes life possible is permanent, intolerable uncertainty. This uncertainty is an invitation to embody the in-between spaces where unknowing becomes a site of knowing.

Unknowing and the Body

> If our understanding comprehends, it is in a mode which remains unknown to it, and it can understand nothing of which it comprehends.
>
> *(Teresa of Avila, 1515–1582)*

Take Saint Teresa, for example, one of the ablest women, in many respects, of whose life we have the record. She had a powerful intellect of the practical order. She wrote admirable descriptive psychology, possessed a will equal to any emergency, great talent for politics and business, a buoyant disposition, and a first-rate literary style. She was tenaciously aspiring, and put her whole life at the service of her religious ideals. Yet so paltry were these, according to our present way of thinking, that I confess that my only feeling in reading her has been pity that so much vitality should have found such poor employment.

(William James, 1902)

Like other medieval mystics, Teresa of Avila's "knowing" coincided with illness in the body. Fainting spells, inexplicable fevers, and mysterious ailments plagued her as she struggled with her banishment as a youth to an Augustinian convent as a result of her "wild" nature. At one point, she slipped into a coma and was about to be pronounced dead when she suddenly pried open her eyes beneath the wax that had already been pressed upon her lids in preparation for burial. Like Julian, her recovery was "deemed miraculous, and the passion of her devotion for God deepened" (Starr, 2003: 9). At age 40 (much like Hildegard), she had a calling from God and began to experience a relentless series of supernatural states. Her raptures were legendary. She would enter into trancelike states that paralyzed her for hours, she experienced levitations, and her most famous rapture was the transverberation (captured by the Italian sculptor Gian Lorenzo Bernini). In this mystical moment, her body experienced total rapture as she is plunged with a flaming sword, leaving her on fire with love for God. Jacques Lacan remarked that "you have only to go and look at Bernini's statue in Rome to understand immediately that she's coming, there's no doubt about it" (Medwick, 1999: xvi). Like Luce Irigaray, I would argue that it is absurd to draw conclusions from a piece of marble, but her expression of complete ecstasy does suggest a profound bodily experience of coming to know.

Like other mystics then, the body as a site of knowing was central to Teresa's theology. She wrote in her autobiography *The Life of St. Teresa Written by Herself*, in 1585, "I, who have gone through so much, am sorry for those who begin with books; for there is a strange difference between that which we learn by reading and that which we learn by experience" (Lewis, 1997: 101).[18] For Teresa, trusting one's own experience as given to one by God is the essence of her theory of knowing. While she took up a narrative of deferral like other women mystics, she perhaps went farthest in claiming personal experience as central to experiencing union with God. Her books *Way of Perfection* and *The Interior Castle* are guides to an epistemology that centers on prayer and contemplation as the path to personal experience with the divine.

Teresa's focus on the interior of the body was no coincidence. Her lifetime was one in which the Catholic Church faced one of its greatest challenges, the Reformation. The Counter Reformation was characterized by a shift in authority. If the Catholic Church was to continue to convert souls, the Church had to be made more accessible to individuals. This shift included the increased focus on Christ's humanity and people's ability to experience Christ's love. Yet, those embracing this individual agency walked a fine line, one that was kept in line by the Inquisition. Teresa was not exempt from the gaze of the authority of the Church. "From the moment that she had her first mystical rapture to the night she drew her last breath, Teresa lived in fear of the Spanish Inquisition" (Starr, 2003: 16). Her narrative strategies of deferring her agency as well as continual disclaimers of her authority must be interpreted within this context in which they were scrutinized by Church officials for heresy. Teresa deftly manages to make her points, and her criticisms, while never offending the Church.

Despite this scrutiny, she went on to write in 1577, the mystical masterpiece, *Interior Castle*, as a teaching guide for her Carmelite nuns in the life of contemplation and prayer. In this sense the book has a more formal tone compared to *Way of Perfection* which had a tone of intimacy as she spoke about humility, detachment, and love for one another. This book, like all her others, begins with a vision—the image of a magnificent castle inside our souls, at the center of which dwells God himself. According to Starr (2003), "outside of this vision, Teresa saw the whole book unfold in a flash" (p. 22). What was potentially threatening to the Church was the concept that God dwelled inside the body, in the soul. In contrast to dominant theological norms of the time that saw the body as evil, Teresa's view of the body is such that it is so glorious that God himself chooses to dwell in it. There is no mention of transcending the body as a means to enlightenment, but on the contrary the journey to union with God is one of self-discovery. Her theology might very well have gotten her burned at the stake since it did not require ritual or authority figures. *Any-body* had access to the divine.

This journey to the union with God is described by Teresa as follows: "Consider our soul to be like a castle made entirely out of a diamond or of very clear crystal, in which there are many rooms" (Flinders, 1993: 186). She then describes the castle as having seven "dwelling places" that represent the seven stages of prayer. These stages (although not always linear) include initiatory, transition to the supernatural, the union of the soul with the God, purification, and, lastly, the dwelling place. This last dwelling is where the "greatest of all mystical paradoxes unfolds" (Starr, 2003: 26). When union with the divine (or what Teresa calls the Beloved) is achieved, the separate self is annihilated; the subject–object distinction is replaced by love. Ultimately, the soul returns to the ordinary world. And then, this new soul, forever transformed by love, returns to the everyday world to be of service to others. Like the bodhisattvas in Buddhism, they return to earth, staying embodied, until all others have found liberation (Hendry, 2007).

Enclosure in the body (she compares it to a cocoon that dies and then is reborn into a white butterfly) is synonymous with freedom. Paradoxically, it is through being enclosed in the body, not experiencing freedom, that eventually one discovers freedom. For women of the late medieval period whose lives were increasingly bound by enclosure either in the household or the convent, reading Teresa would have provided a profound rereading of the female body not as a prison, but as a labyrinth of joy. This transformation in love, according to Starr

(2003) "creates an unshakable sanctuary of peace inside of her so that no matter what challenges life in the world may present, she can weather them joyfully, knowing that her Beloved dwells inside her and he will never, ever leave her" (p. 27).

Teresa was perhaps the last of the great female mystics. Although religion would continue to be the dominant narrative through which social life was organized for another 100 to 200 years, new narratives based in science and colonization would begin to challenge the Church (and a spiritual epistemology) as the absolute source of authority. This spiritual loss paralleled the loss of visible authority for women. Reason, not love, would eventually emerge as the locus of "knowledge." This was not done without struggle. As we have seen over and over again in this chapter, the body is always a contested site of regulation. By the 16th century the embodied knowing of female mystics was no longer understood as the work of the divine, but as the work of the devil. With the spread of the witchhunts and the onset of the Reformation, there was a sharp drop in the number of female mystics. Their books and their writings, went underground, in some cases not to surface again until centuries later. These profound writings, though varied and shaped by differing historical contexts, suggest the complex ways in which women have authorized themselves as knowers. Working within and through the dominant religious and gender discourses of their day, they understood the body as a site of knowing. Against the normative theology of Christianity which posited women (read "body") as the source of evil and sin, these women reinterpret the creation story not as one of "fall," or leaving the body, but as one of creation, as a site of generativity. Human experience is not to focus on sin, but on love. Knowing is not a result of transcending the body, but staying embodied, trusting our lived experience. For these women mystics, embodied knowing reflects a holistic rather than hierarchical cosmology. The body is not just a conduit, but produces a transgendered epistemology that disrupts binary understandings of gender thereby creating a space in which women and men can be knowers through trusting their experience.

Reflections

The time is right for a shift of emphasis in our theories of knowledge and learning and therefore to focus our aim towards the embodied organic, intellectual, inclusive "outlaw" emotions and the affective domain.

(Sheila Macrine, 2002)

Bodies always already are cultural artifacts, the product of the interaction of flesh and meaning. The body is a terrain of the flesh in which meaning is inscribed, constructed and reconstituted . . . our body is as much constituted by flesh as by words and symbols.

(Gert Biesta, 1994)

The body remains a contested site. Feminists (Bordo, 1993; Butler, 1993; Jaggar, 1989) continue to work to unravel the bound and gagged body from Cartesian chains without reifying it into an essentialized female body. The raptures, visions, meditations on Christ, mystical lactations, and other bodily experiences of medieval women religious might seem "bizarre" from a contemporary point of view. Yet, as Judith Butler suggests, the body constitutes a ludic arena of linguistic performance, a public proscenium of "play" where the categories of male and female act out dramas of misrecognition (as quoted in Cruz & McClaren, 2002). The body continues to be a site of "play" (tattoos, piercings, sculpting) and acting out (anorexia, bulimia). In fact, I would argue the obsession with the body in postmodern culture speaks to the deep desire to acknowledge this neglected space. We are not "talking heads"; we are fully enfleshed. This flesh has a long history. As Raymond Williams has suggested, there has always been an historically rooted counternarrative that has resisted the dualisms of mind and body, experience and knowledge, feeling and reason, a narrative that embraces wholeness, human integrity, and sensual being (see Shapiro, 2002). A transgendered and transgressive epistemology is one that is embodied in a holistic (mind, body, and soul) under-standing of the human experience that acknowledges the profound and complex ways in which we come to know. Embodied knowing requires a rethinking of dominant metaphors that situate learning as ends and objectives and students as products.

Curriculum theorists are engaged in claiming the body as a site of knowing as a way to envision an embodied self that disrupts notions of a unitary individual that is the product of humanist thought (Guillory, 2010; Jaramillo, 2010; Lesko, 1998; Macrine, 2002; Morris, 2008; Orner, 2002; Wear, 1994). A "bodied" cur-riculum as Stephanie Springgay and Debra Freedman (2010) suggest "opens up subjectivity to the in-between of corporeality, materiality, and difference shifting the perception of embodiment as universal, toward an understanding of bodies and knowledges as difference" (p. 229). This disruption of a unitary subjectivity is central to reconceiving the docile student body that is the focus of continual surveillance and monitoring. Not unlike the medieval mystics, young student bodies seek to experience their bodies, to reinscribe their experience as a site of knowing, to claim their experience as a site of embodied knowing. While medieval women engaged starvation, flagellation, and other types of bodily manipulations to reclaim bodily experiences, youth culture's engagement with sports, drugs, sex, body art, and illness (obesity, anorexia, etc.) signals a response to the ways in which bodies are being "subject" to complex and contradictory discourses of identity.

I would maintain that the contemporary "medicated body" (Pinar, 2002) and "posthuman body" (Weaver, 2010) signify a desire to reconstitute the body and embody a body as one of infinite possibilities. For men, rejecting the body as a site for knowing (starting with Descartes) has been critical to maintaining a gender binary that situates men as knowers. According to Pinar (2006) this engendering of knowledge has also been racialized through a process in which "keeping the brain (and power and money) for himself and giving away the body to the black man, the white man gave away his manhood, became castrated, became a dead man hung on a cross" (p. 76). Pinar asks "Is the fetishized body of Christ the substitute for the body we have lost historically, through embourgeoisement, as Pasolini suggested?" (p. 77). This desire for the body as a site for transgendering knowledge as a means to embrace fully the lived experiences of eros, pleasure, rapture, and contemplation is the work of embodiment that many women mystics undertook.

Women mystics never "gave away the body" and at the close of the Middle Ages many died at the stake because they refused to give it up. The loving, erotic, passionate meditations women religious had with Christ on and off the cross was for women, in contrast to men, a way in which to remain embodied. The desire for union is not about merger or sublimation but about transgendering. In the end, St. Paul was right, women transgressed. Reading, exploring, studying, experiencing their bodies they embodied knowing by transgressing the boundaries of gender. The focus on the illness, sufferings, and self-mutilation of these women is not meant to glorify these acts or intended as an indictment. However, they signal, like the many women and men today engaging in cutting, drugs, and other forms of embodying that the body continues to be a powerful site for transgression. For women mystics, knowledge was not separate from the body. More importantly, their epistemology was one of "unknowing." Through the use of contemplation, prayer, meditation, silence, as well as illness, flagellation, and mutilation they sought to "let go" of the illusion of control that was central to emerging understandings of knowledge. Instead, "unknowing" becomes the prerequisite for learning and education. As Dwayne Huebner (1999) so eloquently states, "There is more than we know, can know, will ever know. It is a 'moreness' that takes us by surprise when we are at the edge and end of our knowing" (p. 403). This "moreness" is the spirit of education that embraces our embodied knowing as a site of love, compassion, and wisdom as well as pain and suffering.

4

DECOLONIZING CURRICULUM

Please enlighten me again, whether it has ever pleased God, who has
bestowed so many favors on women, to honor the feminine sex with the
privilege of the virtue of high understanding and great learning and whether
women ever have a clever enough mind for this. I wish very much to know
this because men maintain that the mind of women can learn only a little.

She [Lady Reason] answered, My daughter . . . I tell you again . . . if it
were customary to send daughters to school like sons, and if they were taught
the natural sciences, they would learn as thoroughly and understand the
subtleties of all the arts and sciences as well as men.

(Christine de Pizan, 1405, The Book of the City of Ladies)

In this allegory, Christine de Pizan (1365–1430) struggles to understand the tension between her own self-understanding as a learned woman and the cultural
norms of the day which denied women not only equality but situated them as
objects of knowledge. Humanist scholars pondered: Were women fully human?
Were women capable of absorbing education, exercising reason, and controlling
their feelings? *The Book of the City of Ladies* addresses these questions in a dialogue
in which three ladies, Reason, Rectitude, and Justice, comfort Pizan and explain
why men have so universally attacked and slandered women (Lerner, 1993).[1]
Reason explains that clearly nature provided men and women with the same
natural qualities, but it is the social constraints placed on women's activities that
have resulted in their lack of learnedness. Reason then goes on to offer examples
of the stories of "learned women of Antiquity, including Sappho the poet,
Nicostrata, who invented the Latin alphabet; Minervas, who invented Greek script
and cloth-making; Ceres, who invented agriculture; Isis, who discovered the art
of planting gardens" (Lerner, 1993: 194). Pizan's book is a history of women

written from an entirely women-centered point of view. According to Gerda Lerner, it is the "first consistent effort by a woman at constructing Women's History as a means of creating collective consciousness" (p. 261).

Had the book gained wide circulation, it might have informed the debates in Europe over women's education. However, the belief that women were incapable of reason and were intellectually inferior to men was, ironically, to become the dominant ideology of the "Renaissance" and "Enlightenment." This ideology, in which women are to be objects of knowledge, but never subjects, is I argue throughout this chapter a form of colonization. Pizan's writing clearly suggests that women of the period were situated as objects through the emerging discourses of reason and rationality, discourses that functioned to colonize gender and construct it as a binary. Despite the attempts of Christine de Pizan, and other women theorists discussed in this chapter, to "decolonize" women from their positionality as objects of knowledge, they remained the "subjects" of colonizing ideologies.

This ideological colonization of women and "others" as *objects* of knowledge, not *subjects*, was central to epistemological shifts in the "knowing subject" as rational, logical, and disembodied as opposed to a medieval understanding of the subject as holistic and dialogical. As Bernadette Baker (2001) reminds us "the dominant model of understanding personhood within Western cultures prior to the 15th century was the neo-Platonic and Judeo-Christian depiction of a perpetual struggle between different conditions of the soul/mind/body" (p. 124). The body, or the subject, could not be understood as a discrete entity; it could only be made sense of as part of a whole ontology. Women religious of the medieval period (discussed in the previous chapter) saw the body not as separate, but as part of a complex discursive space in which they continually engendered their experiences. While the 12th through the 15thcenturies had seen a flourishing of women's ways of knowing and being in the world, the emergence in the fifteenth and sixteenth centuries of "rationalism" and "scientific method" as dominant ideologies, dependent on a body/mind binary, functioned to "colonize" not only women's bodies, but all bodies. To construct the body as a distinct interior space was to construct a new territory in which a binary view of body/mind as a "real" space was necessary. It is this binary that is the precondition for the colonization of this new territory that becomes known as the "*the* body."

This would resonate w/ Donald Blumenfeld Jones

Colonization, as Nina Asher (2010) reminds us, is not just the occupation, control, and economic exploitation of one nation by another, but requires the physical and psychic occupation and control of a people. This occupation of the "subject" is only possible when the "subject" is constructed as having an interior space that is conceptualized as able to be worked upon or filled. This transformation of the "subject" as having an interior and exterior is one that is a product of modernity. It is this binary construction of subjectivity that becomes central to the corollary concepts of body/mind, subject/object, male/female, public/private, state/citizen, and self/other. Thus, colonialism is not only the conquering of foreign lands and the domination of one country over another for economic purposes, but is the internalization of the colonizer by the oppressed (Fanon, 1967). Colonization becomes not so much an "act" of conquest, as the attempt to infiltrate and impose an internal "mapping" of submission and subordination.

Consequently, I engage the concept of colonization as one in which this new interior is the territory of colonization, in the sense that this new subjectivity must be learned. And, I will argue that this imposition of a new "subject" identity, which was deeply gendered, was, in part, learned through the discursive practices of the new education—"schooling." This chapter maintains that this ideological colonization of the subject is predicated on a binary construction of gender in which men are subjects of knowledge and women objects of knowledge. This colonization would be the site of both resistance and accommodation.

A central theme throughout this chapter is that it is no coincidence that "education" as a formalized institution (schooling) went hand in hand with colonization. The term "school" emerged at the beginning of the 17th century in England and marked what would become mass education (Davis, 2004). This institutionalization of learning was radically different from ancient and medieval understandings of education in which the liberal arts (geometry, astronomy, arithmetic, music, grammar, logic, and rhetoric) were the heart of the curriculum as opposed to the practical arts (math, reading, writing). These "disciplines," which reflected the emerging scientific view of the world marked a radical episte-mological shift in which knowledge was no longer understood as critical to meaning-making, but as a tool or object for mastery of the world. This shift in knowledge corresponded to changes in subjectivity and contributed to new understandings of the autonomous individual. As a consequence new constructions of identity, including those of the "child," "mother," and "other," became depen-dent on organizing social relations through forms of classification that ensured stratification and categories that reinforced hierarchical, gender, and class structures. Mass education with its focus on control, method, order, and discipline was critical to shaping this new identity. Colonization would not have been possible without it. And, as William Doll (2002) and Claudia Eppert (2007) argue, the "haunting spirit of control" continues to pervade the contemporary curriculum as a means to avoid the fear of uncertainty and the unknown.

Thus, colonization did not begin in faraway lands but in ideologies and dis-courses, starting in the 15th century and spanning the Renaissance, Enlightenment, Scientific Revolution, and Reformation, that reconstructed knowledge as the product of reason, rationality, and natural rights. These epistemological revolutions were predicated on the emergence of a "new" subject whose identity was the product in part of a binary view of gender in which male was associated with reason, intellect, and the public sphere, and female was relegated to irrationality, emotion, and the domestic sphere. This dichotomy was central to creating a dualistic, binary worldview that resulted in categories of self/other, subject/object, male/female, private/public, and state/citizen. A prerequisite for this binary construction of subjectivity was the reconceptualization of space as distinct and discrete which made possible a "subject." These identity narratives were central preconditions to colonization and not only had to be learned, but they required a new subject.

What was revolutionary about this learning were the means through which these new subject identities were self-regulated. Schools as institutions emerged in the 16th century as one of the primary institutions through which the "self" as masculine, rational, and self-controlling was learned. Thus colonization is as much a way in which power and knowledge were codified to limit ways of knowing and who could be a knower as it was a historical fact. Consequently, a discussion of colonization and education must begin with the effects of the Renaissance, Scientific Revolution, Reformation, and Enlightenment on gender relations. These discourses functioned to legitimate the colonizing of the "New World" by European powers. Women were central to this effort. Ironically, colonization provided them with sites for both resistance and accommodation.

The beginnings of this chapter trace the radical epistemological shifts embedded in the discourses of the Renaissance, Enlightenment, and Reformation as well as how these were intimately intertwined with colonization. How these discourses were gendered and how women of the period contested and appropriated these discourses to construct their own understandings of gender will be discussed. In part two of this chapter, the project of colonization in North America is examined from the perspective of women who saw the "New World" not as a site of exploitation but as a site for creating a "New Eden" in which gender relations would take on new meanings. While not negating the impositional and violent act of colonization, this chapter seeks to reinscribe colonial history in more complicated ways that highlight how the work of women (Maria of the Incarnation, Anne Hutchinson, the Ursuline Sisters, Ann Lee, and Henriette Delille) sought to simultaneously engage in colonization as a means to decolonize the gendered subject identities that had been imposed on them.

Did Women have a Renaissance?

This question posed by Joan Kelly (1999) calls into question accepted schemes of historical periodization. According to Kelly, "to take the emancipation of women as a vantage point is to discover that events that further the historical development of men, liberating them from natural, social, or ideological constraints, have quite different, even opposite, effects on women" (p. 21). As Kelly suggests, the changes brought on by the Renaissance culminated in the "state" emerging as the primary organizer of society rather than the feudal system. Although women were clearly subordinate within the feudal system, its more decentralized organization of power allowed ruptures in which women participated in the politics, economy, and cultural traditions of the day. In effect, gender relations as exemplified by courtly love displayed in feudal relations were predicated on reciprocal personal dependence (Kelly, 1999).[2] While medieval and feudal institutions had used social relations to work out a "genuine concern with sexual love," the denial of the right and power of women to love, the transformation of women into passive "others" who serve resulted in new social relationships that mirrored relations to the emerging nation-state. This "colonization" of women as "objects" and men as "subjects," whose primary bond was with the state, not personal relations, was central to the division of personal and public life that was to organize society. With this division, the modern relation of the sexes made its appearance. The task of how to educate men to take up identities as "subjects" of the "state" (with the corresponding discourses of "enlightenment" and "natural rights" that were to emerge) and how to educate women to take up the identity of "object" of knowledge (embedded in the discourses of "republican motherhood" and "cult of domesticity" that were to emerge) was the task of the day.[3] The colonization of men's and women's bodies to subordinate themselves to the state was central to the emergence of capitalism, the nation-state, and colonization. The shift from the medieval period to the beginning of the "modern" era resulted in gender being relegated to the private sphere and shaped all subsequent gender relations and social ideas regarding who could be a knower and what could be known.

Central to this new way of thinking was the rationalism of René Descartes, who, according to Lerner (1993), "had a liberating effect on women because he assumed that the mind, not the body, was the instrument for sensation and knowledge. And that men and women had the same potential for understanding" (p. 210). Although the long-term impact of Descartes' philosophy has been the hegemony of dualistic thinking and essentialized rationalism, it did function for women in the Renaissance as an argument against the essentializing discourses of gender, by arguing that it was the mind and not the body that was the site of knowledge. While women of the medieval period had argued through "embodied knowing" that they were moral creatures under God and thus entitled to equality, the dominant argument for women's education and women as knowers now shifted to one grounded in the "contract" and "natural rights" in which they would become more virtuous citizens.[4] Both Sir Thomas More and Desiderius Erasmus argued that since learning and morals go together, educating women would make them better women (Glenn, 1997). However, while the traditional humanist educational program emphasized Latin, grammar, rhetoric, history, poetry, and moral philosophy, the curricula for women focused on how learning would increase women's virtues—chastity, obedience, and humility. Woman's education was directed toward enhancing their womanliness. While education was opened to women, it was to be done in the home and the university was closed to all female students. Thus, the educated woman was one who was silent, obedient, and pious.

Isotta Nogarola of Verona, a 15th-century humanist, expressed her anxiety regarding her learnedness:

> Do not hold it against me, if I have transgressed those rules of silence especially imposed on women, and seem scarcely to have read that precept

of Vergerio's, which warns against encouraging articulateness in the young, since in plentiful speech there is always that which may be censured. And Sophocles too called silence a woman's greatest ornament.

(Jardine, 1999: 56)

In fact, women who spoke out as public intellectuals or were loose with their tongues were seen as immodest and naturally unchaste, vain, and promiscuous. According to Jardine (1999), "the charge that she is unchaste challenges the view that as a woman she can be a prominent humanist and remain a right living person" (p. 57). The sanction or stain of impropriety resulted in the censure of women's public voices. Consequently, a humanist education for women was not a preparation for public life, but was an end in itself; it had no purpose, but was merely a sign of cultivation. For men, a humanist education "provided a fictional identity of rank and worth on which the precarious edifice of fifteenth-century Italian city state's power structure depended. It read as 'valour,' 'manliness,' 'fortitude' . . ." (p. 70). So for ladies who aspired to be learned, the convent provided the guise of a private, chaste space in which the temptations of knowledge did not have to be resisted but could be indulged. To the convent they went.

While there were clearly learned women, "it was not customary for a woman to pursue advanced humanistic studies" (p. 50). It is in this climate that several women challenged the emerging epistemological shift based on gender. Christine de Pizan, as noted above, was a pioneer in advocating for women's education. *The Book of the City of Ladies*, by reconstructing the contributions of women to history, clearly establishes the innate intellectual capacity of women. Her educational treatise, *Le Livre des trios vertus*, outlined a plan for female education. Although she insisted that women's intellect and moral judgment were equal to men's, she assumed that men and women would have separate duties to perform. In fact, she did not contest the traditional role of women as wives and mothers, nor the traditional qualities of humility, patience, steadfastness, piety, modesty, and most of all "discretion" (Anderson & Zinsser, 1988). Women's primary role, according to Pizan, was to please her husband. In order to do this however, education was required. For Pizan, women's moral character was not innate, it had to be cultivated. Thus, the purpose of education for both men and women was to be the same: "the development of the whole person into a virtuous and moral human being" (Lerner, 1993: 194). However, because men and women had different duties to perform in everyday life, their education would have to be different. Only boys would receive instruction in Latin and speculative training; however, both boys and girls would learn mathematics. Young girls would also have instruction in sewing, knitting, embroidery, and weaving.

Throughout the 17th century, English, French, Dutch, and German women argued that it was not women's inherent intellectual inferiority that resulted in their lack of knowledge, but rather their educational deprivation. Their responses were varied, but one thing is clear: there was a movement to gain education. Margaret

Cavendish (1623–1674), the Duchess of Newcastle, was a strong advocate for women's education. Although self-educated, she wrote five "scientific" treatises, five collections of poetry, two books of essays and letters, and two volumes of plays. She attributed women's inferior status to the cruelty of men, and although married, was perhaps the first advocate for separate women's education as well as a utopian vision of a female community. A contemporary of Cavendish's, Mary Astell (1666–1731), a British intellectual, unlike Cavendish, spent most of her life in genteel poverty and chose a life of celibacy. Her major work, *A Serious Proposal to the Ladies, For the Advancement of their true and great Interest, By a Lover of Her Sex*, advocated that "God should be the only object of our Love" (Lerner, 1993: 203). This moral commitment became the rationale for her celibacy and platonic friendships with women and the foundation for educational reform. Specifically concerned with the education of women who were single, she proposed the founding of a college and home for women so that they might withdraw temporarily to educate and fortify themselves before returning to the world. For Astell, women were absolutely and inherently equal to men. Education would serve to raise women's consciousness "of their own situation so that they might better protect themselves from abusive male power" (p. 206). Her dream was of an independent intellectual women's community that would be its own colony, one in which women would be free of the colonizer. While this dream was never to materialize, she inspired women across Europe to challenge their subordination.[5]

According to Lerner (1993), "there was a theme of independent womanhood by the pioneers of feminist thought in 17th-century England and France" (p. 136). These women—Sarah Fyge, Bathsua Pell Makin, Mary Astell, Lady Mary Chudleigh, and Marie de Gournay in France, often referred to as the "Blue Stockings"—shared a commitment to the development of social roles of women outside of marriage and motherhood. Education that promoted the intellectual advancement of women was central to that vision. Across Europe in the salons of France, England, and Germany the "Blue Stockings" met for intellectual discussion, support in writing and publishing, and friendship. In London, the first group composed of Elizabeth Carter, Elizabeth Montagu, Catherine Talbot, Hester Chapone, Samuel Johnson, Samuel Pepys, George Berkeley, the Rev. Thomas Birch, and Samuel Richardson supported the publications of Elizabeth Carter's translation of the Stoic philosopher Epictetus through advance subscriptions and a generation later, Fanny Burney's third novel, *Camilla*, was supported based on the subscription list gathered by the Blue Stockings. While excluded from formal sites of education, women found sites, like the salons, in which to pursue their intellectual activities. These activities, as well as those of women religious to found schools for girls and women, signified women's desire to provide a counternarrative to the dominant ideologies that maintained that women were not capable of intellectual thought. While many women of the medieval period sought agency through the body, women of the Renaissance, given the focus on reason, were compelled to justify their intellectual capacity in ways that extended the discourses of the body.

The process by which feudal independence and reciprocity yielded to the state, and its corollary dependency in gender relations, occurred over several centuries and at different rates in different countries. Although seen as a "Renaissance" for men, for women these social relations had dire implications, especially in the realm of education.[6] Positioned as "objects," women were constructed as passive, emotional, and incapable of reason.[7] The reemergence of classical Greek thought, in particular Aristotle, further reinforced beliefs that women were inferior. Ironically, the "Renaissance" is depicted in traditional histories as the period in which the individual emerged from a site of oppression in a feudal, medieval period better known as the "dark ages." The concept of the "individual" as a reasoned and rational subject, as opposed to the medieval inter-subjective and holistic subject, was the precondition for the first formal schooling and education. There was nothing natural about constituting subject identity as a gendered binary in which maleness required one to take up the discourses of reason, rationality, and individuality and femaleness required the discourses of virtue, piety, and obedience. The inscription of the concept of "an" individual with a determined interiority (a spatial concept) that is occupied by a particular version of the self was essential to the production of "the" rational subject which was the precondition for the corollary concepts of "citizen" and "state." According to Bernadette Baker (2001) "this version of the subject was comported to be reflective, had a transparent and visible self, had techniques of the self, and was able to pivot back and glance at that self from other vantagepoints of the person" (p. 19). There is a subject because a certain type of "relationship with the self" comes into being in a culture. While traditional histories have highlighted this new subject as one that is capable of rationality and reason, Baker suggests that this new rational "subject" is only possible due to a simultaneous reconfiguring of space. The subject, previously constituted, or understood as intersubjective, or as being in relation, now is understood as inhabiting a space. In other words, the subject now had an "inside that could be impacted to some extent by what was outside" (p. 63). This new reconfiguration of the subject requires a spatial reconstruction of the subject that includes an interiority and exteriority. I would suggest that the "renaissance" had not so much to do with "new" or "renewed" knowledge, but with a new subjectivity that was predicated on a binary understanding of interiority/exteriority, male/female, reason/emotion, self/other, and subject/object. This binary view of subjectivity is the precondition for, and makes possible, the discursive power relations of colonization.

Because these new discursive identities were not "natural," they had to be learned. At the heart of this new identity was a *subject* who took itself as an *object* of possible knowledge (Baker, 2001). This new subject, predicated on an imagined interior space, which was conceived as an empty space to be filled, could now be colonized because it functioned as an "object." Formal education, or schooling, became part of the technologies through which this colonization took place. While this period is commonly understood as an advance or progress toward "enlightenment," this obscures the ways in which the discourses of education were central to the production of subjectivity and gender as a binary that functioned in both liberatory and oppressive modes. That "education" became central to the discursive practices that were critical to the construction of a gendered subject identity is in direct opposition to the dominant narrative of curriculum that maintains that this was a period of "enlightenment." In the following section, I examine how several women "enlightenment" thinkers negotiated their sub-jectivities within these new discourses of gender, identity, space, and power. Again, I do not mean to "recuperate" women in order to fill in an incomplete "enlighten-ment" narrative. Conversely, I seek to re-member how particular women at this particular moment negotiated new subjectivities and spaces within complex colonizing discourses.

Enlightenment? For Whom?

> It is an absurd notion that the education of females should be of an opposite kind to males . . . education should be the same for all rational beings.
>
> *(Catherine Macaulay, 1790)*

The Renaissance was the prelude to a burgeoning of educational "enlightenment" philosophies including the writings of John Locke (1632–1704) and Jean Jacques Rousseau (1712–1778). Central to the educational philosophies of these two thinkers was a radical epistemological shift that was part of a larger paradigm shift. This shift, prompted by the "Age of Reason" and the "Scientific Revolution," posited that knowledge was not the result of spiritual, divine, or embodied know-ledge, but the direct result of the inductive study of nature through experience and experiment (Smith & Smith, 1994). According to Locke, "No man's knowledge can go beyond his experience" (Davis, 2004: 89). Locke formulated a *tabula rasa* theory of the mind: the mind was a blank slate (or empty space) ready to be filled with experience. Smith and Smith (1994) identify six themes that characterize the enlightenment: rationality, scientific naturalism, anticlericalism, human happiness, experience, and learning effectiveness. While these ideas under-pinned the growing belief that educational opportunity should be available to all individuals and groups, the emerging beliefs regarding social and gender binaries resulted in a differentiated curriculum that contributed to the emergence of a colonizing curriculum.

Although Rousseau and Locke advocated education for women, they clearly prescribed a curriculum for girls that would prepare them solely for the roles of housewife and mother. Locke, who was to influence the revolutionary thinkers in colonial America, advocated that each individual is endowed with inalienable rights that were to be protected by a social contract with the state.[8] Women, because they were "naturally" subordinate to men, were excluded from this con-tract. Rousseau, although advocating education as the prime site from which to educate the self-reliant, autonomous, and rational citizen of the state, also prescribed a woman's role as that of tending the male and making his life pleasant. Jane Roland Martin (1985) maintains that "Emile is to be educated for the role of citizen, and hence the political realm, Sophie is not . . . does this not mean that Emile's education will be governed by one set of principles and Sophie's by another?" (p. 51). These separate gender-bound ideals of education were central to Rousseau's philosophy and relegated women to the private sphere. For Martin, the critical issue is not only that women were not seen as suited to the public sphere but, more importantly, the private sphere of women which constitutes the work of mothering, child rearing, and domestic duties is seen to be of no value in constituting definitions of citizenship.

The Age of Enlightenment can be credited with the emergence of modern schooling as a right of all "citizens." Thus, the idea of schooling (rather than family, church, or community) as a primary apparatus for shaping cultural norms and ideologies of morality and civic knowledge emerged in this time period. While the liberating effects of this expansion of education cannot be underestimated, when we look more closely at the emergence of "schooling" and its corollary discourses of "rationality," it had profound colonizing effects.[9] Education became the primary way in which the new social relations of gender as separate domains of public/private, subject/object, reason/emotion were codified. Although the term "enlightenment" has been used to signify progress because education became available to more people, the reification of a gender dichotomy that functioned as essentialized and disadvantaged both genders, has been obscured. Men's education was grounded in rationality, while women whose powers of reason were seen as "less," were limited to an education that prepared them for their domestic roles. This binary separation of intellectual capacities based on gender imposed through dominant educational narratives of the time was negotiated by women thinkers in a variety of ways.

Mary Wollstonecraft (1759–1797), a British intellectual, would be the first to "put the claims for women's rights and equality in the context of a broader liberationist theory for all of society" (Lerner, 1993: 211). By 1790, Wollstonecraft considered herself one of the apostles of the Enlightenment who championed a new philosophy which rejected arbitrary power, as manifested in the Divine Right of Kings, and instead saw civil and religious liberties as part of one's birthright. These rights were "natural" but required an educated and reasoned mind. Power did not dwell in the monarchy or aristocracy, but in a political community which derived authority from the consent of each individual governed by it (Brody, 2004). The individuals in the community would exercise their sovereign power by virtue of the capacity to reason intelligently, a capacity that was strengthened by proper education. Education was central to this new social contract.

Wollstonecraft's philosophical evolution was in part the product of her experi- ences as an educator. Born into a middle-class family and desiring to stay single, she established in 1784 a school at Newington Green, a center for intellectual writers and reformers in London. In 1787, she published *Thoughts on the Education of Daughters*, which did not challenge the traditional domestic sphere for women, but criticized the lack of seriousness with which most women, especially those of the upper classes, gave to their duties as mothers and wives. For Wollstonecraft, virtue and moral character were the product of hard work. For women who indulged in vanity and frivolous behavior, Wollstonecraft had little patience. Her stint as a governess for Lady Kingsborough in Ireland reinforced her belief in the need to educate girls not in elite boarding schools or through private tutors, but in an atmosphere where their self-indulgence and vanity would be redirected to the "intellectual and moral development of their own children" by administering to the suffering poor around them (Brody, 2004: xv). Influenced by her intellectual community in London, she increasingly developed the belief that it was an educated mind that resulted in virtue and thus was a necessity for women.[10] Consequently she published *The Female Reader*—which might be considered the first textbook for girls and would imprint useful lessons on the mind. The reader included selections from the Bible and Shakespeare as well as a preface and four prayers which she wrote herself.

Her most radical work and the one which laid out in most detail her philosophy of education was *A Vindication of the Rights of Women*, published in 1790. In this work, she dared to take the liberal doctrine of inalienable rights as articulated by John Locke and Jean Jacques Rousseau and assumed these rights for her own sex. In *A Vindication of the Rights of Women* she argued for the equal education of women. Her primary premise was that better educated women would make better wives and mothers, and thus produce better citizens. Educated motherhood provided an ideology that left intact the gender norms of separate spheres for men and women, but argued that if motherhood was so important, it could not be left to the uneducated. This concept would appear as Republican Motherhood in America.

And while many other women had advocated for education for women, Wollstonecraft was singular in her analysis of the role economic and social systems played in the subordination of women (Brody, 2004). Women would never be "equal" if they could not be seen as independent human beings.[11] Gender ideologies in the 18th century were based on notions of women as dependent, passive, submissive, and the "weaker" vessel. For Wollstonecraft, equality did not mean that women and men would not have different social roles. In fact, she embraced an essentialized ideology that elevated women's greatest work to mothering the virtuous citizens of the republic. By taking up an essentialized subject identity, this appropriation of dominant gender ideologies functions to legitimate the education of women.

Wollstonecraft was the first to advocate for a "national" education program for both girls and boys. This program would replace traditional boarding-school education for girls that emphasized dance, music, and decorum, with a rigorous curriculum that included history, philosophy, classical languages, botany, and physical education. Central to her educational vision was the "equal" education of the sexes. Gender inequality, in her analysis, had been the result of unequal education in which men had been educated to be rational, which she believed was vital to doing everything from running the government to disciplining a child (Smith & Smith, 1994). It was the lack of training in rationality that had resulted in women's servitude. Consequently, Wollstonecraft proposed a national system of education in which a system of coeducation would produce independent women capable of making rational decisions. In her vision, elementary schools would serve all children from all classes between ages of five and nine. Girls and boys would dress alike so that teachers would have difficulty in distinguishing by sex or class. After age nine, working-class boys and girls would be separated so that they could learn appropriate skills and trades. Wollstonecraft was especially adamant that working-class girls learn skills so they could be financially independent. Middle-class children, both boys and girls, would receive an education that prepared them for university study and professional careers. While class distinctions were made, gender differences were to be eradicated in her vision of education. The result of this coeducation would be equality of the sexes.

The radical nature of this proposal can be understood by the sweeping criticism it engendered from both women and men. Hannah More, a contemporary of Wollstonecraft and advocate for women's education, vehemently opposed the view that women and men were equal. She wrote in *Strictures on the Modern System of Female Education* (1799) that "Far be it from me to make scholastic ladies or female dialecticians, it is only the vulgar and ill informed who struggle most vehemently for power" (Brody, 2004: xxxix). While More advocated for women's education, and like Wollstonecraft criticized the contemporary curriculum that focused on fashion and manners, she parted ways with Wollstonecraft's view that women given the same education as men would also become intellectuals. For More, morality and virtue were spiritually derived and not a product of "reason." Reason threatened to undermine the force of Christian humanism as well as corrupt women by indoctrinating them to a worldview that was focused on worldly power and pursuits rather than spiritual ones. Wollstonecraft became the target of much criticism for her radical view on women's intellectual capacities. This critique suggests that women philosophers of the time did not act in unison, but that there was a variety of responses to the complex array of gender-social ideologies that had to be negotiated. Not all women thinkers embraced "rationality" or "reason." While Wollstonecraft garners much attention in regard to educational philosophy and history, women philosophers responded in a variety of ways to the colonizing effects of education.

Elizabeth Hamilton (1758–1816) exemplifies the complex negotiations in which women Enlightenment philosophers engaged as they articulated a philosophy of education. Born in Belfast, she lived much of her life in Edinburgh and moved in the circles of the Scottish Enlightenment philosophers. According to Martin and Goodman (2004),

The fundamental building block of Hamilton's educational theory—the centrality of the education of the heart to the education of the intellect—followed closely the aims of Scottish Enlightenment philosophers of the common-sense school to build a "science of the human mind" based on the writing of John Locke. (p. 35)

While drawing on Locke, Hamilton departed from him in that she did not believe that all ideas were formed solely by external stimuli. Drawing on the writings of Johann Heinrich Pestalozzi (1746–1827), the Swiss pedagogue who is credited as the father of child-centered learning that focuses on objects and children's experiences, rather than on books, she theorized that the development of the mind and of ideas was not solely a rational process but one which engaged intuition and the heart. Thus, Hamilton rejected the rigid dichotomy of reason/emotion or mind/body which was central to the construction of gendered identities in dominant Enlightenment thought as well as in the thought of Wollstonecraft.

In *Hints Addressed to the Patrons and Directors of Schools*, published in 1815, Hamilton outlined the practical applications of Pestalozzi's method and argued for a child-centered, active, experiential learning method. Rejecting both the educational philosophies of Locke and Rousseau, she was drawn to Pestalozzi's "method" because it was both empirical (based on the observation of children) and philosophical. His critique of rote learning was based on his view of children as active seekers, not blank slates. *Hints* outlines the basic principles of education she formulated, many of which she shared with Pestalozzi: interest in the science of the mind; a view of education in which aspects of affect, morality, and reason were viewed holistically; a stress on the importance of early education; an active experimental pedagogy; and a critique of rote learning.

Unlike Wollstonecraft, Hamilton rejected the notion of reason as the source of knowledge. Alternatively, she articulated a philosophy that resisted the dualisms of reason/mind and instead posited a theory of knowledge that engaged heart, body, and mind. In her publication *A Series of Popular Essays: Illustrative of Principles Connected with the Improvement of Understanding* (1813), she discussed the relationship between understanding, imagination, and the heart. She believed that the heart was central to the later development of the intellect; this had a great impact on shaping her vision of the role of mothers as the master-key to the minds of children. Mothers were central to the moral development of children as well as to national interests. She put forward a view that domestic virtue constructed national identity. Mothers were central to the regeneration of the nation, and if they were to do their job well, they needed to be educated as intellectuals. Thus Hamilton combined domesticity and intellectual work and did not see these as mutually exclusive or essentialized. In *Letter on Education* she begins by offering herself "as a model for the new intellectual-domestic woman" (Kelly, 1993: 265). She represented the "domestic woman" as the professionalized custodian of the national conscience, culture, and destiny.

While most women philosophers during this time argued that it was not women's innate inferiority that resulted in their educational disadvantage, but their lack of educational opportunity; it was the question of what kind of education women should receive that was debated. Most agreed that "motherhood" was the role for which women should be educated. "Motherhood" was central to the project of building the nation state by virtue of their role in rearing "citizens." This construct of the citizen as a rational, autonomous, individual was central to the ongoing ideologies of public/private and the "state" as the center of identity formation. Imposition of this gendered subjectivity required a form of colonization that required men to become "virtuous citizens," women to become "mothers," and the construction of the "child" (Baker, 2001). These subject identities were, I would argue, the primary curricular goal of the emergent notion of national education and a corollary of the colonization of bodies as male/female, public/private, and self/other. Thus, despite notions of education as liberating women and men and as central to "enlightenment," I argue that education also becomes a form of colonization.

Implicit in several women theorists' critiques of the role of education during this time is an articulation of the role of the "new" citizen as part of the hegemony of the state. Catherine Macaulay (1731–1791), although best known as a British political historian and philosopher, was also a theorist who advocated for the education of young people (Titone, 1999). Her theory of education is best articulated in her work *Letters on Education*, published in 1790.[12] Macaulay reflected a growing number of women professional writers: increased education, resulted in a more literate population, urbanization resulted in newspapers and magazines, more leisure time resulted in the growth of a female readership. Macaulay exemplified the modern woman and philosopher. Her most well read work, the *History of England*, was published in 1763. This was the first political history written by an English woman and was widely read throughout Europe and in the American colonies where leading thinkers such as John Adams, Benjamin Franklin, Mercy Otis Warren, and George Washington praised it.

Macaulay's political theory in which she engaged with the ideas of the "enlightenment," and the new concept of the "citizen," were a prelude to her larger preoccupation with the role of education in shaping the ideal citizen. Shaped by the dominant ideologies of the Enlightenment with its focus on man as a rationale being, whose contract with the state would result in the natural liberties guaranteed to each citizen, she was an unabashed proponent of rationality. Where she departed with thinkers such as Locke and Rousseau was that for Macaulay (like her younger contemporary Wollstonecraft), rationality was not solely the domain of men. She argued that human nature was not biologically determined but that "human nature—the essential wholeness of the human being—is separate and distinct from the exhibited set of properties of boys and girls as observed in society" (Titone, 1999: 8). Gender traits as exhibited in 18th-century Europe were socially constructed not biological, not essentialized. This radical departure from the dominant gender ideologies of two separate natures was the fundamental foundation for her philosophy of education. The purpose of education was to achieve wholeness as a human being, for only in so doing could one become the rational and moral human being that was the prerequisite for citizenship.

Most educational efforts during this time, including Wollstonecraft's, as noted above focused on women receiving an education like men. Rationality (male) was understood as central to knowledge and women could only become rational (and thus knowing subjects) by having an education like men. Thus, Macaulay's vision of education was not merely compensatory (adding women to men's education), but truly revolutionary in that she advocated that education should encourage the full expression of both what we consider feminine and masculine qualities. Without this integration of masculine and feminine, human beings would be distorted, necessarily crippled. The improvement of society depended on both men and women perceiving themselves and functioning as complete intellectual and emotional co-equals. This was the essence of becoming more fully educated and more fully human. Education would be radically reshaped. For Macaulay it was education, not the family, legal system, or Church that was the critical context for addressing and changing beliefs and behaviors (Titone, 1999).

Macaulay was radical in maintaining that the fundamental premise of education needed to be rethought by redefining gender not as dualistic and essentialized. While embracing rationality as one trait of what it meant to be human, she was unlike Wollstonecraft who saw rationality as the sole source of knowledge. While both embraced "enlightenment" ideas of rationality, Wollstonecraft maintained an essentialized view of gender in which women could become rational beings like men through equal education. And for Wollstonecraft, rationality for women was to be used to enhance their skills as mothers. While many women of the time argued for the education of women based on the notion that education was essential to "good" motherhood and the raising of virtuous citizens, others rejected this essentializing rationale as the grounds for women's education.

In summary, women of the Enlightenment resisted the notion that they were intellectually inferior. They did so by writing and arguing that it was not the lack of intelligence but the lack of education. Most advocated that women have access to the education of men. This compensatory step accepted the dominant curriculum with its focus on rationality, the classics, and rote learning. Catherine Macaulay was perhaps the only theorist to challenge the very foundations of the curriculum by proposing an epistemology that conceptualized education without drawing on a gender dichotomy as its basis. This was a step toward the decolonization of subject identities that were imposed through rigid gender dichotomies. While most reforms focused on adding women to men's schools, this essentially required women to internalize the colonizer's binary worldview under the guise of "equality." Yet, there were women thinkers who rejected the concept of "equality" as defined by the state. For women religious, "equality" was a man-made concept that was inherently flawed because it presumed earthly matters as central to "freedom" and "liberty." The emergence of numerous Catholic women's communities (as well as some Protestant) during the 17th century was in part not only a consequence of the Counter-Reformation and Reformation, but I would argue a response to emerging notions of subjectivity grounded in the rational/reasoned/ public/citizen subject whose primary allegiance was to the state. For women religious "enlightenment" was theorized from the premise of spiritual universalism that rejected a binary view of subjectivity. Thus, throughout the Renaissance and Enlightenment women religious also advocated for the education of women, yet they did so on very different grounds as humanist women and women of the "enlightenment."

(Re)forming Women: Women Religious and Curriculum Theory

The Reformation has been understood as a "reform" movement in which the corruption and hierarchical nature of the Catholic Church was critiqued. The "new" Protestant denominations sought to eliminate the "Church" as an institution that mediated one's experience and instead posited that individuals could have a direct relationship with God. While this clearly was liberatory in light of the excesses of the Catholic Church and its hegemony, and might also be seen as a form of decolonization, the Reformation worked in complex and contradictory ways in relation to education. For both Catholic and Protestant male clerics the dominant belief regarding women was that they were by definition inferior to men and therefore must be subordinate. Consequently, the "reformation" did not reform the Church for women by validating their personal experience of the divine or their expression of this through public speaking or preaching. Both Martin Luther and John Calvin believed unequivocally that women could not perform any aspect of the ministry (Anderson & Zinsser, 1988). Like the "renaissance," the "reformation" did not reform ideas about gender, "the active, the intellect, the reason is man; the lesser, the passive, the material, the body is woman" (p. 254). This "natural" hierarchy, taken from the metaphor of the patriarchal family found in the Jewish Bible (or Old Testament), was the foundation of the family in which the father was the patriarch and the woman the model child. These gender relations did not fulfill the democratic promise of the Reformation for either men or women. For men, this position of power precluded any possibility of a mutually interdependent relationship and imposed modes of masculinity and heterosexuality that were essentialized and circumscribed. For women, the Reformation held even less potential for "reform." According to Anderson and Zinsser (1988), "woman found herself defined in relation to a man, given no identity outside of that relationship" (p. 257). This was in stark contrast to the medieval religious experience where women religious claimed a direct relationship with God.

While the Reformation maintained dominant gender roles, like all ideologies there were spaces for rupture, resistance, and appropriation. One of these was that the model Christian wife needed to know how to read. According to Lerner (1993), "the protestant reformation was the major intellectual watershed for women in a variety of ways" (p. 129). Central to the Reformation of Martin Luther was making the "word of God" accessible to all. No longer would a select clergy have a monopoly on the Bible. The Bible was to be available to all and this required fundamental literacy. Thus, Protestantism fostered the development of public education by making rudimentary education available to all girls and boys. Women in particular were expected not only to be able to read the Bible, but to teach their children to read and write so they could acquire religious knowledge. Male Christian humanists such as More and Erasmus argued that because learning and morals go together, educating women would make them even more virtuous; they would be even more chaste, obedient, and humble. The education of women was thus promoted, but not for the public roles that male priests or intellectuals undertook. Women's education was clearly to serve and honor men. It was a private matter intended for the purposes of educating children and in some cases for the pleasure of the father and/or husband.

For Protestant Reformers who sought to make the Bible accessible to all, the purposes of education differed from those of Renaissance humanists. Reformist instruction had a narrow, vernacular, biblical education as its focus as compared to that of the humanists which was characterized by a broad, intellectual, multilingual education for the purposes of cultivating the intellect, primarily of upper-class women. The focus of Reformation education was on the education of all girls and boys for the purposes of moral and social "domination inherent in the Christianization of society" (Glenn, 1997: 150). The focus on the return of purity of the early Christian Church marked it as a spiritual movement that extended equality to all followers. This egalitarian worldview necessitated a much broader educational program while the humanists promoted a more intensive intellectual program to a more elite segment of society. Thus, while the Reformation ushered in education that was to be extended to all, it was clearly less intellectual and reproduced a patriarchical worldview in which women and non-Protestants were objects of colonization.

There were also dissidents from the mainstream of Calvinist and Lutheran Protestant reform who sought to embody the true potential of the Reformation. The reformist group that most clearly embodied a vision of equality and education were the Quakers.[13] Led by George Fox, the Quakers believed that the "inner light" made Quaker women equal to men, and women were embraced as equals in the struggle for the new world of "brotherhood" (Anderson & Zinsser, 1988). Fox's pamphlet *The Woman Learning in Silence* (1656) articulated the basic principles of Quakerism that were based on the belief that all human beings had been created by God by implanting the Indwelling Spirit in everyone. This included both men and women. Quaker women were better educated than most of their contemporaries and unlike other Protestant Reform groups they had a tradition of public speaking and of religious leadership.

Margaret Fell (1614–1692) exemplified this new religious woman and had an active public career as a missionary, teacher, preacher, and writer. She and George Fox eventually married and were imprisoned for not taking the Oath of Allegiance to the Crown. While in prison, she wrote *Women's Speaking Justified* (1667) which was a fully developed scriptural argument justifying women's active role in biblical history and their right to participate in public religious life (Lerner, 1993). She wrote (Fell, 1667):

> Those that speak against the Power of the Lord, and the Spirit of the Lord speaking in woman, simply, by reason of her Sex, or because she is a Woman, not regarding the Seed, and Spirit, and Power that is in her; such speak against the Christ, and his Church, and are the Seed of the Serpent. (p. 5)

Fell advocated the resistance of gender norms and expectations of the "Renaissance" which situated women as subordinate to men. But, perhaps even more radical was her epistemological position, shared by the Quakers, that all individuals were capable of constructing knowledge. Knowledge was not "out" there, but was a personal, relational experience that was grounded in self-awareness and spiritual transformation (reminiscent of the Gnostics). This view of knowledge differed radically from the dominant notions of rationality that were deeply embedded in gender relations of the 17th and 18th centuries. Women, as well as men, were not objects of knowledge, but were subjects: subjects who were resisting the colonizing effects of subject identities that constructed the individual with clearly distinct gendered roles. As a religious philosopher, Fell articulated an early form of feminist pedagogy that situated the individual as an active agent in constructing knowledge.

Anna Maria von Schurman (1607–1678), a learned German Protestant, also challenged the denigration and subordination of women in her classically inspired arguments for female education. Her treatise of 1638, *Whether the Study of Letters Is Fitting to a Christian Woman?*, was published in the Netherlands, France, and England. In this work she raised questions about the "traditional views of women's limited roles, and by its very existence proved how learned a female could become" (Anderson & Zinsser, 1988: 265). Although her early work was pre-occupied with the role of study and learning, her later theories eventually questioned the role study and learning played in "true knowledge" and perfection. She is credited with having developed the form and structure of the Pietist "house church" which gave women unusual opportunities for religious leadership. Her vision shifted from one of isolated scholarship to a communal life which combined practical knowledge and spiritual growth.

Ironically, her promotion of the education of women was not free from colonizing tendencies. In her Latin treatise *The Learned Maid or, Whether a Maid May Be a Scholar* (1641), she advocated education for only those who could afford the means of instruction and who were free from domestic cares (Lerner, 1993).

As a celibate woman, she was free from the tension between domesticity and intellectual pursuits that functioned to inhibit many women from pursuing education. However, Anna Maria von Schurman had a profound impact on the renowned intellectuals of the day, including René Descartes (who greatly admired her) and Cardinal Richelieu, as well as inspiring many women of her time and serving as a role model for many generations to come.

While this flourishing of women's active agency was welcomed in the early stages of the Reformation, as women took up roles as preachers, teachers, and interpreters of the Scripture, their roles as "equals" were questioned. By 1698, six years after Fell's death, women were effectively excluded from the administration of the Quaker sect and by 1701 women who attended the yearly Quaker meetings had to give prior notice if they wanted to speak. Protestant women prophets found that when they acknowledged the inferiority of their sex, spoke of themselves as vessels of the divine, and echoed the views of the male leaders of their faith, their prophecies were acknowledged and they avoided persecution (similar to the narrative strategies medieval women mystics used). While many women negotiated these shifting gender expectations by embracing the rhetoric of submission, some like Anna Trapnell, the mystical English poet, did not. In 1654, she was imprisoned by Cromwell. Jane Lead (1624–1704) was deemed unorthodox for her writings. She envisaged a soul united with Sophia, the feminine Wisdom, a union more awesome than anything promised in other faiths. Much like the Gnostics, she made Eve her heroine. Thus, while the Reformation ushered in a time in which there was promise that women could be knowers and interpreters of their own experience, this was a brief period. And while Fell was eventually released from prison, others were not as fortunate and were burned at the stake when their transgressions went too far.[14] Negotiating the complex rhetoric of "reform" was a delicate balancing act. While the Reformation initiated a mass movement in educating boys and girls, most reformers, like followers of Luther and Calvin, criticized women for speaking too eloquently and believed that no woman should perform any tasks of public teaching or ministry.

In the end, Protestant reformers, like many of the Enlightenment philosophers, took up the ideology of "motherhood," which resulted in the essentializing of women's role and solidifying a binary framing of gender. Female literacy was not advocated out of any sense of equality, but was strictly seen as women's proper role, thus reinforcing dominant gender roles. In addition, the intense religious struggles of the day required that each denomination find means of maintaining and perpetuating their particular faith. If women and mothers could be educated they would more likely ensure that the next generation would be trained and indoctrinated into the respective faith. The desire to make and keep converts to the faith became a major force in the push for public education—a form of colonization. Women reformers were both colonized and colonizer. They were colonized by gender norms that continued to regulate women's roles in the Church to private, domestic activities in which women were clearly "carrying" out the word of others, but never their own ideas or experiences. At the same time, as mothers responsible for teaching reading and writing, they participated in the colonizing act of reinforcing a binary view of male/female, subject/object, and self/other. Embedded in this dualistic ontology was a corollary epistemology, one in which knowledge was viewed as external, fixed, and in need of being transmitted from the outside into an internal state. This exterior and interior reconfiguration of space and subjectivity was essential to the colonization that would eventually extend to the "New World."

On the one hand, the Reformation did provide a site of self-authorization for women. Despite its restrictions on women and rhetoric of inferiority and sub-servience, the new Protestant denominations called on women religious to promote their faith through education and even preaching. This space opened a floodgate through which numerous women organized institutions and spaces in which to educate women. Women religious went so far as to participate as active colonizers in the "New World" as a means of not only spreading the faith but of creating a "New Eden," a world that would embody the "true" vision of Christianity in which gender was not the defining category. Before looking at one example of the transformation of Protestantism in the "New World," I turn to the theorizing of Catholic women religious during the time of the Reformation. Ironically, the focus of much hatred among male Protestant reformers was the convent. This space, which provided women a place of their own, like the centers of learning at Whitby, Bingen, and Helfta discussed in the last chapter, were clearly a threat to Protestant reformers who sought to colonize women.[15]

In the Shadow of God: Catholic Women Religious

Threatened by the zeal of the Protestant Reformation, the Catholic Church allowed new groups of nuns to be organized that were allowed to teach, tend to the sick and poor, and manage their own convents. Unlike the Protestants, the Catholics could not go so far as to let women preach.[16] Catholic women religious wasted no time in organizing orders for the purposes of education. Catholic women religious, like those of the medieval period, were at the forefront of advocating for the education of women. The first order for teaching was the Ursuline order founded in Italy in 1535 by St. Angela Merici. Whereas previously, female orders had been cloistered and engaged in a single activity—prayer— Merici's Ursulines lived in the outside world and engaged in the public activity of teaching girls. They justified this radical departure by arguing that it was mothers who gave children their first religious training and, therefore, young girls who were to become mothers needed to read and write and be educated in church doctrine. And because Protestantism promoted literacy for women, the Catholic Church recognized that they must also do so.

By 1598 after 40 years of religious warfare that granted religious freedom to the Protestant Huguenots, ardent French Catholics were committed to return France to Catholicism. A massive missionary campaign was needed. Throughout 16th–century France, small groups of pious laywomen offered instruction in Catholic doctrine and over time they became Ursulines. By 1610 there were 29 Ursuline communities. By 1700 there were more than 300 communities and 10% of all French women lived as avowed religious in this teaching order (Rapley, 1990). French Ursulines were essentially missionaries dedicated to restoring France to the "true faith" by a program of universal education for women.[17] The Ursulines spread to Catholic Germany, Belgium, and Holland and provided lower and secondary education for rich and poor girls alike. The curriculum emphasized Catholic motherhood and homemaking, thus instilling in young women a sense of their importance in being active agents of the faith. It was these Ursulines who would venture to the "New World" in 1727 to continue their vision of universal female education.

Another Catholic educator, Mary Ward (1585–1645), born in Yorkshire, England, was a lay sister of the Poor Clares, and in 1609 she established a religious community of women in France that ran a school for girls. This was followed by the founding of nearly a dozen schools throughout Europe that served both English boarding students and a day school for the children of the poor. The academic standards of the schools were very high, being modeled on the Jesuits' school for boys and included the study of Latin and other foreign languages. These convent schools for girls were highly recognized and several Mary Ward schools are still in existence in Germany today.

The Counter-Reformation, like the Reformation, extended education to girls and boys, and sought to educate all in the basic rudiments of reading and writing as a means of making the Bible accessible to all, not just an exclusive group within the Church. This democratization of religious life clearly extended literacy to the masses and signaled that one's personal experience of the "Word" was a legitimate form of knowledge. According to Lerner (1993), "Education was no longer only a necessity for economic and class advancement, it was now for Protestants the direct means for reaching salvation, a religious responsibility for the individual and the community" (p. 198). At the same time, this extension of who could be a knower and what could be known was clearly inscribed by gender. Least women abandon their maternal and domestic spaces, it was argued that women's education was to improve their roles as mothers, wives, and helpmates. Men were ultimately the interpreters of the word, while women were to "teach" the interpretations of men. Silence, submission, and piety were the characteristics of good Christian women. Consequently, education functioned to colonize the female into a role of submission and the realm of the private, and the male into one of dominator whose realm was the public arena. Thus, the notion of separate spheres, predicated on dualistic subject identities of who could and could not be a knower was brought to the "New World" and was, in fact, central to the colonization process by making possible the concept of the "other." While women religious were inscribed within these colonial relations and shifting subjectivities, I maintain that they were not passive pawns of the Church, but to the contrary, they were active agents in negotiating the complex and contradictory discourses as a means to inscribe their own understandings of the education necessary to achieve spiritual universalism.

The "New Eden": Colonizing the "New World"

While the Reformation resulted in new sects and the flourishing of new experiments in religious life in Europe, the potential for the fulfillment of a truly spiritual reform would require new soil, soil untainted by the legacy of corruption, greed, and politics of religious institutions both Catholic and Protestant. The "New World" became the site on which both Protestant reformers and Catholic visionaries sought to construct their "New Edens." Ironically, this colonization would entail the submission of indigenous peoples (Ng-a-fook, 2006). For women religious, this new space provided a place to enact true reform. This vision of a "New Eden" was one based on a spiritual universalism in which the knowledge of God was to be extended to all. This "education" was the task of women. For women religious the "New World" brought the promise of challenging the ideology of separate spheres that relegated them to objects of knowledge and never knowers in their own right. I will focus on two examples of what I suggest are decolonizing curriculum theorists—the Puritan, Anne Hutchinson, and the Ursuline Sisters who settled in colonial Louisiana. While these two clearly inhabit contradictory spaces in relation to their role as both colonized and colonizer, they obviously disrupted the colonial gender norms that were central to the ideologies of domination and submission inherent in colonization.

The New Eve and American Jezebel—Anne Hutchinson

Founded as the "city on the hill," this image of the Puritan "New World," as they called it, was to be the true embodiment of God's vision for humankind. While leaving behind what they saw as the excesses of the Church (even the reformed Church), the Puritans were convinced that they were the "chosen" people of God. At the heart of the Puritan ideology was the belief in the doctrines of predestination and the conversion experience. They saw themselves as an elect and they knew the truth. Jonathan Winthrop, the colonies' first governor, saw his exodus from England as part of a second Protestant Reformation (LaPlante, 2004). As the Church of England had withdrawn from the Church of Rome, he in turn was withdrawing from the Church of England. In 1630, 11 ships sailed for the New World with the goal of purifying the Church—thus the name *New* England. How they would define the central institutions of Church, government, and school would inevitably reflect how the individual was understood. For the Puritans, the individual was a moral being, not an economic or political being. According to McKnight (2003), "Puritans had always sought methods toward morality, reasoned approaches toward certain behaviors. However, it was up to each individual to develop the method through prayer, contemplation, and Biblical interpretation, as long as one eye carefully attended to the moral conventions of the day" (p. 33). One might term this an epistemology of "reasoned spirituality," a combination of reason/rationality and faith/spirituality. This epistemology was central to the Puritan critique of the Catholic Church whose absolute control over theological interpretation had excluded any possibility of individual insight or knowledge of God. Control thus shifted to the individual as the locus of knowledge, not the Church. With this shift came the negotiation between individual agency and maintaining group identity (i.e., control). This tension was clearly exemplified by the controversy of the relationship between the individual and God as evidenced by the case of the trial of Anne Hutchinson and later the Salem Witch trials. These events were pedagogical acts that determined the relationship between gender, knowledge, the individual, and the community. The Puritans initially drew on both reason and faith as interrelated sites of knowledge. Faith revealed the ultimate mystery of God and God was the source of reason.[18] The balance between faith and reason was to be tested as the Puritans set out on their "errand." Inevitably this balance was a gendered one and was pushed to its limits by Anne Hutchinson.

Anne Hutchinson was 43 years old when she arrived with her husband William in Massachusetts in 1634. She quickly became known as one who was skilled in the "healing arts" and became part of the community of women who helped each other during childbirth and times of illness (Collins, 2003). Her work as midwife and nurse provided an opportunity to discuss theological matters with women and later hold meetings in her home. These meetings were conducted in direct disregard to the injunction by St. Paul, "I permit not woman to teach" (Woody, 1929: 129). Her critique of outward signs of salvation such as wealth and good works, which would exclude women, functioned to deconstruct the boundaries between the public and private. In contrast, Anne maintained that God's grace could be shown not only through outward signs but also through inner experience (similar to the medieval mystics and the Gnostics). This interpretation enabled women to claim salvation, but more importantly to have a relationship with the eternal and to be knowers. In sanctioning the voicing of women's own religious authority, Anne undermined clerical authority.

The solace and comfort she brought to women extended to the weekly meetings in which she interpreted the Bible in ways that helped the women to deal with the trials and tribulations of a frontier life in which they often birthed as many as 15 children and lost many of them. Her words of comfort and reassurances that one could trust one's own judgment of salvation imbued her with an authority and reverence that male ministers coveted. As well as extending her belief of personal salvation to women she also extended this to Native Americans. She had opposed the Pequot War, in which almost every Pequot was massacred. Anne saw it not as a "divine slaughter," but, like Roger Williams, refused to support the forced conversion of Indians. Anne, like Roger, believed in the concept of freedom of conscience. Individuals, including women and Native Americans, were imbued by God with the capability to discern their spiritual beliefs and relationship with the divine. The fact that her views encouraged her male followers to be the first "conscientious objectors" contributed to her being viewed as a woman whose influence was beyond the prescribed norms of women. While the Puritans had left behind the Great Whore of Babylon, the Catholic Church, they now confronted a new "Jezebel." This could not be tolerated.

Like her father before her, who had stood trial in 1578 in St. Paul's Cathedral in London on the charge of heresy, she entered the courtroom in November 1637. Charges had not been brought. Since women could not speak in public, preach in public, or hold office there were few charges that could be launched against her. Her quick wit, intelligence, and knowledge of the Bible made it difficult for Governor Winthrop to find any plausible reasons for charging her with a crime. In the end though she was convicted of heresy and banished from the colony.

According to LaPlante (2004), Anne Hutchinson was "an American visionary, pioneer, and explorer who epitomized the religious freedom and tolerance that are essential to the nation's character" (p. xvi). In a time when no woman could vote, teach outside the home, or hold public office, she had the intellect, courage, and will to challenge the ministers and judges who had founded the Massachusetts colony. Her radical theology, which took Puritanism to its logical conclusion, maintained that each individual could interpret the word of God and discern its meaning. This unmediated action made each person a knower, man and woman alike. To speak with authority about her interpretations of the Bible, as she did in the meetings in her home, threatened the authority of the ministers and their errand in the wilderness. This errand, or jeremiad, ironically necessitated a firm guiding vision to fulfill its mission; dissension was a necessary evil but only when it did not threaten the very foundation of reform—male hierarchy. For John Winthrop, Anne Hutchinson was the second Eve, a source of evil temptation who lured women and men to transgress normative gender boundaries. Anne threatened the very power relations on which the "city on the hill" was built. For Anne the "New Eden" would be the fulfillment of God's original paradise, a garden in which knowledge of God would be accessible to all. For Winthrop and the other Puritan ministers, the "New Eden" would bring the fulfillment of God's moral imperative which, according to their interpretation of the Bible, required the submission of women to men. Ironically, the Puritans had been rebels themselves, but now in order for their "city" to survive, they had to eliminate all rebels.

Anne Hutchinson might be seen as America's first European woman curriculum theorist. She posited an epistemological worldview that acknowledged each individual—male, female, European, or Native American—as a subject who could come to know. For Hutchinson, knowledge was a spiritual matter, and what one came to know was determined by one's relationship with the divine. Revelation, inspiration, interpretation of the Bible, and prayer were all ways in which to discern one's relationship or calling from God. Her faith in the process of grace—not in the predetermination of being "chosen"—made her theology a radical departure from many of her contemporaries whose epistemology was grounded in predetermination (reminiscent of the caste system of education we have today) and the outward sign of works that signified the chosen.[19] For Anne, the ultimate source of knowledge was in relationship with the divine. No minister, father, or husband was above Christ and one's personal relationship with the divine. Her moral imperative or "errand in the wilderness" was not one of creating a "city on the hill" in which God had a covenant with a chosen group. For Anne, all were potential chosen people of God. Rather than a "city on the hill" Anne sought to create a "New Eden" in which there was freedom of religion such that each individual could taste of the "tree of life."[20] Like contemporary debates in educational theory, the central issue then as now, is the question of who can be a knower and how do we come to know. For Winthrop and many other Puritans, knowledge, albeit accessible to all, was a form of control. For Anne Hutchinson, knowledge was freedom of individual conscious. That she dared to speak this viewpoint in public threatened the very foundation of the "city on the hill." She was eventually convicted as a heretic and was exiled to Rhode Island. From there she wandered to New York where, in 1640, she and her family were massacred by a group of Indians who were revenging the slaughter of 80 members of their tribe by the Dutch.

The Puritan legacy or, as Douglas McKnight (2003) has suggested, the "gift"— the symbolic/secular narrative of an "errand in the wilderness" to become a "city on the hill"—has been largely ignored by educational historians who assume that the Puritans were "merely concerned with theological truth and autocratic government" (p. 3). However, their passionate faith in education and its role in shaping America as a chosen place is central to the relationship between culture, identity, and the American narrative. Every crisis in America is coupled with reforms (or as McKnight suggests jeremiads) in education. Education is seen as central to "saving" America in times of economic, moral, and political upheaval. The legacy of the jeremiad—"the call for reform"—is one of control. Control over who determines what counts as knowledge and who can be a knower. The case of Anne Hutchinson exemplifies the beginning of this legacy of control (particularly over women educators) over who determines epistemological norms. While the Puritans have left a legacy of universal literacy, the purposes for which that literacy is used has been continually contested.[21] While the 17th-century Puritans saw literacy as central to a moral imperative of creating a "city on the hill," Anne Hutchinson redefined that moral imperative of literacy as one of individual conscious. Her ultimate vision was a process of decolonizing the self from the social imperatives of a patriarchal society through reclaiming an Eden based not on worldly gender norms, but a moral imperative based on individual conscience in which knowledge was profound and accessible to all.

Catholic Women in the "New World"

> The ardent desire we had to see this promised land made us endure every-
> thing with joy.
>
> *(Ursuline Sister, 1727, quoted in Emily Clark, 1998)*

These words, written from colonial Louisiana to loved ones in France, reflect like her Protestant sisters, a vision of the "New World" as a promised land. This "promised land," unlike the "city on the hill," would be Catholic. However, this Catholicism would be unlike any other. It would be a Catholicism built on a spiritual tradition that saw women as the central agents of conversion and salvation. This "promised land," or "New Eden," would be guided by a female-centered focus on education as well as a female devotional practice that centered on the Virgin Mary. In other words, the Ursulines who arrived in New Orleans, Louisiana in 1727 would have as their goal the transformation of *every* woman into an agent to propagate the faith. Their promised land was not one in which earthly riches would be attained or nations would dominate; their goal was neither economic nor political. In fact, their vision of a "New World" stood in sharp contrast to the emerging mercantile, nation-building focus of most European states. Contesting the emphasis on earthly goods, they sought to use their position as Catholic women religious to shape a radically different society that would elevate "spirituality" above all other pursuits. Education would be the primary vehicle for fulfilling this mission.

Because education played a significant role in colonial policy as a way to achieve social and cultural dominance, it is uncontested that the Ursulines were central to the project of colonization. Yet, while they clearly functioned as colonizers, the vision of Catholicism they would try to impose was one that functioned to decolonize women, Indians, and enslaved Africans as mere "objects." They appropriated the Catholic faith and institution in ways that situated them as subjects. In fact, their story is an exemplar of the ways in which women during this time period used the institutions at hand to craft roles for themselves as active agents within the circumscribed gender norms of the day as a means to impose their own vision. For the Ursulines, their vision was one that transcended earthly concerns; the impermanence of the world relegated it to a marginal status. Their quest was for spiritual universalism. While perhaps difficult for us to understand, living in the secular world as we do, the role of religion was still a primary organizing agent in society during this time. The Ursulines took up the curricular task of "reforming" the Catholic Church to focus on the spiritual equality of all human beings. At a time when Africans and Native Americans were seen as savages and even nonhuman this was indeed a radical vision.

The unique educational vision and agency of the Ursulines has been obscured for several reasons. First, it has been argued that the Ursulines (as well as other missionaries) merely carried out colonial policy by transforming "barbarians" into loyal subjects of the the king. Specifically, according to Robenstine (1992), the Ursulines aided in the colonial project by educating women who were central to the establishment of families, which in turn was essential to establishing French culture, French society, and French family life. The Ursulines are seen as mere pawns in the development of the colonies' economic and strategic development and the transmission of French culture but with no agency of their own. What is neglected is that the Ursulines did not merely reconstruct French life in the colonies; they advanced their own vision.

Second, Catholic women religious have often been portrayed as "handmaidens" of the Church (Coburn & Smith, 1999). Historians (Davis, 1965; Roelker, 1972) have argued that in contrast to the Catholic Church, the Protestant Church empowered women through the "introduction of a vernacular, participatory liturgy, promotion of literacy, and exhortation to recognize spiritual equality" (Clark, 1997: 770). However, despite the rhetoric of spiritual equality, the story of colonial Puritan women, as described above, illustrates that a "sophisticated ideology grew up to support the gendered division of labor that excluded women from roles of public authority, such as preaching and church governance" (p. 772). Protestant women prayed, listened, reflected, and obeyed. They did not lead religious organizations. In fact, at the close of the 18th century, Protestant women were increasingly enclosed within the bounds of the family and lived in a state of dependency in a male-dominated republic. This would lay the groundwork for the "cult of domesticity." For the Puritans, this would be the way to resolve the tension between an ungendered spirituality and a gendered world. For the Ursulines, this was unacceptable. As Emily Clark (1997) suggests, "In the very era when Protestant women gave up this separate institutional heritage in favor of a richer congregational life that joined the sexes, Catholic women not only retained their single-sex organizations but expanded them" (p. 773). And expand them they did. The dearth of research on Catholic women educators has not only reinforced the stereotype of the Catholic woman religious as "handmaiden," but distorted the history of education by neglecting one of the longest surviving continuous educational institutions in the United States.

Like the Puritans who saw themselves as leaving a "corrupt" civilization to create a "New Eden," Catholic women religious also saw the "New World" as one in which they would actualize an ideal society. The first Ursuline convent founded in the New World was in 1639 in Quebec by the widow Marie Guyart, known as Marie de l'Incarnation. Her letters, published in the late 17th century, describing her work among the Native Americans and her education of French girls, were an inspiration to other Ursulines who saw vision and purpose in missionary work in the New World. Like Anne Hutchinson and Roger Williams, she did not believe in the forced conversion of the Indians. In fact, she acted much like an ethnographer in the sense that she tried to understand the worldview of the Iroquois and Algonquins as exhibited by the rich descriptions of Native life in her letters.[22]

In August of 1727, 12 Ursuline sisters arrived in New Orleans. At the time the majority of the population were enslaved Africans, Native Americans, indentured servants, soldiers, and forced exiles. There were only 2,228 French inhabitants. The sisters' first task was to set up a school. By November of 1727, the first students arrived. When they opened their doors, they admitted French, Native American, free Black and enslaved African girls who attended the free catechism classes offered during the day. In essence, the sisters were complying with Article II of the Code Noir of 1724, which mandated that "all slaves who will be in our province, shall be instructed in the Catholic, Apostolic and Roman religion, and baptized" (Clark, 1998: 123). The nuns applied a "spiritual universalism that blurred social and racial distinction in favor of a hierarchy of pious belief and practice" (p. 59). For the Ursulines, who were clearly aware of the inequities of race, gender, and class, equality was not a matter of worldly social change. The impermanence of the material world directed their worldview to the larger goal of liberation through spiritual transformation. This said, their focus on educating enslaved Africans and Free People of Color (FPC) made them unique in the American colonies.[23] Anglican clergy in the Northern colonies, in contrast, largely ignored or avoided the conversion of the enslaved.

By 1734, the Ursuline sisters had moved to their first permanent location on Chartres Street where they continued to have French day scholars and boarders and on Sunday and weekday evenings they educated Indian and African women and girls. In addition to catechesis, the curriculum included French, Latin, reading, geography, stitchery, flower making, writing, and arithmetic. By focusing on self-activity, learning by experience, and the interests of the child, they anticipated the humanist and romanticist pedagogies of Pestalozzi and Froebel.

In addition to running the convent school, the Ursulines extended their influence on education in a variety of ways. Ironically, as slaveholders themselves, they set an example for other slaveholders. In 1770, they were among the top 6% of slaveholders among those plantations on the lower Mississippi River. The public position of the Ursulines in colonial society, the size of their slave population, and the sisters' prominence as major slaveholders meant that the nuns' slave community was a conspicuous example to slave and slaveholder in the New Orleans area (Clark, 2007). As mistresses of the plantation, the Ursulines departed from colonial law by encouraging marriage among the slaves. The sacraments, of both baptism and matrimony, that were "enjoined upon their slaves offered bondspeople opportunities to construct cultural mechanisms that strengthened community and recalled familiar African social arrangements" (Clark, 1998: 12). Among the Ursuline slaves there was a predominance of nuclear families living under the official blessing of a sacramental marriage. The advancement of these social conditions among enslaved Africans was in contrast to other colonies where families were separated as a means of maintaining control and destabilizing enslaved communities. The Ursulines, while never contesting slavery, clearly worked within the institution by drawing on Catholic doctrine and French legal codes to decolonize the most oppressive aspects of slavery. Their efforts to educate enslaved persons and create stable family units resulted in a rich tradition of African-Creole Catholic families in New Orleans, many of whom were FPC, that went on to develop their own educational institutions in the antebellum period.

A second way in which they extended education was through confraternities, groups of laywomen who organized to carry out an active campaign of catechesis among the young and unconverted of the colony. In 1730, the first of these was formed, known as the Ladies Congregation of the Children of Mary. This organization allowed women to express their religiosity as organized communities with elaborate internal governance structures, female-led devotional routines, and independently administered sources of wealth and programs of charity. As promoters of education, they visited families to encourage instruction of their children as well as the baptism and catechesis of slaves and FPC. In this regard they were responsible for promoting basic religious literacy among large numbers of slaves. Both White and African women were members of the Children of Mary. Thousands of women of African descent in New Orleans became Catholic. According to Clark and Gould (2002) the Afro-Catholic women "eventually employed their religious affiliation to transform themselves from nearly powerless objects of coercion into powerful agents" (p. 4).

By the early 19th century this community of Afro-Catholic women would draw on the original vision of the Ursulines of spiritual equality as a means to promote their education, culture, and position (Porche-Frilot & Hendry, 2010). This unique religious creolization that resulted in both the feminization and the Africanization of the New Orleans' Catholic Church can be attributed to the eventual development of some of the earliest educational institutions for African-Americans in the United States. The St. Claude Street School and convent established in 1824 had been specifically erected for the education of free girls of color. In the 1830s, Henriette Delille, a free woman of color, formed a confra-ternity named the Sisters of the Congregation of the Presentation of the Blessed Virgin Mary. According to Clark and Gould (2002) this agency by women of the Afro-Catholic tradition to "move into the publicly acceptable arena of religious activism" was directly related to the universalist ideals brought by 18th-century French missionaries. By 1842, under the leadership of Henriette Delille, they had established themselves as the Sisters of the Holy Family, the second Black order of nuns in the United States. Their primary mission was the education of enslaved girls and free women of color. St. Mary's School (as well as 67 other schools) continues today to shape an Afro-Catholic legacy of spiritual universalism. Ironically, the Sisters of the Holy Family claimed the French Catholic tradition in order to defy the social and racial conventions of antebellum New Orleans. By promoting education they contested the racist ideology that denied basic humanity to enslaved Africans (Porche-Frilot, 2006). The Sisters of the Holy Family exemplify more than any other group the complex contradictory posi-tionalities of being both colonizer and colonized. As promoters of the Catholic faith and slaveholders themselves they took up subject identities that constituted them as colonizers; yet as promoters of education for women and enslaved Africans, they decolonized the very subject positions on which colonialism was predicated.[24]

Ironically, despite popular notions that the South lagged behind the North in education, through their educational work the Ursulines raised the literacy rate of women in New Orleans to one of the highest in early America. The literacy rate for women in New Orleans in 1750 was 71%—slightly higher than the literacy for men (Clark & Gould, 2002: 4). In the 13 colonies, the literacy rate for women was generally half what it was for men. The Ursulines not only advanced education for all women, but were central to shaping a public role for women in the Catholic Church. Unlike their Protestant counterparts, Catholic religious communities allowed women to live in autonomous female communities, manage significant financial resources, and administer institutions in the public realm. This way of life contrasted sharply with the Protestant religious experience of women whose influence was firmly within the household and who had no public leadership role in the Church. As noted earlier, Protestant women who overstepped the bounds of domesticity were banished. Catholic women, however, not only had a visible public presence in French colonial Louisiana, they were at the forefront of shaping that society. As the Ursulines approach their 300-year anniversary, they are still a viable educational institution, as are the Sisters of the Holy Family. Each of these institutions reflects a larger tradition of women's educational agency. As proselytizers of the Catholic faith, they were complicit in the colonial project. At the same time, they extended education, helped shape an Afro-Catholic female culture which endures today and signifies a unique Creole community that embodies many African traditions, and contributed to shaping a female culture in New Orleans that valued education and spiritual universalism.

While colonialism in America was deeply shaped by religious beliefs that prompted visions of an ideal society, religious ideologies and subjectivities increasingly were challenged by the new "enlightenment" ideologies of liberal democracy. The state, rather than the Church, was emerging as the central organizing institution of society. In fact, these women religious were to some degree the last of a generation of women who drew on religion as the source for their epistemology and worldview. The Enlightenment ideas of equality, brotherhood, and citizenship were to emerge as central in shaping colonization. How these Enlightenment philosophies were brought to the New World to shape education would radically alter foundational ideas about the nature of education. No longer would moral or spiritual goals shape education, but a secular view of education for good "citizenship" would come to dominate educational discourses.

Prior to the Enlightenment the locus of power was the divine king and the feudal state. Monarchy was seen as absolutism. The Enlightenment rejected this absolutism in favor of the "rights" of each individual to enter into a contract with the state with the inherent rights of citizenship. The locus of the individual shifted from one grounded in an interdependent state of relationships in which gender was much more fluid, to one of a dependent relationship with the state that was dependent on gender binaries. Social relations between the sexes mirrored those of the citizen to the state. The trade off for men's "new" power as citizens was their dependence on the state. In return for this dependence, women were to be dependent on men. According to Juster (1994), "Female dependency and male independence were yoked together in republican visions of the political family" (p. 12). This dependence severely constrained women's behavior by restricting their public roles. Thus, while under colonial rule women had played a role in shaping society through their activities in religion, dame schools, and the domestic economy, the American Revolution imposed new roles on women that required dependence and submission. "Disorderly Women" were not tolerated (Juster, 1994).

This new relationship between the individual and the state was encoded in the concept of the citizen. Republics rested on the virtue and intelligence of their citizens. The new state required a well-educated citizenry and this required the expansion of education. The virtuous citizen was loyal to the state. Of course, this citizen was a male one. In fact, central to the construction of this loyal citizen was ensuring that women did not attract men's attentions away from the state (male). Women competed with the state's attention (perhaps a threat to homoerotic desire) and in some measure counteracted the state's claim on men's emotions and loyalty.[25] A critical element to dissuade this type of seduction was the indoctrination of men into citizenship through public education (representing the state) in which good republican virtues could be developed. These virtues were, in fact, often contrasted to those of women whose female qualities were the measure of what a good citizen should avoid. According to Kerber (1980), "Samuel Adams warned against the undermining of public virtue by the effeminate refinements of the theater" (p. 31). Effeminacy was associated with timidity, dependence, luxury, and self-indulgence, even homosexuality. If Americans lived in a world of the political imagination in which virtue was ever threatened by corruption, it must be added that the overtones of virtue were male, and those of corruption were female (Kerber, 1980). Enlightenment political thought culminated in the American Revolution of 1776. And revolutionary it was. While many women hoped the revolution would uncouple the essentialized binary gender roles that had shaped 18th-century political and educational thought, this was not to be the case. Ironically, the revolution functioned to solidify and reinforce gender conceptualizations. As Joan Landes (1988) suggests, "avenues for women's freedom were foreclosed rather than expanded with the rise of the modern nation state, secular culture, private property, and even Protestantism" (p. 21). Gendered subjectivity, grounded in a binary that was by now for all practical purposes understood as "natural," would be irrevocably linked to the construction of citizenship and the "public" sphere of the state. The public/private, self/other, male/female, subject/object binaries were constructed as "real" through the discourses of "natural rights," "the contract," and "Republican Motherhood."

How these colonizing discourses worked in complex and contradictory ways to determine who could be knower, what could be known, and what constituted knowledge would be the focus of generations of educational theorists.

Enlightening America

It is a measure of the conservatism of the Revolution that women remained on the periphery of political community; it is possible to read the subsequent political history of women in American as the story of women's efforts to accomplish for themselves what the Revolution had failed to do.

(Linda Kerber, 1980)

I expect to see our young women forming a new era in female history.

(Judith Sargent Murray, 1798)

While Judith Sargent Murray was optimistic about the impact of the Revolution on women, the American Revolution was not a revolution for women. The focus on individual rights central to the virtuous citizen whose primary relationship was with the state—the public realm—functioned to exclude women more than ever from having a voice in shaping American culture and society. Enlightenment notions of citizenship were exclusively male, drawing their political "vocabulary from Aristotle, who believed that the good life could be realized only in the context of the public sector, a strictly male arena" (Kerber, 1980: 7). "Women were thought to make their moral choices in the context of the household, a woman's domain that Aristotle understood to be a non-public, lesser institution that served the polis" (p. 7). Politics (defined as public) was the affair of men.

Thomas Jefferson, Benjamin Franklin, and Noah Webster heralded the notion that human society and conditions could be improved by extending education to all. Well, almost all. Like their European brothers, they advocated education for women as a means for preparation for motherhood and, in the case of slaves, education was strictly forbidden and severely punished (Beale, 1975). Drawing on the ideas of Locke, Rousseau, and Voltaire, the "founding fathers" embraced Enlightenment notions that privileged reason and rationality as central to good citizenship. The construction of the citizen, whose primary relationship was with the state, not God, family, or community required a new type of education. Reason and rationality required the suppression of emotion, a binary way of thinking, and an inherent understanding of knowledge as separate from the self.

Jefferson did promote three years of education for White children of all classes at community expense. After the three years, the most advanced boys would be selected to attend grammar schools for another two years after which the "best geniuses will be raked from the rubbish annually, and instructed at public expense" to finish the college preparatory courses (Smith & Smith, 1994: 232). Half would then be selected to attend college at public expense. Thus, while the Enlightenment ideas of extending education to the masses took root in America, it did so while maintaining a gender dichotomy in which the private sphere was the domain of women and the public sphere the realm of men.

In essence, the American Revolution completed the colonization of women. The only way in which women could serve the republic was through educating virtuous male citizens on whom the health of the republic depended. Republican Motherhood, in which women were to be dedicated to the "nurture of public-spirited male citizens," became the central political role that women took on. This essentialized ideology of Republican Motherhood relegated women once and for all to the domestic sphere. To prepare men for the public sphere it was seen as essential that men be taken from their mothers (the private sphere) to be raised by the state (men/public) because women could not be trusted with the task of educating for citizenship. The project of mass, public education, what has been referred to as the Common School Movement, was central to the construction of the individual as male, rational, and free (see Chapter 1 for a more detailed discussion). This subject identity was made possible by its corollary concept of female, irrational, and dependent. From this perspective the project of democracy and public schooling can be seen not as enlightenment or progressive, but as central to the project of colonization.

Ironically, this ideology would become the starting point for advocating for women's education. First, if women were to have the important responsibility of rearing the future sons, they themselves would need to be educated. Second, women took up a political role, although in the home. According to Kerber (1980), "this new identity had the advantage of appearing to reconcile politics and domesticity; it justified continued political education and political sensibility" (p. 12). Women (Emma Hart Willard, Margaret Fuller) took up the colonizers' ideology of "Republican Motherhood," rooted in the separate sphere of domesticity, and politicized it. This is exemplified by the work of Catharine Beecher (see Chapter 1), in particular, who argued that women were best suited to be "teachers" due to their natural maternal instincts. Drawing on the ideology of teaching as "women's true profession," a generation of women theorists embraced this essentialist ideology in order to justify the role of women in the public sphere. This appropriation of the ideology of Republican Motherhood as a means to disrupt the colonization of women's subject identities as passive, docile, submissive, and maternal would become the basis for arguing for women's education throughout the 19th century. Yes, women argued, if motherhood is so important we must be educated. Thus, the work of decolonization proceeded in complex and contradictory ways. By the end of the 19th century many in the first generation of college-educated women sought to take up public positions that extended beyond teaching in order to actually define and shape alternative understandings of education and the institution of schooling. They sought to contribute to philosophy and public policy regarding the very nature of what constitutes education. This would require the redefinition of "citizenship" as well as the public/private, male/female binary that was central to its construction. This "unsettling" of the dominant ideologies of citizenship and gender would take place, in part, in the settlement house movement. It is to that story that I turn in the next chapter.

Reflections

> Maybe we are all exiles in a dehumanizing educational process.
>
> *(Cameron McCarthy, 1998)*

> The work of decolonization is necessarily a collective effort which involves thinking oneself out of the spaces of domination.
>
> *(Nina Asher, 2002)*

Is all education colonizing? Postcolonial theorists such as Asher (2002, 2005), Fanon (1967), McCarthy (1998), and Minh-ha (1991) maintain that identity politics must be conceptualized in ways that resist the imposition of subject identities that privilege the binary of a subject–object duality through male/female, self/other, Black/White, and colonizer/colonized. These colonial identities continue to be produced through contemporary educational discourses such as tracking, multiculturalism, "at-risk," special education and, thus, schools continue in the project of colonizing students by imposing subject identities. We have traversed three centuries and multiple ideologies that I suggest were not inherently liberatory or enlightened but, to the contrary, were central to the project of colonization. While education, particularly mass public education, has taken on almost mythic status in regards to its role in a democratic society, as Merle Curti (1935) maintained there has always been a "cleavage" between the fact and the ideal in education. As Michael Katz (1968) suggests, schools are "imperial institutions designed to civilize the natives" (p. xvi). This tension between the role of education as reproducing social relations and the status quo versus functioning as a primary institution in the process of democracy is an ongoing one that postcolonial educators address. At the center of this work is an understanding of the deeply implicated intersections between the project of "identity" and the project of "schooling."

Postcolonial education seeks ways in which we can think in more "hybrid" ways that allow us to understand the "other" in relation to, rather than apart from ourselves and vice versa (Asher, 2002: 82). Deconstructing this binary is difficult work. The deeply normative nature of this way of thinking, as this chapter has shown, is hundreds of years in the making. I have shown numerous resistances that specifically have challenged notions of an essentialized gender binary. These ruptures suggest that education as colonization has been unsuccessful. Failure, in this case, is a good thing. Some, such as Anne Hutchinson, Catherine Macaulay, and Henriette Delille, have refused to be colonized and take up a position as "object" of knowledge. And, in fact, many of the women discussed worked in the "in-between" spaces in which they were simultaneously colonized and colonizer. Central to the project of decolonizing curriculum history is recapturing these spaces that have been marginalized in educational history because they do not fit neatly into the grand narrative of educational history as progress and progression from "unenlightened" to "enlightened."

By ignoring the social thought of women curriculum theorists, it has been possible to construct a tidy historical narrative that privileges reason, citizenship, the public sphere, and public education as normative. The writings of women in this chapter attest to different visions of education, ones not grounded in classical liberal democracy, ones not predicated on the binary of gender, reason/emotion, body/spirit, and self/other. The ongoing colonization of bodies and minds continues to be deconstructed by the work of contemporary curriculum theorists (Asher, 2005). This work disrupts the dangerous notion that colonization is a time period in history that can be relegated to the past, that it is something we are beyond. The current imperialism of the United States to create a world safe for democracy echoes the European colonizers (Chomsky, 2007). Colonization is a *not* a thing of the past. It continues to be a "massive effort to coordinate dominant identities by pasting over breaks and contradictions within hegemonic cultural form" (McCarthy, 1998: 259). Over 500 years ago, Christine de Pizan asked "what has made exclusion possible?" We continue to ask the same question today.

5

UNSETTLING CURRICULUM

There are many indications that this conception of Democracy is growing among us. We have come to have an enormous interest in human life as such, accompanied by confidence in its essential soundness. We do not believe that genuine experience can lead us astray any more than scientific data can.

(Jane Addams, 1902, Democracy and Social Ethics*)*

Equilibrium, not repression among conflicting forces is the condition of natural harmony, of permanent progress, and of universal freedom. That exclusiveness and selfishness in a family, in a community, or in a nation is suicidal to progress. Caste and prejudice mean immobility. One race predominance means death. The community that closes its gates against foreign talent can never hope to advance beyond a certain point.

(Anna Julia Cooper, 1892, A Voice From the South*)*

For Anna Julia Cooper and Jane Addams the notions of "progress" and "progressivism" were understood as the degree to which society saw itself as a community that embraced the diverse experiences all its members. The essence of democracy was, according to Addams (1902), the product of "diversified human experience and its resultant sympathy" (p. 12). Likewise for Cooper, the warning that repression and prejudice were tantamount to "death" is a poignant reminder that the "progressive" era (1890–1920) coincided with one of the most savage periods of White repression in the history of the United States, as Whites strove to ensure their supremacy through segregation, immigration quotas, disenfranchisement, eugenics, and racial violence.

In contrast to the dominant ideologies, which argued that immigrants and African-Americans were uncivilized and responsible for the decay of the moral fiber of America, Addams maintained that it was the "common lot" who could regenerate a decaying America (Rudnick, 1991). She argued that democracy should be a flexible and expansive form of government enriched by a diverse culture that saw all members as "citizens." Addams's conception of democracy was grounded in the necessity of recognizing the social capacity and efficiency of the popular will, including immigrants, African-Americans, women, and the working poor. Her notion of "radical" democracy embraced the experiences of women, African-Americans, and immigrants by bringing their values into the community, not by erasing their ethnic culture and lifestyle. Thus, "the identification with the common lot, which is the essential idea of democracy, becomes the source and expression of social ethics" (Addams, 1902: 11).

The naming of this time period as "progressive" in dominant curriculum histories has masked its deeply troubling nature.[1] Canonical texts such as Lawrence Cremin's (1961) *The Transformation of the School* and Patricia Graham's (1967) *Progressive Education: From Arcady to Academe,* resist definitive definitions of "progressivism." Cremin (1961) wrote in regard to definitions of progressivism: "None exists, and none ever will; for throughout its history progressive education meant different things to different people" (p. x). Historians have, however, attempted to classify various strands of progressives. According to Kridel and Bullough (2007), these classifications include Cremin's designation of progressives as scientists, sentimentalists, and radicals; Kliebard's addition of social meliorists; Tyack's administrative and pedagogical progressives; and Rugg's "scientific methodists" and "project methodists." Kathleen Weiler (2005) has suggested that rather than seek unity, we need to focus on the disparate ways in which progressivism functioned. Looking at the different strands and phases of progressive education "not as a linear progression, but as a series of breaks and shifts" opens new spaces in which to "unsettle" dominant readings of progressivism as either inherently liberatory or oppressive (p. 4).

Baker (2001), Marshall (1995), Walkerdine (1990), and Weiler (2005) have articulated the complex and contradictory ways in which "progressive" discourses have functioned. Embedded within progressivism was the vision of "the child," freed by a new education, who would build a new social order. The subject identity central to the progressive project was, according to Valerie Walkerdine (1990), the self-regulating individual who was free from overt control. This emergence of the "child" as a "subject" was both a rejection of Reformation notions of the child as sinful and morally corrupt in need of discipline *and* a direct response to the underlying social anxieties of "race suicide" and "mongrelization" that were present at the turn of the century which required a subject whose identity was naturalized as superior (White, middle class, and male). Thus, the focus on freedom and empowerment can also be understood to "serve the ends of those who control and benefit from existing arrangements of society by teaching middle-class children to be self-directed, to prepare them for future class positions, and to encourage them to believe in the goodness of their society rather than be critical and questioning" (Weiler, 2005: 8). While the nature of the "subject" within progressive discourse is contested, my purpose in this chapter is not resolution. In fact, it is the proliferation of identities that provides a rupture and break to the traditional progressive narratives and opens spaces to examine counternarratives of identity that disrupt binary views of progressivism as either liberatory or oppressive.

This chapter presents the work of curriculum theorists who sought to "unsettle" curriculum by disrupting the subject identities embedded in dominant discourses of gender, race, and ethnicity that were grounded in social Darwinism and its corollary "White supremacy." Popularized by the English philosopher Herbert Spencer and his American counterpart, William Graham Sumner of Yale, the doctrine of "survival of the fittest" recast civic virtue as a reflection of material success that was the result of superior capacity for hard work and self-denial. The "fittest" were by nature the most evolved and those who were poor were clearly less developed. Because "survival" was based on natural selection it should not be interfered with. Consequently, both Spencer and Sumner argued against any government interference that might infringe on the laws of nature. This laissez-faire approach reinforced notions of ethnic, racial, and gender differences grounded in biological determinism and science that focused on the individual (not the community) as the site of progress. In education, social Darwinism became the foundation for an ideology of racial, ethnic, and gender superiority that would translate into progressive ideologies of "practical" knowledge, curriculum differentiation, testing, and tracking as a means to promote "democracy" through social efficiency. These "progressive" ideologies, grounded in an emerging "science" of education, were understood as critical to social stability and social uplift. Simultaneously, an alternative reading of Darwin's theory of evolution "demonstrated the continuity of human being with nature, and shifted interest from speculations about transcendence, permanence, necessity, invariance, and certitude to reflections on finitude, temporality, relativity, chance and fallibility" (Seigfried, 1996: 176). A philosophical worldview emerged that sought not absolute understandings of a fixed world but one that focused on the human potential for "change" and "adaptability" in which diversity was understood not as a threat but as key to civic virtue. "Unsettling" the grip of biological determinism and racial superiority, many social reformers and activists (Lester Frank Ward, Jane Addams, William C. Bagley) drew on Darwin's theory of evolution to underscore "change" and "evolution" in the natural world as indicative of the potential of "growth" and "change" rather than innate and predetermined human dispositions. These curriculum theorists posited a "subject" that was fluid, mutable, and an agent of change.

By positing an oppositional "identity politics," they contested the dominant ideologies of racial superiority that were linked to the emerging ideals of the "perfect man" and "new woman" that went hand in hand with the triumphing over the challenges of immigration, modernization, and industrialization (Kasson, 2001). These "ideals" drew on Darwinian ideas of bodily perfection that were represented as White, Anglo-Saxon, muscular bodies for men, and fragile, weak, and pale bodies for women as the imagined summit of race, gender, and social class. These cultural fantasies expressed not only "supremacy," but also expressed anxiety about the "new immigration" (Catholics and Jews from Eastern Europe) and "darker bodies" (Kasson, 2001). Evolutionary theory posited, as Bederman (1995a) explains,

> The most advanced races were the ones who had evolved the most perfect manliness and womanliness. Civilized women were exempt from heavy labor and ensconced in the home. Civilized men provided for their families and steadfastly protected their delicate women and children from the rigors of the workday world. (p. 28)

The Darwinian idea of evolution of the "perfect race" was also reinforced by the Eugenics movement—a social "movement concerned with the improvement of the human gene pool by controlling the proliferation of inferior types: Jews, poor people, blacks, people with disabilities and homosexuals" (Griffin, 1998: 31). According to Winfield (2007), eugenicists posited solutions to social problems and reinterpreted social Darwinism in progressive language such that they were able to appeal to a broad audience of Progressives. In education this included the so-called "Father of Curriculum" John Franklin Bobbitt, G.S. Hall, and Edward Thorndike. Eugenics, or "scientific racism," in tandem with practices of "true womanhood," were ideologies that were central to reinforcing and reconstituting "White masculinity" and the corresponding construct of "White femininity" forming a hierarchy of ability and human worth based on gender, race, and ethnicity. These racial and gendered constructions of identity were critical to defining citizenship, human rights, and, in the realm of education, who was considered "educable" and what type of education they should receive.

Central to this ideology were strands of progressivism that focused on "intelligence" testing whose purpose was to develop homogenous groups as a means for increasing school efficiency through tracking and curricular differentiation. By the end of World War I, the testing movement, begun in France and Great Britain by Binet and Simon, that was seen as central to the project of social engineering, had been adapted and modified in the United States with funding from the General Education Board, a foundation created by John D. Rockefeller, in order that all the nation's schools could test children to determine their intelligence. Developed by Lewis M. Terman, an educational psychologist at Stanford, the Stanford Achievement Test, was based on his belief in genetic determinism in which testing was critical to the "understanding of race differences, mental growth, genius, and insanity" (Lagemann, 2000: 93). This strand of progressivism attracted many researchers and reformers (including Edward Thorndike and Franklin Bobbitt) who believed that "human racial stock" might be improved (Ravitch, 2000: 134). Critical to these "progressive" educators was the belief that IQ testing would allow for more efficient curriculum differentiation in which testing would be used to group students, define what they would learn, and determine their future vocation. Ironically, they saw "differentiation" as more "democratic" since learning was individualized to student needs rather than having a "common" curriculum that would ultimately fail to meet the needs of many students.[2] That contemporary educational testing, as well as tracking, is the direct outgrowth of the eugenics movement is often obscured when this strand of the progressive movement is deemed merely as "social efficiency" or is obscured by the traditional focus on "child-centered" or "social reconstructionist" battles.

This chapter maintains that the work of curriculum theorists such as Jane Addams, W.E.B. Du Bois, Charlotte Perkins Gilman, Ida B. Wells, Anna Julia Cooper, Carter G. Woodson, Mary Church Terrell, Lavinia Dock, and Lillian Wald, was in part a response to this "eugenics" movement and "crisis of masculinity" (Kimmel, 1996). This "crisis" was the result of a nexus of social conditions that included, according to Pinar (2001), "1) industrialization, 2) the entry of women into the public spheres in growing numbers, 3) the Emancipation of blacks, 4) a massive influx of immigrants, and 5) the closing of the frontier" (p. 322). Confused about the nature of male power, men searched for a means to fortify their manliness. It is no coincidence that bodybuilding, sports, alcohol, and drug consumption as well as lynching emerged at this time.[3] Race in particular became the focus of the male gaze as a mechanism for asserting masculine superiority. By invoking White supremacy, men sought power and control, thereby reasserting their masculinity. The 1890s were a time of "virulent racism and racially conceived nativism, a time of lynching, black disenfranchisement, xenophobia, and imperialism" (Pinar, 2001: 324). The sexual mutilation of Black men's bodies as part of lynchings reveals how the process of demasculinating the "other" served to feed White men's fantasy of masculinity (always assumed to be heterosexual).

This fantasy of masculinity was further bolstered by women's relegation to the domestic sphere. Discourses of domesticity relegated women not only to the home, but maintained that coeducation was dangerous because it distorted the natures of boys and girls. Women's sphere was to be in the home where they focused on child rearing. The subject identities of the "perfect woman"—domesticity, submissiveness, piety, and passiveness—were embedded in the ideology of "separate spheres." Of course, this construct was reserved for White women (and upper-class ones at that), whereas Black women faced a sexualized identity that made it impossible for them to fulfill this ideal (Guillory, 2010). How women constructed a subject identity against and within these imagined and abstract ideas that "white men fashioned for them" (Pinar, 2001: 301) is the unsettling of "progress" that I seek to explore.

The anxiety over the loss of manliness and racial superiority found its corollary in the increased need for social control and regulation. Education (in fact, schooling became mandatory during this time) was a primary avenue through which this control and regulation of identity was exercised. As I have suggested earlier in Chapter 1, the narrative construction of curriculum history during this time as the story of the struggle between various forms of progressivism, including social efficiency, child-centeredness, and social reconstruction functions to obscure the degree to which education functioned as regulation. In regards to gender and race, social efficiency reconstituted masculinity through the ideology of the "expert" and through its sub-discourse of "differentiation." Simultaneously, child-centered and social reconstructionist progressives re-constituted masculinity as normative through the narrative of the family plot by situating the teacher (i.e., woman) in the role of facilitator, never as constructor of knowledge in her own right. In writing the history of progressivism as a "struggle" and binary of social efficiency and child-centeredness/social reconstruction, it has functioned to obscure the work of other curriculum theorists who sought to "unsettle" the imposition of gendered and racial identities.

The remainder of this chapter focuses on the work of Jane Addams and Ida B. Wells as exemplars of curriculum theorists whose "settlement" work posited a radical critique of racist and sexist ideologies that were predicated on beliefs of innate superiority. In contrast, their unique vision of "progressivism" saw "difference" as central to democracy. They posited a vision of radical "democracy" through deconstructing its corollary discourses of citizenship (embedded in liberal democracy as male, White, public) and domesticity (embedded in liberal democracy as female, White, private). This deconstruction by settlement house workers would reveal the insufficiency of categories such as race, gender, and class to capture, by themselves, the complexities of experience that were central to understanding democracy as a "living, breathing organism." Education was to be the key to radicalizing America, and the settlement house (not the school) was to be the site for this learning. For these women, the settlement house, as well as women's clubs, were sites of democratic education where they attempted to address the growing inequities of America's urban culture.[4] While their work was part of a much larger movement of social change that included numerous reform efforts, this chapter will focus specifically on the settlement house movement because of its radical reconstruction of education as community-based, holistic, life-long, and based in the experiences of all citizens. Many settlement communities emerged at the turn of the century (Henry Street in New York, etc.). However the Hull House Settlement and the Negro Fellowship Room in Chicago provide the richest source of historic information due to the prolific writings of Jane Addams, as well as the writings of Ida B. Wells. Consequently, I focus on their work.[5] While much of their work was directed toward social reform, the deconstruction of the subject identities, made available through the dominant discourses of citizenship and domesticity, was the focus of their theoretical work on which I draw.

Unsettling Citizenship

> Addams thought of those who came and went to Hull-House as citizens, or
> citizens-in-the-making, not as clients or receivers of services.
>
> *(Jean Elshtain, 2002)*

Jane Addams was a social philosopher whose gender, race, and class analyses
provided a radical critique of the fundamental assumptions of "Enlightenment"
discourses of classical liberal democracy. Addams's vision of "social democracy"
challenged dominant discourses of Enlightenment political thought by exposing
the deeply gendered and racial categories of political theory that conceptualized
rights as universal, individual, natural, and inalienable. Addams was engaged in
revising conceptions of politics and power by viewing them through the lens of
gender, ethnicity, class, and race. She articulated the ways in which the political
sphere was demarcated as public/private, how concepts such as citizenship
appeared to be gender neutral, and how liberal political discourse excluded the
experiences of immigrants and women, especially the experiences of women's
collective action. In widening the circle to redefine citizenship including the
experiences of women, Blacks, and immigrants, Jane Addams showed herself to
be an astute social critic and theorist who anticipated many of the critiques of
contemporary feminist political theorists (Bock & James, 1992; Eisenstein, 1994;
Laslett, Brenner, & Arat, 1995).

For Addams, democracy would not be achieved until every human being's
experiences had full expression in society. Rejecting a universalistic or equality
oriented view of democracy as devaluing of women and minorities, Addams
maintained that recognizing difference, not minimizing it, was essential to
democracy. For Addams, the social ethic that was democracy was the responsibility
to undertake a "wide reading of human life" (Knight, 2005: 401). The ethical
ideals of liberal democracy grounded in rights and responsibilities were for Addams,
remnants of an out-of-date ethics, an ethics that undermined true cooperation,
dialogue, and sympathic understanding. The rhetoric of equality obscured the real
lived experience of every day life as well as cloaked the contextual and interpretative nature of "equality."[6] For Addams, as for many contemporary feminists,
gender "equality" ultimately meant the assimilation of women to men under the
guise of gender "neutral" politics (Bloom, 1998; Pateman, 1992). As Virginia Held
(2005), Nel Noddings (1992, 2002), and Susan Okin (1989) have argued, the
paradoxical nature of liberalism highlights how the concept of equality functions
as oppressive rather than liberatory by keeping women subject to male-defined
values and institutions that masquerade as universal. Like late 20th-century social
theorists grappling with the shifting meaning of democracy in a post-Cold War,
postmodern, multicultural, and global society, Addams confronted complex questions (Fraser, 1996; Mouffe, 1995; Whitson & Stanley, 1996): Does democracy
require a recognition of difference? What role does social equality play in

democracy? How should we frame a political theory based on "multiple inter-secting differences"? (Fraser, 1996). Can this be accomplished without either the loss of political agency or the balkanization of identity politics?

I will focus on Addams's critique of the fundamental assumptions of classical liberal democracy. For Addams, the concept of universal, individual rights and its corollary concepts of natural man and inalienable rights ultimately functioned to obscure difference and thus neglected the experiences of women and immigrants. Liberal democracy's focus on inalienable rights assumed a static view of the political process and threatened to impose conformity of political behavior. For Addams, who saw democracy as a living, breathing social organism, liberal democracy failed to provide the flexibility to respond to social change. In addition, Addams critiqued the focus of classical democracy on political rights at the expense of the social and economic dimensions of democracy. Classical liberal democracy would be insuffi-cient to address the social problems of the day because it was incapable of creating social equality. The alleviation of economic inequalities was a prerequisite for the social interaction that was democracy. Democracy was a collective, not an individual, act.

Democracy as a Social Organism

> To attain individual morality in an age demanding social morality, to pride one's self on the results of personal effort when the time demands social adjustment, is utterly to fail to apprehend the situation.
>
> *(Jane Addams, 1902,* Democracy and Social Ethics*)*

Addams's focus on social adjustment, rather than individual accommodation, as a remedy for social ills compels me to nominate her as a neglected social critic of bourgeois individualism and liberal democracy. Influenced by John Stuart Mill's view of individual morality as a part of a "social organism," Addams (1902: 268) rejected the notion of universal, individual, natural rights as antithetical to the very foundations of democracy She argued that much of the "ethical maladjustment in social affairs arises from the fact that we are acting upon a code of ethics adapted to individual relationships but not the larger social relationships" (p. 221). Classical democracy, based on the concepts of natural man and the doctrine of inalienable rights, reinforced political participation as individual and thus actively undermined the social interaction on which democracy was predicated. The focus on the individual as foundational to democracy hindered the very social relations that Jane Addams saw as central to developing the sense of social responsibility necessary for democracy.

No progressive reformer, according to Lois Rudnick, understood better than Jane Addams the cognitive dissonance Americans experienced as they applied 19th-century rural values and standards of behavior to 20th-century urban, industrialized society (Rudnick, 1991: 145–167) In *Newer Ideals of Peace,* Addams (1911) critiqued the doctrines of liberal democracy as framed by the "founding fathers," especially Thomas Jefferson. For Addams, these philosophies were no longer viable. She maintains that although these

> men are strongly under the influence of peace ideals which were earnestly advocated . . . their idealism, after all, was founded upon theories concerning "the natural man," a creature of the sympathetic imagination.
>
> Because their idealism was of the type that is afraid of experience, these founders refused to look at the difficulties and blunders which a self-governing people were sure to encounter, and insisted that, if only the people had freedom they would walk continuously in the paths of justice and righteousness. It was inevitable, therefore, that they should have remained quite untouched by the worldly wisdom which counsels us to know life as it is, by that very modern belief that if the world is ever to go right at all, it must go right in its own way. (pp. 31–32)

A political system in which the founders of the republic talked of "natural man" but conceptualized citizens as abstract, disembodied beings would be incapable of "substituting a machine of newer invention and greater capacity" (p. 34). Consequently, democracy as invisioned by the founding fathers would no longer suffice to meet the conditions of turn-of-the-century American society.

In *Democracy and Social Ethics*, Addams maintained that the emerging democratic nation-states of the 18th century were dependent on "penalties, coercion, compulsion, [and] remnants of military codes" (1902: 37). The very concepts of natural rights and inalienable rights were rooted in the relation "between sovereign and subject, between the lawmaker and those whom the law restrains, which has traditionally concerned itself more with the guarding of prerogative and with the rights of property than with the spontaneous life of the people" (Adams, 1902: 33). In other words, classical liberal democracy was based on mistrust of the masses. The democratic nation-state with its rhetoric of natural rights, was based not on true belief in equality but on suspicion and the interests of the upper classes. For Addams, these inherent foundational premises made liberal democracy an unacceptable form of government.

According to Addams, the concepts of inalienable and natural rights were inherently problematic because they ignored the reality that "rights are not 'inalienable' but are hard-won in the tragic processes of experience" (pp. 32–33). If the experiences of women and immigrants were to count as political, the notion of natural and inalienable rights needed to be reconceptualized as socially produced, not static, and as historically and contextually situated, not as God-given. That static view of rights embedded in liberal notions of democracy threatened to impose a conformity of political behavior that restricted the flexibility of democracy to respond to social change and oppression. Like contemporary feminists, Addams was also concerned that the concepts of universal and natural rights, on which notions of the political, especially citizenship, were founded, made invisible gendered and ethnic experiences (Eisenstein, 1994: 36–53; Young, 1995: 99–124). As Iris Marion Young maintains, the "discourse of liberal individualism denies the reality of groups . . . and in fact obscures oppression" (1995: 104).[7] For Addams, the experiences of women and immigrants as a site for theorizing the political were undermined by the discourses of liberal democracy.

If democracy was to function as a living, breathing, social organism, then radical changes in its very premises were needed. Addams's critique of liberal democracy as obscuring the experiences of women and immigrants through the discourse of universal natural rights is exemplified in two major social issues of the day—the so-called immigrant problem and women's suffrage.

Democracy as "Diversified Human Experience"

A central focus of Addams's theorizing about democracy emerged out of her experiences living at the Hull House, in the heart of Chicago's immigrant community. The exploitation, oppression, and manipulation of immigrants by industry, the educational system, and politicians reinforced for Addams the limitations of liberal democracy. The roots of civic corruption that plagued turn-of-the-century cities could be traced to the belief "that our early democracy was a moral romanticism, rather than a well-grounded belief in social capacity and in the efficiency of the popular will" (Addams, 1911: 34).

Ironically, the discourse of universal experience embedded in liberal democracy legitimated the "othering" and marginalization of immigrants. This mistrust of immigrant culture and experience was manifested in dominant ideologies of assimilation and Americanization that emerged in response to immigration. Ignoring a critique of the capitalist/industrial order, many Americans focused on the racial and ethnic differences as the cause of social turbulence and moral decay. A proponent of Americanization, Stanford Professor Ellwood P. Cubberley (1909), described the southern and Eastern European immigrant:

> illiterate, docile, lacking in self-reliance and initiative and not possessing the Anglo-Teutonic conceptions of law, order, and government, their coming has served to dilute tremendously our national stock and to corrupt our civic life. (pp. 15–16)

For Cubberley, the first task was to break up ghettos and assimilate immigrants by divesting them of their ethnic character.

This ideology of Americanization reached its peak during World War I and in the early 1920s, when nationalist and xenophobic sentiments were extremely strong. At the height of the "red scare," Hull House provided a safe house for immigrants accused of "radical" and "un-American thinking." Early on,

Addams (1911) opposed immigration quotas, thereby adopting another controversial stance. She was critical of the narrowness of Americans:

> As Spain in the sixteenth century was obsessed by the necessity of achieving national unity, above the variety of religions, so Twentieth Century America is obsessed by the need of national unity above all else. (p. 296)

She was unwavering in her stance against the nativism expressed in the war fever prior to, during, and immediately following World War I.

Addams staunchly rejected Americanization and assimilation. Instead, her conception of democracy was grounded in the necessity of recognizing the "social capacity and efficiency of the popular will," particularly that of immigrants, women, and the working poor. Rather than corrupt American culture and society, immigrants, according to Addams, could teach Americans a great deal. In contrast to the dominant ideologies arguing that immigrants were responsible for the decay of the moral fiber of America, Addams maintained that it was the immigrant who could regenerate a decaying America (Rudnick, 1991: 151). Democracy should be a flexible and expansive form of government that could grow and be enriched by immigrant culture. In fact, democracy was the product of "diversified human experience and its resultant sympathy" (Addams, 1902: 12). For Addams, social democracy embraced immigrants by bringing their values into the community, not by erasing their ethnic culture and lifestyle. Thus, she stated that "the identification with the common lot, which is the essential idea of democracy, becomes the source and expression of social ethics" (p. 11). Her belief that the "common man" had something to teach Americans was evident in the following statement:

> It is no easy task to detect and to follow the tiny paths of progress which the unencumbered proletarian, with nothing but his life and capacity for labor, is pointing out for us. These paths lead to a type of government founded upon peace and fellowship as contrasted with restraint and defense. They can never be discovered with the eyes of doctrinaire. From the nature of these cases, he who would walk these paths must walk with the poor and oppressed, and can only approach them through affection and understanding. The ideas of militarism would forever shut him out from this new fellowship.
>
> *(Addams, 1911: 30)*

Despite her naive idealization and romanticization of the immigrants, Addams again reinforces the notion that democracy must be flexible enough to take into account the experiences of others rather than be locked into a system of universal, natural rights. Difference, not equality, becomes the basis for a true democracy.

To reduce Addams's motivations to maternalism or "noblesse oblige," as has often been done, is to simplify and decontextualize her complex relationship with the local communities in which she lived. In fact, rather than having a condescending view of immigrants, she saw them as playing a central role in shaping democracy. She stated in *Democracy and Social Ethics* (1902):

> We know instinctively that if we grow contemptuous of our fellows and consciously limit our intercourse to certain kinds of people whom we have previously decided to respect, we not only tremendously circumscribe our range of life, but limit the scope of our ethics. (p. 10)

It was her belief that "to know all sorts of men, in an indefinite way is preparation for better social adjustment—for the remedying of social ills" (p. 8). This outlook was the basis for her work at Hull House.

Addams's vision of radical democracy as a social organism took seriously the experiences of immigrants and African-Americans as a site for theorizing the political. Embracing difference through acknowledging collective experience, not universal, abstract individualism, was paramount if democracy was to avoid the supposed neutrality and objectivity that cloaked the experiences of specific groups such as African-Americans, immigrants, and women.

Uneasy Sisterhood

> The colored people of America find themselves today in the most trying period of all their trying history in this land of their trial and bondage. As the trials and responsibilities of the man weigh more heavily than do those of the infant, so the Negro under free labor and cut throat competition today has to vindicate his fitness to survive in face of a colorphobia that heeds neither reason nor religion and a prejudice that shows no quarter and allows not mitigating circumstances.
>
> *(Anna Julia Cooper, 1892)*

Lemert and Bhan (1998) maintain that Anna Julia Cooper's book *A Voice from the South* is the "first systematic working out of the insistence that no one social category can capture the reality of colored women" (p. 14). Cooper, like other Black women, including Mary Church Terrell and Frances Grimke, were trustees of the Colored Settlement House in Washington DC. While a teacher and principal at the M Street High School, Cooper began to volunteer her time in supervising settlement house programs. She noted in 1913 in the Oberlin College alumni journal that "paradoxically enough, the very period of the world that witnesses the most widespread uplift movements and intensest devotion to social service finds in America the hard wall of race prejudice against Negroes" (Lemert & Bhan, 1998: 219). While she lauds the work of Hull House and the work of settlements in addressing issues of class and race, it is clear that she recognizes the immense challenges that racism presents in building community. In part, this difficulty is brilliantly expressed in Cooper's work in her articulation of the insufficiency of such categories as race or gender, even class, to capture, by themselves, the complexities of women's experiences. Unsettling these categories, destabilizing the notions of "Whiteness," "womanhood," and "masculinity" were central to her work as well as to the work of Ida B. Wells and Jane Addams. And while Addams did not fully grasp the complexities of racism in the 1890s, she did understand that racial prejudice was a critical social issue (Knight, 2005). Interracial reform work in the settlement house movement became a major focus.

Although it is unclear when Wells and Addams first met, once they did so they sustained a working relationship throughout the course of their lives. After Wells moved to Chicago in 1895, Addams and Wells joined forces regularly to address issues of injustice. Knight suggests that Ida B. Wells first met Addams when Addams called her for assistance in organizing a luncheon for the biennial meeting of the National Council of Colored Women. While clubwork was increasingly attractive to both Black and White women as a mode of organized reform, the ideology of segregation and subordination penetrated its policies and practices. At the same time, Black women's clubs were not solely reactions to discrimination or an imitation of white women's groups. They had different priorities and the separation of clubs, and, for that matter, the settlements, was often desired. Despite differences, attempts to "speak together" did occur, as when Jane Addams nominated the first African-American woman, Fanny Barrier Williams to join the Chicago Woman's Club. While Addams was not always aware of or understood all the complexities of White privilege, she was committed to racial equality (Knight, 2005). In her autobiography, Wells (1970) characterizes Jane Addams as the "greatest woman in the United States" (p. 259). These two women were committed activists whose vision of a more just society made them allies in numerous causes, including women's suffrage, improved race relations, women's rights, and civil rights.

Despite common commitments to many social movements, Addams and Wells differed in their fundamental analysis of the causes of racism. For Addams, African- Americans suffered from cultural deprivation as a result of slavery. Consequently, their needs differed from those of immigrants and required, in part, unique and separate institutions. Wells advocated separate institutions for African-Americans that would address and take into account their particular social and cultural realities. Simultaneously, both Addams and Wells worked for the integration of schools, the women's club movement, and the National Association for the Advancement of Colored People (NAACP). They shared the belief that both separate and integrated institutions were necessary—that no single policy regarding race relations would be sufficient to address the complexities of race, gender, and class.

Although the African-American population was small in Chicago until the

1920s and the Hull House neighborhood did not contain a large Black population until the 1930s, Hull House sponsored meetings for Black women and supported the Black clubwomen's movement; furthermore, Hull House had one Black resident in the 1890s, Dr. Harriet Rice, who was in charge of the dispensary (Stebner, 1997). Lugenia Hope, the founder of the Atlanta Neighborhood Union, a Black settlement, worked for a benevolent society in Chicago and spent time at Hull House.

In 1899, when the National Association of Colored Women's Clubs met in Chicago, Addams called Wells in order to set up a meeting with the Association and its President, Mary Church Terrell. The officers of the National Association accepted the invitation to meet at Hull House (Duster, 1970), and in that same year Addams attended the 1899 biennial meeting of the National Association of Colored Women. In 1909 she was named to the executive committee of the NAACP and a member of the Chicago Urban League. In Chicago, the Urban League was formed to address the social problems of Black migration. While it was initially supported by the conservative leadership of the Chicago Black community (those supportive of Booker T. Washington), the enthusiastic response of Black women and the Chicago Federation of Colored Women's Clubs expanded the work of the league in regards to programmatic outreach, as well as supporting the Wendell Philips Settlement and Douglas House. However, the Black community was not united in its support of the Urban League. Wells was suspicious of the pro-Washington leadership in the league, as well as its reliance on White philanthropy which differed from Wells's confrontation and protest tactics with White reformers (Salem, 1990). Like the differences in the White community, there was no monolithic Black community activist group. While Wells was clearly a radical, many Blacks adopted a more assimilationist policy in part due to the nature of race relations and the severe consequences of contra-dicting dominant racial and gender norms.

In 1910, Wells sought out to get support for putting an end to a series of articles in the *Chicago Tribune* that advocated the segregation of the public schools. In her autobiography, Wells (1970) recalled:

> I went to the phone and called up Miss Jane Addams of Hull House and asked if she would see me. When I called upon her and explained the situation I said, "Miss Addams, there are plenty of people in Chicago who would not sanction such a move if they knew about it. Will you undertake to reach those of influence who would be willing to do for us what we cannot do for ourselves?" She very readily agreed to do so, and the following Sunday evening there were gathered at Hull House representative men and women of the White race, who listened to my story. (p. 276)

Wells addressed the group and emphasized how separate schools always meant inferior education for Black children. After the meeting, Addams went to see the editors of the *Tribune* with a White delegation. The series of articles was stopped (Wertheimer, 1977).

In 1901, Addams and Wells had an exchange regarding lynching in *The Independent*. Wells believed that lynching was a "primary means of controlling Black social and economic life" (Ware, 1996: 179). Her investigations showed that Black men accused of rape were often the same men who were seen as a threat to White businesses. She also asserted that many accusations of rape were unfounded, since relations between Black men and White women were often consensual. In fact, fewer than one-third of lynching victims were even accused of rape. In Wells's view, "Black men lynched for 'rape,' far from embodying uncontrolled lust, were innocent victims, seduced into having consensual sex with carnal White women" (Bederman, 1995b: 415). In attributing sexuality to White women, rather than to Black men, she reversed both gender and racial stereotypes (Schechter, 1998). In particular, she construed White women as having agency, albeit of a sexualized nature, in opposition to the discourse around Victorian womanhood, which celebrated true women as pious, pure, and maternal guardians of virtue and domesticity. Although she attributed agency to White women, she simultaneously set them up to take the blame for lynching. Not only did she debunk the myth of the Black rapist, but also she contradicted the stereotype of the Black savage by arguing that lynching should be interpreted as White barbarism destroying Black manliness.

Not surprisingly, the American press rejected the radical implications of her argument. She then took her anti-lynching campaign to England, where the English were shocked to hear of the mob rule that had replaced law and order in American society. Wells's appeal to English citizens was framed as that of "one civilized race to another for protection from violent White barbarians" (Bederman, 1995b: 417). Her goal was to mobilize Americans against lynching as the work of unmanly savages. In appropriating the discourse of "civilization," a discourse central to legitimating racial discrimination, she was able to subvert it and insist on the womanliness of Black women and the manliness of Black men. By appropriating White, middle-class gender norms for Black men and women, Wells attempted to subvert racial discrimination and violence.

Although Addams also spoke out against lynching, she did so on the grounds that this method of punishment set aside due process of law and trial by jury. In other words, she did accept the argument that Black men were guilty of rape. What she abhorred was the lack of justice, not the racial prejudice inherent in the act of lynching. Addams also strongly opposed the argument that this type of brutal and public punishment would deter future crimes. In the January 3, 1907 *Independent* article she wrote, "the suppression of the bestial cannot be accomplished by the counter exhibition of the brutal only" (as quoted in Aptheker, 1977: 27). Ironically, while Wells upheld normative gender roles of manliness and femininity, Addams disrupted them. Addams suggested that White women reject the argument that lynching protected them because lynching was another form of protective paternalism that kept women subordinate to men and ultimately debased women. She called on women to testify that only where law and order ruled could the rights of women be secured. For Addams, women had the responsibility, as the morally superior sex, to convince the public of the horrors of lynching. These differences in analysis highlight the complex ways in which Wells and Addams took up race, class, and gender to subvert injustice through arguments that simultaneously reified dominant gender and race discourses. In her response to Addams's article, Wells lauded Addams for decrying lynching, but she questioned how the "distinguished writer" could make the absolutely unwarrantable assumption that Blacks had committed these alleged crimes (Wells, 1901).

This dialogue between Addams and Wells was part of an ongoing relationship in which their different understandings of the causes of social injustice did not impede joint work. Addams and Wells were both active supporters of W.E.B. Du Bois. Addams had invited Du Bois to speak at Hull House in February 1907. In 1908, Wells and Addams worked together on a mass meeting at Orchestra Hall that featured Du Bois as a guest speaker. This meeting was designed as a call to action against lynching, the convict-lease systems, and segregation. Addams and Wells were founders of the NAACP. Both were involved in the Illinois suffrage campaign, the Chicago Woman's Club, and the Political Equality League. As committed activists, they were dedicated to social change that required a rethinking of dominant gender and race relations.

Addams's and Wells's vision of radical democracy took seriously the experiences of immigrants, women, and African-Americans as a site for theorizing about politics. They believed that difference—not universal, abstract individualism—was paramount for democracy. Only by embracing difference could the experiences of specific groups such as immigrants and women come to light. Addams's analysis of gender, as manifested in her views on suffrage, reflects parallel lines of thinking.

Women's Suffrage as "Means to an End"

Addams's critique of universal natural rights was seen most readily in her belief that women's suffrage was not a goal in and of itself but part of a larger vision of social change. While active in the work of the National American Women Suffrage Association (NAWSA) and serving as its first vice president, Addams nonetheless recognized the limitations of suffrage in bringing about radical change in social relations.[8] Like other social reformers, including Margaret Haley, Jane Addams believed that involvement in political activities and community organizing did more than the ballot to teach them about citizenship (Rousmaniere, 2005). The full realization of democratic ideas would require more than granting suffrage to all citizens. In effect, focusing on suffrage reinforced the notions of natural rights and democracy as public and individual. As Alasdair MacIntyre suggests, the doctrine of rights is "tradition bound, not a discovery of something universal" (MacIntyre, 1984: 230). An understanding of citizenship as public and individual not only obscures the political nature of the everyday work of women (such as teaching, mothering, housework, and community and union activities) but also negates alternative epistemological foundations of citizenship based on women's experiences.

For Addams, democracy entailed not only the recognition of women as citizens but also a redefinition of citizenship. Historically, women could not be full citizens. Carol Pateman reminds us that "women, our bodies and distinctive capacities, represented all that citizenship and equality are not. Citizenship has gained its meaning through the exclusion of women, that is to say (sexual) difference" (Pateman, 1992: 19). The very concept of citizenship was dependent on subordination. The exclusion of women from citizenship did not, however, mean that a woman had no political duties. The 18th-century doctrine of "republican motherhood" maintained that women's political duty (not right) was to bear children (sons) and rear them as virtuous citizens. Demanding that women's role as mothers not be seen as subordinate to citizenship, Mary Wollstonecraft, in *A Vindication of the Rights of Women*, and Olympe de Gouges, in *Declaration of the Rights of Women and the Female Citizen*, both argued that female difference, especially motherhood, should be the basis of equal citizenship. To claim the special role of women as mothers as the rationale for citizenship is, as Pateman asserts, to "demand the impossible; such difference is precisely what patriarchal citizenship excludes" (Pateman, 1992: 20). And in fact, fuller citizenship for women, when it did come in the form of voting rights, was justified ultimately on the basis of difference, even though writers such as Elizabeth Cady Stanton had argued for suffrage from the standpoint of equality. In the end, women's claim to higher moral ground was more compelling to legislators than the claim to the vote based on equity. Alice Paul's frustrations during the 1920s in building a base of support for the Equal Rights Amendment and the difficult victory of the Nineteenth Amendment indicated just how tenuous public support was for women's claims to equality with men.

Addams used the notion of gender difference as manifested in the ideology of separate spheres to argue for women's role in the public sphere. However, she broadened the conception of women's experience beyond mothering and housekeeping. Elevating suffrage as a symbol of citizenship in a democracy reified masculinist conceptions of "politics," thereby obscuring the ways in which women saw themselves as political actors, particularly the work of women's collective action.[9] She included women's collective action and women's pacifism as sites from which to redefine the political. Although Addams has been critiqued as essentializing women's innate moral nature, Victoria Brown maintains that Addams's conception of the differences in the political values of men and women were attributable to women's experiences, not innate habits of instincts (Brown, 1995: 179–202). In fact, for middle-class and upper-middle-class women, the rhetoric of women's innate feminine altruism and motherly charity was embraced as the cloak under which even the most forceful social and political actions were advanced (Ryan, 1979). Brown (1995) maintains that Addams's focus on women's collective duty to reform was a "function of the very particular emphasis Addams placed on economic democracy, [rather] than an accommodation to conservative nostalgia for selfless womanhood" (p. 183).

Addams's vision of "radical democracy" conceptualized citizenship, not as private and individual, but as an ongoing, determining of "ideals by our daily actions and decisions not only for ourselves, but largely for each other" (Addams, 1910: 256). In this sense, Addams did not put the classical liberal emphasis on women's individual right to the vote. If democracy was to function as a "social organism," citizenship needed to be reconceptualized as a collective act not an individual one. Citizenship that focused on the right to vote functioned to define the political as public and individual. This thrust of classical democracy toward political rights alone reinforced abstract individualism and failed to develop a notion of individual rights as a product of collective life. It was the social responsibility to the collective, not the individual that characterized Addams's vision of radical democracy as a social organism. Her commitment to honoring difference, not equality, as central to democracy has yet to be taken seriously as a site for rethinking the political.

According to Addams (1911), liberal democracy, with its roots in a preindustrial agrarian society, had not been designed for the needs and conditions of an emerging industrial society. The radical changes brought on by industrialization required a reinvisioning of democracy in which "changes could be considered as belonging to the community as a whole" (p. 124). For Addams, democracy was dependent on social interaction in which diversity was seen as a strength. She rejected a vision of society based on the notion that citizenship was grounded in "White supremacy" or "masculinity." Her deconstruction of liberal democracy sought to expose how citizenship as individual, male, White, and public functioned not as liberatory but as a mechanism for exclusion. In revealing the limited subject identities made available she also addressed class. Social interaction was hampered by a class system that created large gaps in economic conditions. Without economic equality, democracy could not flourish. Addams maintained that until class and gender barriers were removed, the social interactions that were the heart of democracy could not occur. In fact, the reduction of democracy to secure the "rights of man" obscured the "duties to humanity," in particular duties to the working classes (p. 29). In formulating a philosophy of social justice based on economic equality, Addams drew from a variety of social theories, including socialism, Marxism, Fabianism, and cultural feminism. Influenced by Marx, Tolstoy, Ruskin, Ward, Perkins, and others, Addams's pragmatism incorporated a critique of capitalism and gender relations. According to Jill Conway (1971), Addams's social critique "was free from the usual progressive concern with institutionalizing middle-class values. It was future oriented, ready to accept radical change and optimistic about the potential of the American city to become a genuinely creative, pluralistic community" (pp. 164–177).

A Peaceful Working-Class Revolution

Addams had an abiding faith in the working classes. In the Pullman strike of 1894, in which she acted as an arbitrator, her sympathies clearly were with the workers, as evidenced by her comments in her publication *A Modern Lear:*

> We are all practically agreed that the social passion of the age is directed toward the emancipation of the wage-worker; that a great accumulation of moral force is overmastering man and making for this emancipation as in another time it has made for the emancipation of the slave; that nothing will satisfy the aroused conscience of men short of the complete participation of the working classes in the spiritual, intellectual, and material inheritance of the human race.[10]

Social democracy was predicated on the recognition and valuing of the experiences of the working classes. Addams was arguing that in a democracy middle- and upper-class citizens had not only a responsibility to understand the views of working-class people and avoid judgment, but that they had to somehow "incorporate those views into their own evolving, shared, democratic ethic" (Knight, 2005: 386). Her experiences with the Pullman strike resulted in a profound shift in her understanding that benevolence is always oppressive (Hendry, in press). The reform of society through democratic decision-making necessitated that the *experiences* of all groups be validated, not that they be pitied (Procknow, 2007). According to Kathryn Sklar (1995): "At the core of Addams' considerable genius lay a Darwinian belief in the vitality of the human species as expressed in working-class people and a determination to join these people, whatever the cost" (p. 176). Sklar characterizes well the absolute belief that Addams invested in the working class. However, despite Addams's support for the working poor and labor unions, as well as strikes, her commitment to nonviolence resulted in equating class struggle with war. Class struggle, as articulated in Marxist-socialist thought, was, for Addams, a form of militarism that ultimately undermined the building of community and thus hindered democracy (Munro, 1999).

A social theory such as Marxism that described society as composed of monolithic groups like "proletariat" and "bourgeoisie" threatened to solidify differences; it failed to recognize the communitarian threads that connected groups. Addams rejected the Marxist assumption that class antagonism was the impelling force leading to social revolution. For Addams, the struggle for economic, political, and social advantages was not rooted solely in material needs and limited by the modes of production. Rather, it was also rooted in the militarism inherent in notions of "struggle" and "revolution," to which Addams objected on the grounds that military values were "destructive, masculine, and inferior to the more socially advanced feminine values of cooperation and pacifism" (Deegan, 1990: 226).

At the same time, Addams shared with Marxist analysis a firm belief in economic equality.[11] Her ongoing struggle with Marxist thought is recalled in *Twenty Years at Hull-House* (1910), in which she reflects that she "longed for the comfort of a social creed which should afford at one and the same time an explanation of the social chaos and the logical steps towards its better understandings" (p. 187). And yet Addams was suspicious of totalizing social theories. In the case of Marxist–socialist thought, Addams critiqued the theory of class conflict as solidifying a monolithic, static view of class that over–simplified and obscured the differences among the working poor. The idea that members of the working class were ignorant of their oppression (suffering from false consciousness) and its causes reinforced conceptions of the working class as disempowered and thus ultimately reproduced the very hierarchies that Addams was contesting.

Despite her criticism of Marxism, Addams supported the work of labor unions, although she continually sought nonviolent methods of resolution. In the 1895 publication *Hull-House Maps and Paper*, Addams discussed her commitment to laborers and support of their efforts to break the cycle of poverty. Addams was especially interested in supporting trade unions for women. Women's labor unions in Chicago were organized primarily through Hull House and included the Cloakmakers' Union, the Shirtmakers' Union, and the Chicago Women's Trade Union League. Mary Kenney, a union organizer, accepted Addams's invitation for the Bookbinders' Union to meet at Hull House. Kenney eventually formed the Jane Club, a rented residence for self-supporting working women. Addams advocated for the workers' goal of shorter workdays, increased wages, better industrial and general education, and workers' protection in the marketplace. Ultimately, though, Addams was committed to a trade union movement oriented toward large-scale social change, not the limited economic benefits of a short-term contract. In fact, she believed labor unions were ultimately a tool of capitalists because they reduced negotiations to single industry issues rather than systematic change.

Addams's unwavering commitment to a cooperative society was deeply embedded in her belief that a social analysis based on a conflict model of society reinforced the conflict process.[12] In this sense, the "radical" nature of her thought, in which social change was dependent on cooperation and peace rather than on conflict and aggression, clearly delineated her from other progressives and pragmatists. Addams's rejection of militarism and her adoption of a "cooperative-democratic" model of criticism and analysis differed radically from Marxist analysis (Deegan, 1990: 275). Social change for a democratic society was contingent on the rejection of militarism in all its forms, including class struggle. Her understanding of democracy was predicated on cooperation and pacifism, approaches that Addams saw as specifically linked to women's nature and values that were denied expression in a patriarchal society.

Cultural Feminism, Pacifism, and Democracy

Addams's problem with socialist thought stemmed not only from its militarism but also from its rigid orthodoxy and truncated analysis of women's status and values.

She believed that social theories predicated on militarism necessarily excluded women. As a consequence, "there was no place for woman and her possible contribution in international affairs under the old diplomacy" (Addams, 1902: 81). Until women's values had full expression, society could not be democratic. Like contemporaries Charlotte Perkins Gilman and Mary Ritter Beard, Addams based her analysis of social relations on women's subjugation as the primary form of oppression. Furthermore, she argued that the oppression of women retarded all human progress.

As a cultural feminist, Addams believed in the superiority of women's values, worldviews, and behaviors. This view was not out of line with the dominant ideology of separate spheres in which women were seen as morally superior to men, providing them with a "specialized feminine perception of social injustice . . . [coming] from women's innate passivity and from women's ability to empathize with the weak and dependent."[13] From Addams this ideology could not be carried to its logical extreme because women were denied full expression in a patriarchal society. Addams carried the ideology of separate spheres to the extreme where she held that the exploiters of society were masculine and that women held the true vision of a democratic society (Conway, 1971: 171). Rather than interpret this as complicity with the gender ideology of separate spheres, I would argue that Addams's standpoint functioned as a form of strategic essentialism (Spivak, 1988). Embracing dominant gender ideologies, she simultaneously resignified them. This was perhaps nowhere more apparent that in her staunch belief in the natural humanitarian and pacifist traits of women.

Drawn to the cooperative philosophies of Tolstoy and Kropotkin, Addams embraced the concepts of nonresistance and pacifism as central to defining and changing class exploitation (Deegan, 1990: 275). Although Addams eventually criticized Tolstoy as being too utopian and individualistic, she was drawn to his vision of "bread labor," which positioned a simple life connected to the soil as central to a philosophy of nonresistance.[14] This concept appealed to Addams because of the positive connotation associated with making and creating food, traditionally the work of women. The connection between food production and pacifism provided Addams with a conceptual framework for using women's experiences as central to shaping public policy and international affairs.

Addams's commitment to nonviolence and pacifism was evidenced in her staunch opposition to World War I. Addams traced this opposition to the early fall of 1914 when a small group of social workers held a series of meetings at the Henry Street Settlement in New York with the goal of formulating a reaction to war. From these meetings, several organizations emerged, including the Union Against Militarism and the Women's Peace Party, in which Addams served as chairman. Three thousand people attended the first convention of the Women's Peace Party in January 1915. Among other demands for limiting arms production and the substitution of economic pressure for warfare, the platform called for the education of youth in the ideals of peace, the further humanizing of governments by the extension of suffrage to women, and the investigation of the economic causes of war. This articulation of the connections between education, economics, and gender in addressing militarism as a form of oppression reflected the gendered analysis of change that was undertheorized in traditional Marxist-socialist thought. Most important, her vision of democracy extended the notion of equality to incorporate not only political equality but also social and economic equality. Without economic equality, political and social democracy could not be achieved. In this regard, Addams provided a radical critique of liberal classical democracy with it emphasis on political rights.

For Addams, social democracy would not be realized until women's culture had full expression. Hull House became the realization of women's culture and the manifestation of Addams's ideals of social democracy. Addams's concept of "widening the circle" speaks directly to the issue of how to invision a form of democracy that recognized difference while also maintaining a standpoint politics. Addams was ultimately committed to a separatist position, one that rejected liberal, mainstream, heterosexist assumptions regarding social relations. Although men also lived there, Hull House was a woman's collective established to contest the nuclear, patriarchal family, which Addams saw as inherently undemocratic (Sklar, 1995: 130). True democracy would entail a radical restructuring of social relations that honored a multiplicity of modes of association. Hull House thus became the embodiment of Addams's intention to provide an alternative to the male success myth by creating a "paradigm of national character and culture that is predominately female and includes previously excluded racial and ethnic groups" (Rudnick, 1991: 146). According to Anne Scott (1993), settlement houses not only were "miniature republics" in which women learned about politics but also were in themselves institutions that contested politics as usual. By reconstructing normative gender relations which privileged the patriarchal nuclear family, Addams and others provided an alternative vision of social relations grounded in "Republican Motherhood" that was communal, female-centered, and community based. Hull House thus provided a radical reinvisioning of political culture in which community networks, not individual rights were the foundation of democracy.

Unsettling Domesticity

> A settlement wasn't a thing but a way of living—hence it had the same aims as life itself. The settlement wasn't being started from the desire to do good. Philanthropy had been identified with helping instead of with interpretation.
>
> *(John Dewey, 1894)*

In 1891, there were six settlement houses in the United States; but by 1910 there were more than 400 (Davis, 1967). In 1890 there were settlements in New York, Boston, and Chicago; by the turn of the century almost every major city in the

United States had a settlement house. While Addams's understanding of the purpose of the settlement house emerged over time, she was initially influenced by her experience at Toynbee Hall in London in 1887. Europe, like the United States during the 1880s, began to experience the consequences of unregulated economic growth and unprecedented immigration into the cities. The first to respond to these ills were the clergy. English Christian Socialism, and its counter part in American "social Christianity," later known as the "Social Gospel," emerged to provide a persuasive and comfortable intellectual underpinning for social service. What distinguished the Social Gospel of the 1890s from earlier forms of Church activism was precisely its assumption that social injustice contributed to poverty, vice, and urban social dislocation. Because Addams was clearly the product of the Social Gospel, she did not immediately adopt a radical social analysis. It was the emergence of the social sciences with its focus on research that was to move the settlement house movement beyond merely a charity or benevolence model of social aid. To understand the issues of poverty, crime, and delinquency, facts and data were needed to sort out policies made on prejudice from policies based on rational information. One of the settlement's distinctive contributions to social thought was the promoting of social investigation as the basis for public policy. Addams worked closely with her friend and colleague W.E.B. Du Bois to advance a model of sociological research that focused on data collection that was collaborative and began with valuing the experiences of those whose problems were being examined. Thus the new science was combined with the new religion to create a new model of urban reform.

From the beginning, Addams grappled with the contradictions and tensions inherent in her privileged class position with its inclination toward "charity," "philanthropy," and "benevolence." These discourses situated her, the "giver" as superior to and "helping" those who were less educated and inferior. While upper-middle-class Victorian society prided itself on individual virtues such as self-control, sobriety, respect for property, and industriousness, Addams quickly came to realize that this view of social change as based on virtues was clearly out of date. According to Louise Knight (2005), Addams's immersion at Hull House living among immigrants resulted in her proposal to replace those virtues with a broader "social ethic" (p. 355). This broader social ethic took into account not only "character" as the means to improve one's lot in life but analyzed the larger social, economic, and political factors that shaped urban life. Just as important to social justice was an understanding of how these conditions were experienced by immigrants in their everyday lives. Philanthropists relied on their moral superiority and their self-righteousness to guide their policy making. What the times required was the abandonment of a sense of "absolute right" or universal ethics. Her rejection of benevolence and individualism resulted in her understanding that ethics change as society changes; that which is ethical is what society finds ethical in the present. For Addams, it is not just that experience shapes ethics; it is that ethics, that which is true, changes (Knight, 2005). This required an immense shift in her way of being in the world and would be the basis of her pragmatist philosophy. To dislodge and continually question her own positions in regard to Hull House would be the work of "unsettling" in which she would engage for the remainder of her life.

The establishment of Hull House by Jane Addams and Ellen Starr Gates in 1889, and of the Negro Fellowship League Room and Social Center by Ida B. Wells in 1910, must be understood as social experiments and curriculum innovations that challenged the emerging reproductionist nature of schooling. In fact, Addams saw the increasing focus on social efficiency, which relied on experts and standardization, as a holdover from militarism. Far from being progressive or democratic, schools were indoctrinating students to accept hierarchy, conflict, and war as ethical. Jane Addams, as well as other settlement workers such as Lillian Wald and Lavinia Dock, were adamant in rejecting male conceptions of citizenship embedded in liberal democracy that fostered military notions of war as a form of conflict resolution or patriotism that was based on nationalism, thereby reaffirming boundaries between people (Smith, 2002). The new ideal of citizenship, or "newer ideals of peace" advocated by Addams, moved beyond individual and national differences to promote compassion for the entire human race. This pacifist vision was clearly at odds with public schooling's increasing focus on differentiation, standardization, and centralization that were antithetical to Addams's notion of radical democracy. Hull House became a radical experiment in shaping a democratic form of education that was in sharp contrast to public schools.

Hull House

According to Mary Jo Deegan (1990), the 1890s were lively and controversial years at Hull House—anarchist, Marxist, socialist, unionist, and leading social theorists congregated there. The primary purpose of Hull House was to "learn from life itself." This spirit of inquiry was central to Addams's understanding of democracy as a dynamic process of social interaction among all citizens, as a mode of "associated living" (Dewey, 1916). John Dewey, George Herbert Mead, Ida B. Wells, Ella Flagg Young, W.E.B. Du Bois, and Charlotte Perkins Gilman, among others, were frequent visitors and speakers at Hull House, as well as close friends of Addams. Chicago pragmatism was born through their collegial contacts and intellectual exchanges.

For Addams and Wells, the settlement house movement was the embodiment of democracy. Addams liked to think of the work at Hull House as a program of "socialized education"—as ultimately a protest against a restricted view of the school. Cremin (1961) maintains that Addams

> lashed out bitterly against the elitism of the wealthy, who believed the underprivileged had little to contribute to the spiritual life of the community, and the provincialism of the educators, whose own narrow view of culture

kept them from grasping the rich pedagogical possibilities in the productive
life of the city. (pp. 61–62)

At the turn of the century, American schools were characterized by social
efficiency and centralization. In contrast, Addams saw learning as lifelong, as based
in community, and as a reciprocal exchange of knowledge intended to empower
learners and heal social, economic, and ethnic divisions.

Addams (1930) recalled: "We used to say the settlement had a distinct place in
the educational field and we were even bold enough to compare ourselves with
universities and colleges" (p. 404). Charles Beard described the early relationship
between the settlements and universities "as exerting beyond all question a
direct and immediate influence on American thinking about industrial questions,
and on the course of social practice" (as quoted in Addams, 1930: 406). Critical
of the emerging role of schools and formal institutions in reproducing unequal
class relations, Addams believed that education should be organized to enhance
the individual's capacity to engage with others in community affairs, thereby
identifying and advancing the common interests that would foster gradual, yet
continuous, social reform (Lagemann, 1985). In their role as educators, the women
in settlements of the major urban centers at the turn of the century not only
worked to transform social relations for a more equitable society but also sought
to rearticulate the very role of schooling and education in shaping a democratic
society.

Despite the cultural pluralism that Addams promoted, there is debate as
to whether this extended to the incorporation of African-Americans into the
settlement house movement (Lasch-Quinn, 1993). The limited response of the
settlement house movement to African-Americans is attributed to the dominant
depiction of Blacks as somehow maladjusted and their "culture as lacking" (Lasch–
Quinn, 1993: 10). For many turn-of-the-century progressive reformers, the brutal
system of slavery had "obliterated morality, family integrity, social organization,
and even culture and civilization itself" (p. 10). The White settlement house
movement on the whole ignored Blacks and did not address the issue of race.
According to Lasch-Quinn, several individuals, including Jane Addams, stood out
from mainstream settlements due to their interests in the particular problems facing
African-Americans. There is no question that Addams addressed the issue of race
relations. However, the focus of her work remained on the immigrants. Her co-
reformer, Louise de Koven Bowen, a major supporter of Hull House and author
of *The Colored People of Chicago* (1913), criticized Hull House for not taking a
stronger position on bridging race relations. Addams clearly saw a difference
between Blacks and immigrants. Although she rejected any biological explanation
for the subordination of Blacks or immigrants, she did distinguish between their
capacity for the social and moral adjustment that she believed was necessary for
functioning in a democratic society. For Addams, the legacy of slavery that had
undermined the Black family had also left Blacks bereft of a sense of community.

This had resulted in a lack of social foundations and cultural traditions. In essence, many settlement workers and reformers saw Blacks as victimized by slavery and thus having very different needs from immigrants. This difference provided the rationale for a settlement policy based on separate branches for Blacks.

Although acknowledging the horrors of slavery, the focus on deprivation as a consequence of slavery resulted in emphasizing Blacks' personal shortcomings while downplaying ongoing racial discrimination and prejudice. Immigrants, on the other hand, brought with them a sense of cultural identity and community that provided a source of moral and social glue. While astute in her analysis of the difference between immigrant and American minorities, Addams's belief in the cultural deficiency or cultural deprivation of Blacks severely circumscribed her ideas regarding race relations and the nature of social policy toward African-Americans. By contrast, Black settlement workers and settlement houses—including Karamu House in Cleveland, Neighborhood Union in Atlanta, and Phyllis Wheatley House in Minneapolis—all rejected the view that slavery had deprived Blacks of fundamental social and cultural attributes.

Hull House's response to Blacks has been described as inaction (Trolander, 1987). Although the second largest Black neighborhood in Chicago eventually developed around Hull House, few Blacks were represented in the Hull House program until the 1920s. Black migration during World War I and into the 1920s resulted in major shifts in the neighbors around Hull House. As the demographic shifted and more African-Americans moved in to the neighborhood, Hull House did conduct a study of Black needs and Black children did participate in the activities and summer camps offered by Hull House. Addams began a Black mothers' club in 1927, although Blacks' participation in other Hull House activities was limited. In part, this was due to the African-American community's own settlement house movement which specifically addressed the need of Blacks.

Black Settlement House Movement

> The highest development of civilization of the future depends of making a beautiful, healthful, community life that shall afford adequate stimulation to all this struggling, hungry desire of the individual. . . . The healthful growth of our democratic civilization is dependent upon the development of this more completely healthful social environment—the organized community.
> *(Lugenia Hope, 1919–1924, Memoranda,*
> Neighborhood Union Papers, *Atlanta)*

Lugenia Hope, founder of the first African-American settlement house, the Atlanta Neighborhood Union, had been a resident at Hull House prior to moving with her husband to Atlanta to open her own settlement. Her poignant plea for a beautiful community life as the highest development of civilization echoes the call by other settlement workers, especially Addams, that democracy was based on collective not individual rights. Like Addams, she sought to address the needs of the residents in her community. Working with sociologists from Morehouse College, settlement workers were trained in survey and investigative techniques to enhance programs by giving community members a voice.

Although settlement houses like Jane Addams's Hull House provided services for newly arrived immigrants from Europe, few social services were available for newly arriving southern Black migrants (Sterling, 1979). Disturbed by high unemployment among Blacks, due to a lack of job skills as well as racial discrimination, and the growing crime rate, Ida B. Wells started the Negro Fellowship League Room and Social Center in Chicago in 1910. Like other settlement houses, the center served as an employment office, dormitory, and school. Located on State Street, the center sought to educate in numerous ways. Not only were newspapers, books, and games provided, but Wells also focused on teaching the skills and customs Blacks needed to assimilate to a northern, urban setting.

Between 1895 and 1917 more than 68 settlement and neighborhood centers were founded in Chicago. Like most settlements, African-American settlements were primarily concerned with child welfare, wholesome recreational activities for youth, and domestic and manual training. Lectures, mothers' clubs, and employment bureaus were created. However, the African-American settlements were, according to Knupfer (1996), unique "in the ways in which they interconnected social, economic, and educational aspects of the community" (p. 91). For the most part these settlement houses were segregated. Two exceptions were the Abraham Lincoln Center and the Frederick Douglass Center, both multiracial settlement houses. In part, segregated settlements were the result of neighborhood segregation already in place. However, when Hull House opened its nursery in 1925, it did establish a quota for African-American children and redrew the neighborhood lines to ensure that the quota would be maintained.

Numerous Black settlements were founded, including the Institutional Church and Social Settlement and the Wendell Phillips Settlement, led by two African-American social workers, Sophia Boaz and Birdye Haynes, who had studied at the University of Chicago's School of Civics and Philanthropy. The Clotee Scott Settlement house in Hyde Park used University of Chicago student volunteers. The most controversial settlement house was the Frederick Douglass Center, co-founded by Celia Parker Woolley and Ida B. Wells. The center's mission was to promote a "just and amicable relationship" between the White and African-American races (Knupfer, 1996: 44). The center was singular in its objective of promoting interracial amity among middle-class Whites and African-Americans. Located adjacent to the Black Belt (the Black neighborhood directly south of downtown), the center was a site for Whites and African-Americans to join together. The center offered fiction and sociology classes and an opportunity to join the women's club, which not only surveyed fine art and literature but was also active in promoting women's suffrage and integration. The Abraham Lincoln Center stood between Black and White communities. The center, which had a

White director and an integrated staff, fostered equal and integrated participation in all activities. The Frederick Douglass Center, although offering classes to poorer African-Americans, had as its primary goal interracial connections.

Wells's Negro Fellowship League, in the heart of Chicago's Black Belt, provided basic services such as health care, lodging, and employment referral services. The settlement houses in the Black community provided day care, as well as classes for young children and kindergartens. Mothers' meetings, domestic training, and health services were also provided. Youth dances, as well as drama, singing, and sporting clubs, were organized to keep adolescents out of the saloons and engaged in wholesome recreation. Cooking, nursing, and dressmaking courses were offered with the aim of making them legitimate professions through industrial education. Academic courses such as sociology, English literature, and English grammar were also offered.

Knupfer (1996) maintains that there were significant differences between White and Black settlement houses: White settlement workers focused on class and regional differences; White workers formulated African-Americans' maladjustment to urban life as the inability to assimilate, whereas African-Americans framed the issue as one of segregation and discrimination. Lastly, White reformers saw African-Americans as disconnected from their traditions and customs, whereas African-Americans spoke of the loss of dignity and family life in slavery. These differences profoundly shaped the understandings of race, the nature of race relations, and the settlement house movement. Although the settlement house movement has been criticized for neglecting race, and ultimately being assimilationist, I maintain that women educator activists' views of race and ethnicity were highly situated and particularistic. These views worked in complex and contradictory ways to both subvert and reproduce oppressive race relations. Even the most progressive and committed White reformers, like Addams, worked within turn-of-the-century racist discourse. And among Black reformers, class deeply divided and informed views toward Black migrant workers. However, in avoiding a universal theory of race relations, both Addams and Wells stayed attuned to the complex dynamics of the situated nature of race relations. This understanding was central to their belief that alternative educational institutions, like the settlement house, were necessary to meet the diverse needs of Blacks and immigrants.

The Curriculum of the Settlement House

Although settlement houses are primarily remembered for providing social services, Linda Kerber (1983) suggests that they were pioneering, even radical, educational institutions. She states:

> Teachers at settlement houses undertook to teach people who were not welcome in the usual schools. They taught women who had baked their bread in communal village ovens how to cope with American kitchens. Jane

Addams' Hull House had free reading rooms. . . . Teachers from the extension division of the University of Chicago came to teach art and literature classes. Hull House made room for a labor museum and a textile museum, in which work of women's hands was exhibited. If we seek to catalogue the contributions of women to American education, the work of the settlement houses must be included in the list. (p. 29)

The reform impulse of settlement homes has traditionally been interpreted as arising out of religious motivations rather than being a form of political work (Sklar, 1990). Similarly, individual women engaged in ameliorating unequal relations through charity work, have not been understood as social reconstructionists or critics of social relations who were engaged in dynamic social experiments designed to restructure society.

Hull House's educational philosophy, in which a settlement was defined as "an institution attempting to learn from life itself" (Addams, 1930: 408), was grounded in the understanding that meaningful learning and social action occurred only when education allowed learners to define their own needs and acknowledged women, immigrants, and migrants as creators of knowledge. Although Hull House could be characterized originally as a paternalistic endeavor (Farrell, 1967) that included a Shakespeare Club, a Plato Club (which brought academics such as John Dewey to lecture on topics like social psychology), and college extension courses at Rockford Seminary, Addams came to realize that meaningful learning and social action must arise from the needs and knowledge of those they were to serve.

In challenging the reproductionist nature of schooling at the turn of the century, Addams used Hull House as a forum for experimenting in curricular and educational reform. Hull House eventually provided numerous educational activities, including the teaching of English, reading clubs for the adults, mothers' clubs, kindergartens, cooking and dressmaking classes, sex education, theater productions, vocational training in woodworking, an art gallery, a public library, a music school, and the labor museum.

The labor museum, drawing on Dewey's concept of "a continuing reconstruction of experience," was intended to empower urban immigrants through validating their heritage, values, and culture (Deegan, 1990: 251). The museum was a prime example of the successful institutionalization of the collaboration and pragmatism of Addams and Dewey. According to Lois Rudnick (1991), the labor museum epitomized Addams's philosophy of education. It elevated crafts to the status usually reserved for the fine arts. In this sense the museum was a "living definition of Addams's non-elitist theory of culture" (p. 156). By providing an opportunity for immigrants to display their Old World skills, immigrant adults were placed in the role of teachers. This validation of the knowledge of adult immigrants was valuable in combating the prejudice against them.

In essence, the labor museum provided a critique of dominant modes of education. Addams's (1902) critique of traditional education was that it was "usually irrelevant and designed to interest the middle and upper classes, ignoring the culture and beliefs and interests of workers and immigrants" (p. 36). The labor museum was intended as an "educational enterprise, which should build a bridge between European and American experiences in such ways as to give them both more meaning and a sense of relation" (Addams, 1910: 235–236). The labor museum provided those who came an opportunity to understand the multicultural worlds of immigrants from their points of view. The process of being in relation with others was the heart of her understanding of democracy as "diversified human experience and its resultant sympathy" (Addams, 1902: 12).

Although Hull House provided programs and services focused on helping its neighbors, at the same time it worked with neighbors to investigate problems common to all and to seek solutions for those problems. The data collection methods pioneered at Hull House to investigate the working and living conditions of the urban poor were eventually adopted by the Chicago School of Civics and Philanthropy, started in 1903 by Graham Taylor, Addams, and other settlement leaders. Research into the social and economic problems of women and immigrants was an integral part of the settlement house movement. The Hull House residents involved in urban research included Edith Abbott, Sophia Breckenridge, and Florence Kelley. Kelley was an outspoken socialist who, after attending Cornell, did graduate work at the University of Zurich where she translated Engels's book, *The Condition of the Working Class in England in 1844.* In 1893 Kelley began a series of on-site investigations of tenement sweatshops in the Halsted Street neighborhood in Chicago. According to Miller (1997), these pioneering sociological surveys would do more for exploited women and children workers than anything else in the country. Living at Hull House for eight years, she not only radicalized Addams, but in 1895 they published the *Hull-House Maps and Papers,* the first comprehensive study on an American working–class neighborhood. Only by conducting research that documented women's and immigrants' experiences, and thus valued their perspectives as legitimate, could an "objective" assessment of the causes of social problems (primarily economic inequalities) be determined. However, this type of urban research, which focused on interview and survey data from immigrants, was seen by the Chicago School of sociologists (Park and Burgess) as subjective, in part because it was collected by women, who by their very nature could not be objective, and in part because these women lived in the communities they were studying.

Like Dewey, Addams (1902) theorized about the role of education in social amelioration by maintaining that "in education it is necessary to begin with the experiences which the child already has and to use his spontaneous and social activity" (pp. 186–187). A staunch believer in the importance of experience in education, Addams (1902) declared:

> We are impatient with the schools which lay all stress on reading and
> writing, suspecting them to rest upon the assumption that the ordinary

experience of life is worth little, and that all knowledge and interest must be brought to the children through the medium of books. Such an assumption fails to give the child any clew to the life about him, or any power to usefully or intelligently connect himself to it. (pp. 180–181)

The ideas developed in Dewey's *School and Society* (1900) and *Democracy and Education* (1916) were in part products of his contacts with Addams. As Seigfried (1996) has suggested, the two thinkers influenced each other in articulating the role of experience in education.

Yet, unlike Dewey, Addams did not believe schools were real sites for social change. She critiqued public schools as cutting into family loyalties, depreciating manual labor, and separating the classroom from work life—the public school undermined the community and family (Deegan, 1990: 282). She rejected the notion of school as laboratories, a concept borrowed from the sciences. Ultimately education as a form of democracy was social action and ultimately this was outside the domain of "science." And she critiqued the emerging university system, refusing to have Hull House be incorporated into the University of Chicago. She vehemently opposed the segregation of knowledge into the academy and the valuing of such ideas over other forms of knowledge and labor. Although this has sometimes been interpreted as anti-intellectual, she was certainly not anti-intellectual but, as Deegan (1990) suggests, an "anti-elitist intellectual" (p. 285). And in contrast to "child-centered" education, she rarely theorized about young children, but instead focused on adolescents (Addams, 1909). She borrowed Tolstoy's term of the "the snare of preparation" to describe the plight of young teens who were often in a state of inactivity just at the time they should be constructing the world anew. Many of the services like the Jane Club were directed toward young working-class immigrant girls and their needs.

The women's clubs formed at Hull House, which organized the immigrant women who attended the cooking schools or whose children attended the kindergartens, eventually came to have affiliations with the General Federation of Women's Clubs. These interactions between academics, women's clubs, and immigrants served an important educational function by providing a mechanism for people of various classes to "speak together" as a means of widening understandings of different communities and enlarging active involvement in the work of social change. This alliance of labor, schools, and middle-class and African-American women worked to implement wide-ranging reforms, including a variety of progressive programs, such as women's suffrage, labor reform, direct primaries, child welfare, race relations, union organizing, healthcare, playgrounds, libraries, and the peace movement.

The close relationship between Hull House and other groups of women in Chicago reveals that one important feature of settlement women's political effectiveness was their ability to gain the support of middle-class and working-class women. Florence Kelley was particularly active in forging a relationship with the

Chicago Woman's Club (the same group that had supported teachers) to gain support for anti-sweatshop legislation. In 1893, Addams received the support of wealthy clubwomen to lobby for factory legislation, and in 1894 the Club formed a Bureau of Women's Labor, which took over the funding of and responsibility for counseling services provided to working women at Hull House. Thus, middle-class and upper-class women were drawn into the settlement activities.

Hull House also served an important, but ignored, role in women's education. The cooperative and communal living arrangements at Hull House encompassed a holistic view of women's professional and personal lives that contradicted the dominant gender ideology of "separate spheres." In particular, college-educated middle- to upper-middle-class women, who had few opportunities in the public sphere, were provided a space in which to pursue their ideals. The environment at Hull House provided many young women with the opportunity to avoid marriage and commit themselves to establishing a woman's culture. This educational opportunity "to relate learning to life" (Lagemann, 1985: 20), and to participate meaningfully in society, has rarely been acknowledged as a serious aspect of educational history.

The educational philosophy that emerged at Hull House was grounded in the belief that democracy grows out of the continual interaction of theory and practice, individual and community, experience and culture. The men and women who lived at Hull House sought dynamic and reciprocal relationships suffused with a truly humane spirit of inquiry as the basis from which to develop social policies and actions that would result in a more democratic society.

Reflections

> Yet, never has democracy been more necessary. No other path will provide a way out of the fear, insecurity, and domination that permeates our world at war; no other path will lead us to a peaceful life in common.
>
> *(Michael Hardt and Antonio Negri, 2004)*

> Citizens, therefore, become subjects within a symbolic order which is premised on particular notions of rights, duties and responsibilities. At the same time, in order to become a speaking "I" in the symbolic space identified as citizenship, the social processes of identification with others are also significant.
>
> *(Madeleine Arnot and Jo-Anne Dillabough, 2000)*

> It is precisely at the confluence of these contextual elements, Puritan inclinations, Social Darwinism and the Progressive movement that the eugenics movement was able to define itself (and everyone else) such that acceptance of eugenic assumptions occurred practically unchallenged for decades.
>
> *(Ann Winfield, 2007)*

The "unsettling" done by the women curriculum theorists and activists described in this chapter was the disruption of the symbolic space that coded "citizenship" (ultimately the right to be fully human) as the vantage point of a select view. Creating this space of exclusion, as Winfield suggests, is the consequence of an American national identity politics that is based on a hierarchical view of human ability. This ideology is so deeply embedded in our collective memories that it is taken for granted. Testing, tracking, differentiated curriculum, and labeling have become normative, so much so that it is difficult to excavate how education, curriculum and schooling are deeply implicated in the ongoing construction of subject identities that are inherently marked along a continuum of worth. It was precisely this "sorting" function (Spring, 2004) of schooling that Jane Addams anticipated and rejected. And like current curriculum theorists (Arnot & Dillabough, 2000; Stone, 1996; Weiler, 2000) she articulated a critique of citizenship that exposed the deeply gendered, raced, and classed conceptions of citizenship that were produced in schools through a focus on individual ability and identity rather than on a communal ethic that she saw as critical to democracy.

At the heart of Addams's critique of democracy was her rejection of the concept of universal, natural, individual rights, which she ultimately viewed as being assimilationist and obscuring difference. Pluralism was viewed by Addams as enhancing democracy. Yet, in order for citizens to benefit from diversity through interactions across lines of gender, race, class, and ethnicity, there needed to be social and economic equality. Without this, democracy could not come to full fruition. Democracy, as understood by Addams, was a process, a way of life that necessitated interaction between people. Violence of any kind, including class struggle, hindered the relationships between the people that were prerequisite for democracy. Central to the work of both Addams and Wells was a view of democratic education as a dynamic social experiment in which the nature of education was defined both as pluralistic and particularistic, emanating from and responsive to the social contexts of diverse communities. Settlement "houses" were not only curricular innovations but were central to developing community networks across institutional boundaries that were seen as critical to enacting democracy as a mode of associated living. The settlement house movement challenged the compartmentalized, instrumentalist view of the social efficiency movement toward schooling as the exclusive avenue for democratic education.

These collective efforts to build networks of social interaction across class and ethnic boundaries to build a community were a form of democracy in action. Interactions among academics, women's clubs, and immigrants served an important educational function by providing a mechanism for people of various classes to "speak together" as a means for widening understandings of different communities and enlarging active involvement in the work of social change. Like other women historians (Scott, 1993; Sklar, 1995), I maintain that these networks and organizations shaped a woman's culture and identity that was pivotal to America's social and political development. That this development influenced educational reform and theories of curriculum is central to rethinking curriculum history from a gendered perspective.

True democracy was based on community networks, not individual rights (Baker, 1990; Sklar, 1990). As educators, Wells and Addams extended notions of education and democracy beyond schooling to include a restructuring of society along more democratic lines. For these women, the purpose of education was to enhance an individual's capacity to engage with others in community affairs as a means of advancing common interests that would foster continuous social reform. I maintain that this work of community building has been neglected as a site of educational reform that contested gender, class, and racial inequalities. The response of Addams and Wells to these social inequities was to develop alternative sites of education for social change. The settlement house movement was an educational alternative that was community-based, that acknowledged learning as life-long, and that addressed the needs of the marginalized. By providing education (broadly defined) for immigrants, African-Americans, and women, their work was a form of teaching that has been neglected when definitions of education have been limited to schooling.

Central to this collective action was Addams's and Wells's focus on racial and gender diversity as strengthening, not hindering, democracy. The heart of their work was the unsettling of dominant categories of race, gender, and class that were embedded in the discourses of citizenship, manliness, and the eugenics movement (Selden, 1999; Winfield, 2007). Because Addams has been criticized as being assimilationist and paternalistic, her actual efforts challenging racism have been overlooked. Among those who see Addams's work as paternalistic and focusing on assimilation are Mills (1964) and, more recently, Lissak (1989). Scholarship on Wells's anti-lynching and suffrage activities has deflected attention from her educational contributions to the settlement house movements. Most important, the ongoing relationship between these two women has been neglected. For both of these women, the development of community networks through interracial club work and the settlement house movement functioned as a means to educate about race relations as well as to address and challenge racism.

At the heart of this work was the recognition that structural inequality, both social and economic, was at the root of racial and gender inequity. Scott (1993) maintains that this realization moved women beyond the ideology of "municipal housekeeping" that had shaped women's reform efforts at the close of the century. In recognizing that the fundamental structures of society would need to be changed, these women joined a "new stage of women's activism, more radical than anything since antislavery" (Scott, 1993: 159). This radical theorizing of race and gender that was at the center of their deconstruction of citizenship and democracy, has rarely been included in the history of social reconstructionism. It is this exclusion that makes possible the dominant binary narrative of "progressivism" (Weiler, 2000). In fact, much of the theorizing of these women theorists antici-pated and provide a continuum to much of the work of critical and feminist theorists (Apple, 1979; Bowles & Gintis, 1976; Giroux, 1983; Lather, 1991; Weiler, 1988) that continues today to deconstruct how schools function as complex sites for identity formation in which ideologies that construct class, race, and gender are continually negotiated. More recently the work of Perry, Steele, & Hilliard (2003), Selden (1999), and Winfield (2007) have examined the ways in which ideologies of racial superiority and eugenics continue to mask themselves in aspects of education such as tracking and testing. Concepts like "at-risk" and "achievement gap" continue to code identities in ways that maintain a hierarchy based on human ability and worth, while masquerading as aspects of "Progressive reforms." Like Addams and Wells at the turn of the century, the need to unsettle the relationship between the concepts of citizenship, education, and democracy is paramount. How subjectivity is constructed and understood in these discourses is critical to understanding how social relations come to be thought of as "normal" or "real." Ironically, one of the normative assumptions is that "progressive" ideology regarding schooling failed or "lost" out (Larabee, 2010). In the next chapter I deconstruct this notion by examining the educational theorizing of women pragmatist philosophers and activists whose thinking drew on Addams and Wells, but also extended concepts of pragmatism by questioning the very concept of "experience" that had been at the heart of progressive philosophy.

6

EXPERIENCING CURRICULUM

To prove that someone cannot teach unless they possess freedom is not enough; it must be predicated that freedom belongs to that form of activity which characterizes the teacher.

(Ella Flagg Young, 1900, Isolation in the School*)*

In 1909, the Chicago School Board appointed the nation's first woman super-intendent, Ella Flagg Young. Her beliefs in a democratic school administration, the inclusion of teachers' voices in school policy and decision making, the broadening of the curriculum to include vocational, technical, and sex education, and equal rights for women were reflective of her pragmatist philosophy and a direct challenge to the hierarchy and stratification implicit in social efficiency. In 1913, when several members of the School Board tried to unseat her, she and Margaret Haley were both accused by Chicago school board member, John Harding, of being "witches." In December 1913, the *Chicago Record Herald* reported that Harding claimed that he "didn't blame the people of ancient times for hanging witches. I did once, but I don't now."[1] Despite the fact that the board did not re-elect her, the Chicago Woman's Club and other women's organiza-tions, as well as John Dewey, George Herbert Mead, and Jane Addams, called a mass meeting which successfully resulted in the reinstatement of Young. Although reinstated, in 1915 Young became the subject of an Illinois state investigation in which her policies as school superintendent were decried as "Frenzied Feminine Finance" (Murphy, 1990: 82). According to Murphy, critics depicted Young as "virtually giving away the store to public school teachers out of her feminist sentimentality, her Catholic sympathies and her alleged near-senility" (p. 82). Young was accused by the Chicago School Board of breeding rebellion and lack of respect for the school Board's authority. Her belief in democratically run schools was in sharp contrast to the emerging ideology of social efficiency, with its emphasis on the centralization and bureaucratization of schools (Kliebard, 1992b).[2] The efficiency movement led by David Snedden, John Franklin Bobbitt, and W.W. Charters, insisted that "curriculum making was a science and that it was too esoteric and complex to be entrusted to teachers and laymen" (Ravitch, 2000: 164). Young, as well as numerous other women educator activists (Crocco, Munro, & Weiler, 1999), contested the control of education by experts. Instead, they claimed that women teachers' rights to be active agents in decision making in schools was central to shaping democracy. Young's belief in democracy as an ongoing process (which required scientific thinking) rather than a static political system was the embodiment of her pragmatist philosophy. It was this commitment to democracy and the role of education in shaping democracy that scores of pragmatist women educator activists embraced at the turn of the century.

This agency on the part of women educator activists did not go uncontested. Young's persecution and public vilification as a "witch" and "feminist" attest to the threat she posed to dominant notions of educational leadership embedded in social efficiency. This perceived threat to men's traditional places of power resulted in a "backlash" movement in which, according to Blount (1998),

> critics portrayed single women teachers as threats to the masculinity of male educators and students. They accused spinster teachers of contributing to the demise of the (White) race. Finally, they used the works of turn-of-the-century sexologists to link spinsterhood with lesbianism, thus creating a climate where single women teachers seemed socially dangerous. (p. 9)

This backlash has contributed to the exclusion of women educator pragmatists from the narratives of educational history. However, women pragmatists' marginalization from the history of pragmatist philosophy is due to several factors including the larger issue of the marginalization of pragmatism. Seigfried (1996) maintains that the ascendancy of logical positivism after World War II functioned to eclipse pragmatism. In contrast to the purely conceptual philosophical analysis of logical positivism, pragmatism requires praxis. This focus on "action" and the belief that theory unrelated to practice is moribund has contributed to the relegation of pragmatism to the margins of philosophy. Considering that the designation of "philosopher" has been almost exclusively an academic one, those pragmatists who chose to work outside the academy have rarely been included as philosophers. Given that women were excluded from the faculties of philosophy departments these criteria has necessarily resulted in the invisibility of women pragmatists. Lastly, the pragmatist goal of democratic inclusiveness resulted in the rejection of a specialized language and disciplinary jargon accessible only to a specialist elite. Women pragmatists, in particular, wrote in a fashion that was accessible and thus not seen as academic.[3] While there were many women who are considered progressive, not all would be pragmatists. My goal in this chapter is to draw attention to a unique group of women educators who were specifically pragmatist. In choosing the women to include in this chapter I have used the following criteria: 1) they were shaped and involved in a community of scholars and activists who drew on the basic principles of pragmatism as discussed above; 2) they were scholars in that they wrote books and articles; 3) they experimented and conducted research; and 4) they developed and/or lived in innovative educational communities. In addition these women not only "practiced" pragmatism they reflected on its basic assumptions and contributed original ideas that have shaped pragmatist philosophy.

Although the dominant narrative of 20th-century curriculum history suggests that the "struggle" (Kliebard, 1995) over curriculum has been the tension between social efficiency, child-centeredness, and social reconstruction, this chapter maintains that this narrative of conflict is, in part, constituted through and made possible through the subordination of women pragmatists' theorizing of the relationship between education and democratic experience.[4] As discussed in Chapter 1, the construction of 20th-century curriculum history as a "struggle" has functioned to construct a narrative that obscures the role of women by privileging a masculine plot of conflict and rebellion. As a consequence, not only are the contributions of women excluded, but as Kliebard (1995) suggests, this metaphor of struggle functions to reify the notion of a "single progressive movement, whether progressive or not, ever existed" (p. 247). This monolithic view of progressivism critiqued by Ravitch (2000), Kliebard (1995), and Krug (1964), maintains not only that it is progressivism's "fluidity" that is its constitutive property, but that this "struggle" is not so much about "curriculum" but about how "curricular changes 'bear witness' to . . . the domination of one cultural group and the subordination of another" (Gusfield, 1986: 181). For Kliebard (1995) it was a drama of "ritualized dominance and subordination" over whose definitions of democracy and democratic education would prevail and be passed on to the next generation (p. 249). For many women progressive educators, the democratic values they treasured were deeply embedded in their pragmatist philosophy.

This chapter will examine Young's as well as other women educators' contributions to pragmatist philosophy. Young is one exemplar of a generation of women who entered the field of education during the progressive era. As Crocco, Munro, and Weiler (1999) have noted, "as was true of other women in the late nineteenth and early twentieth century, education opened spaces for them to act as agents of change" (p. 83). According to Cremin (1961), "progressive education began as part of a vast humanitarian effort to apply the promise of American life— the idea of government by, of, and for the people—to the puzzling new urban industrial civilization" (p. viii). For Cremin (1961), progressivism in education was "a many sided effort to use the schools to improve the lives of individuals" (p. viii). This meant several things: first, broadening the function of schools to include social issues of health, vocation, and quality of family and community life—not just academic life; second, applying scientific research to pedagogical principles; and third, differentiating the curriculum to address the vast diversity of children. Progressivism implied a radical faith that culture could be democratized. This first generation of women college graduates were committed to addressing the social ills of the times through education. Education was broadly defined to include an "expanded view of the role of the school which included attempts to improve the quality of family and community life, health, and the workplace" (Stanley, 1992: 6). Committed to social justice, their educational work included activism in unions, settlement houses, women's clubs, as well as various social movements including suffrage, socialism, and feminism. What distinguished women pragmatists in this chapter from their progressive sisters was their critique of the totalizing nature of any social theory of social change, as well as the abstract nature and privileged standpoint inherent in contemporary theories. Implicit in their views of social change was the pragmatist principle that the relation of theory and practice takes the continuity of experience as revealed through action as the starting point for reflection. Pragmatism was a living tradition that was holistic, naturalistic, emancipatory, pluralistic, and experimental. In rejecting absolutes, universals, and abstractions pragmatism provided an inclusive philosophy of social change. Consequently, these women pragmatists embraced the idea that schools could not be disconnected from the larger social issues of injustice, that the ongoing reconstruction of experience was the basis of democracy and that shared understanding and communal problem solving rather than individual rationality were the basis of scientific inquiry.

These beliefs of democratic education and social change emerged within that unique American tradition called pragmatism. It is a philosophy that still "evades" definition (West, 1989). As West maintains, "pragmatism is a diverse and heterogeneous tradition," one that evades an "epistemology-centered philosophy" and "results in a conception of philosophy as a form of cultural criticism in which the meaning of 'American' is put forward by intellectuals in response to distinct social and cultural crises" (p. 5). For women educators, the crisis was not only the undemocratic nature of education, but a larger social crisis of maintaining and redefining democracy in light of immigration, poverty, urbanization, industrialization, and racism. This was a crisis that was deeply gendered, raced, and classed. By drawing on pragmatism, with its focus on experience, women curriculum theorists of the 20th century sought to "rethink" not only gender, but experience. The women discussed in this chapter are often associated with the "progressive" movement. However, I would maintain that many rejected the label because it was not radical enough. Having been shaped by pragmatist philosophy they distinguished themselves from other progressives by embracing and extending a uniquely pragmatist view. Women pragmatists "dared" to raise the question of what experience and whose experiences counted as a site of knowledge thereby extending pragmatism to include the experiences of women, the poor, immigrants, and people of color. Women educator activists were shaped by pragmatism, but they also shaped pragmatism. Their contributions to pragmatism are the focus of this chapter.

Pragmatism: America's First Philosophy

> But you see already how democratic she [pragmatism] is. Her manners are as various and flexible, her resources as rich and endless, and her conclusions as friendly as those of mother nature.
>
> *(William James, 1906)*[5]

> The pragmatist as artist cannot escape, it seems, from the fact that she is both effect and cause of her community. She learns from her community what and how to produce what is desirable. Her productions, in turn, shape her community's desires as the circulation of power produces and reproduces her community and society.
>
> *(Cleo Cherryholmes, 1999)*

It seems ironic that two leading pragmatists would refer to pragmatism as feminine in light of the exclusion of women pragmatist philosophers from curriculum history. This "feminization" of pragmatism reflects the complex gendered dynamics and intersections of curriculum theory. While pragmatism can be coded as feminine, this gendering induces a binary in which those who construct the theory are male. What is clear is that the dominant narrative of pragmatism gives credit to Charles Sanders Peirce, William James, John Dewey, and George Herbert Mead as the founding fathers.[6] This representation disregards the "founders" own testaments of their collaborations and work with women pragmatists who found in pragmatism a movement in which they could work for a "new intellectual and social order" (Seigfried, 1996: 19). For example, Jane Addams, John Dewey, George Herbert Mead, and Ella Flagg Young worked together in a variety of projects including women's rights, labor unions for women, the extension of suffrage, and higher education for women (Deegan, 1990).[7] Mead and Young, as well as Mead and Addams, were both professional and personal friends. Mead was at the forefront of the Chicago pragmatists in advocating for more democratic control in the classroom, the rights of teachers to unionize, and teachers' right to control curriculum and certification. When Young came under attack in 1914, Mead wrote an article supporting her superintendency. In "A Heckling School Board and an Educational Stateswoman," Mead (1914) maintained that Young had brought the school into active touch with the growing community at a crucial moment. Mead was adamant in his condemnation of the city for sacrificing one of Chicago's greatest and most competent servants.

Louis Menand (2001) in his recent book *The Metaphysical Club*, a social history of pragmatism, provides a historical context for the emergence of pragmatism which posits that pragmatism was a philosophy that emerged in a community of men and women who sought to grapple with America's inherent contradiction of claiming to be democratic while never reaching that ideal. Menand suggests that:

> The Civil War swept away the slave civilization of the South, but it swept
> away almost the whole intellectual culture of the North along with it. It
> took nearly half a century for the United States to develop a culture to
> replace it, to find a set of ideas, and a way of thinking, that would help
> people cope with the conditions of modern life. (p. x)

That set of ideas would be pragmatism. The disillusionment of the Civil War, the
horrors of industrialization, and the challenges wrought by immigration necessitated a set of ideas that maintained the vision of democracy but accounted for its
fallibility. Maintaining democracy against this backdrop of corporatization and
increasing pluralism was the challenge that pragmatism took on. Democracy could
no longer be a mere ideal—it had to become a way of life.

In his lecture "The Present Dilemma in Philosophy," William James (1907)
maintained that:

> What you want is a philosophy that will not only exercise your powers of
> intellectual abstraction, but that will make some positive connexion with
> this actual world of finite human lives. (p. 8)

He goes on in another lecture, "What Pragmatism Means," to trace the word
pragmatism to the Greek word *payua* meaning action, from which the words
"practice" and "practical" come (1907: 18). Charles Sanders Peirce, who first
introduced the term into philosophy, maintained that "our beliefs are really rules
for action" (as quoted in James, 1907: 18). Women pragmatists embodied Peirce's
principle that the sole significance of a thought's meaning was the conduct it
produced. Taking this principle to heart, women pragmatists of the 20th century
were committed to establishing educational institutions that reflected a philosophy
that validated experience, not only individual, but community and social, as the
starting point for reflection on action. Women pragmatists addressed three areas
central to pragmatist thought: experience as democracy, experimentation as
scientific inquiry, and praxis as communal problem solving. In the following
sections I will first focus on Young as a pragmatist case study for examining women
pragmatists' contributions to theorizing experience, second on women pragmatists
who engaged in experimental schools, and lastly on women whose focus was on
community-based schools.

"Giving the Soul's Touch to the Expression of Thought": Engendering Experience

"Pragmatism is in the Air," wrote Virginia Robinson, a high school teacher who
began studying philosophy at the University of Chicago during her summer break
in 1908 (Seigfried, 1996: 67). Several tenets of pragmatism applied to the first generation of reform-minded college-educated women. These included the emphasis of

pragmatism on experience as the starting point for generating knowledge, experimentation as the interrelationship of theory and praxis, and community-based solutions to social problems. At age 50 when Young entered the University of Chicago in 1895, she joined a growing number of women who were drawn to and contributed to the emerging philosophy of pragmatism.[8] Charlotte Perkins Gilman, Lucy Sprague Mitchell, Jane Addams, and Elsie Clapp Ripley, among others, not only studied with or were influenced by those known as the "founders" of pragmatism (Charles Sanders Peirce, William James, John Dewey, and George Herbert Mead), but they extended the notion of experience within pragmatism to include gender. Although Dewey, Mead, and James often took their examples from spheres traditionally assigned to women, none of the male pragmatists made women's experiences central to their own discourse. Seigfried (1996) points out that Dewey's reevaluation of the domestic sphere as a significant model for educational processes provided a basis for calling into question traditional views of education. Dewey drew on the private to reshape the public; however, he still maintained a gender dichotomy. Young, on the other hand, specifically claimed that women's experiences were central to rethinking the very ways in which gender binaries shaped unequal and undemocratic social relations. In this sense her pragmatist theorizing incorporated a gender analysis that her contemporaries did not.

To claim experience as the source for generating knowledge was among the major contributions of pragmatist thinking. In contrast to the dominant turn-of-the-century beliefs that held that knowledge claims must arise from objective, rational, and abstract thinking, pragmatism posited the impossibility of attaining absolute, universal, empirical knowledge. Because knowledge is based on interests and values, it is developmental and historically contingent. Knowledge claims are thus embedded in experience. Pragmatism takes the continuity of experience and nature as revealed through the outcome of directed action as the starting point for reflection. Experience is the ongoing transaction of organism and environment; in other words, both subject and object are constituted in this process. According to pragmatic theories, truths are beliefs confirmed in the course of experience and are therefore fallible, and always subject to further revision.

The focus on experience highlights the social construction of knowledge. However, a central issue raised by women pragmatists at the turn of the century was the question of what experience and whose experiences counted as a site of knowledge. Pragmatists such as Dewey, Mead, and James assumed that experience was a universal concept. The experiences of women's lives—the domestic sphere, pregnancy, childbearing—or the working classes and immigrants' lives, were not commonly considered sites from which to reflect and generate knowledge. Young was particularly concerned with expanding the notion of experience to take into account the gendered and classed nature of experience especially as it related to education.

By grounding philosophy in the daily life of school experience, Young expanded the definitions of who could and could not count as a philosopher.

In claiming that philosophy should not be the sole province of the philosopher, she addressed the question of "What is the end and aim of this life?" In *Ethics in the School* (Young, 1902) she suggests:

> Interest in this, the greatest question put to the human race for solution, is not limited to a particular type of mind nor to a single class of society. The blacksmith at the forge, as well as the philosopher in his study, discusses the fundamental conditions in the attainment of the good as an ultimate end of his life's activity. The maid in the kitchen, as well as the teacher in the school, weeps over the failures and glows over the victories of the creations of the dramatist and the novelist. . . . Before reaching manhood or woman-hood we all come to know that something called virtue must, by a slow process, be realized in daily life. (pp. 8–9)

Shifting the focus of philosophy from the world of abstraction to an emphasis on "lived experience," Young contributed to a form of pragmatism that included and validated women and the working class as capable of reflective, critical thought. In reconceptualizing philosophy as grounded in the daily lived experience of women and the working class, she expands the notion of whose experience and what experience counts as a site of reflection. Of particular concern to Young was reconceptualizing teaching as a site of experience to be reflected upon as well as the primary site in which reflection on experience was taught as the basis for democratic process. For Young, women teachers were central to shaping school in ways that embodied reflection on experience as democracy.

For women educator activists, who deeply believed that women's experiences were a valuable site on which to draw for shaping the knowledge necessary for informing conceptions of democratic life, pragmatism held much potential. According to Seigfried (1996):

> The thesis that theory arises directly from and is accountable to experience allowed them (women) to trust their own experiences even when those experiences ran counter to accepted dogma. They were able to claim as sources of genuine knowledge those of their insights that had been dismissed throughout their education as merely deviant opinions or untrustworthy female sentiments. (p. 57)

The "accepted dogma" regarding women educators was that teaching was inherently suited to them because they were "naturally" nurturant. If teaching was "natural," it did not require thought or reflection on experience. Essentializing women's nature in this way served to exclude their experience. Consequently, teaching was understood as an act that precluded intellectual thought or reflective agency. Young contested this claim that women's knowledge was the result of an essentialized feminine nature. She claimed that women teachers' experiences, when reflected upon (using scientific method), could provide a site of knowledge. Scientific method, according to Young (1903),

> is the method, the attitude of mind, that makes a search for the principle under which facts observed may be explained in their relations and made significant. The principle or "natural law" sought is a statement or formulation worked out by the scientific imagination in getting at the relations and meanings of conditions and sequences observed. (p. 4)

For Young, scientific method meant a critical process of reflection that acknowledged that all knowledge claims are value laden. This was of particular appeal to women pragmatists, because it suggested that differences in men and women were not biological or essentialized, but were in fact social constructions.

In essence, Young makes two assertions regarding the nature of experience. First, reflection on experience is the source of knowledge. Second, this interpretive act is always temporal, situated, and contingent. Consequently, Young argues that knowledge claims must always be reevaluated. Thus the primary goal of education is to teach this process of reflection and interpretation. Young (1902) provides a specific example in discussing the purpose of reading instruction in *Ethics in the School*. She reminds us that outside of school, people do not read to find out who can read better but instead they ask for "interpretation, or as usually expressed, to find out what different people understand by it" (p. 13). Young writes:

> A little eight-year-old girl, after reading a paragraph said, "I didn't make it mean what I think it means," and then without any remark from her teacher, re-read it to her own satisfaction. This demand by the little child that she should rightly interpret the author; this giving the soul's touch to the expression of thought; this permeating the whole with the spirit of the worker, means an advance in the ethical life far beyond that in the child who is trained according to the model. To train to imitate is to ignore the relation of expression to thought, the relation of will to intellect. (pp. 35–36)

Recognizing and encouraging the individual's own understandings—what Young terms the "soul's touch"—was not only pedagogically sound but was an ethical imperative grounded in her belief that reflection was democracy in action. Young (1902) maintains that it is an ethical duty of the "body politic known as the teaching corps" (p. 11) to embody democracy. In essence, teachers were the "body politic" (p. 11) responsible for endowing students with the ability to understand the dialectic relation between expression/thought, will/intellect, subject/object, self/society. Viewing the goal of education as teaching through modeling reflective practice, she was highly critical of standardized curriculums and training models developed by experts that silenced the expressions of teachers and students. If students were not expected to interpret and question, how could they ever be expected to do so as citizens? If schools did not emulate democratic practices how could students be expected to participate as citizens in society?

A recurring theme in her scholarship is that education needed to mirror the processes and behaviors of the democratic ideal of other social organizations. Her critique focused on the decontextualized nature of schooling in which schools were based on hierarchy, competition, control, regulation, and punishment. For schools to be central to shaping a democratic community, the curriculum and culture of schools had to correspond to other democratic institutions. If we expect adults to be cooperative, to live in a community as the expression of democracy how can we expect this behavior if children are taught using rivalry and jealousy? Young consistently critiqued the binary organization of school/society, child/adult, desire/reason, personal/private, and ethical/intellectual that she saw reproduced in schools.

Because Young claimed schools should be democracy in action with teachers acting as the body politic, it was essential for her that schools embody the ethics and morals required for democratic citizenship. Young (1902) stated "If knowledge acquired in the school is used there only, then it must be viewed as something that has no intrinsic value—has a marking value merely" (p. 35). Schools had to be an essential part of society, not separate from it. All functions of the school, including, for example, modes of discipline, were to be based on the democratic norms that shaped and operated in the rest of society. According to Young, the methods of control and regulation of student behavior were to be judged on the basis of whether they helped students to recognize the needs and rights of classmates and teachers, not as a means of encouraging the students to gain the good standing of teachers.

For Young, democracy was a moral imperative that was an active, reflective, interpretive, and communal act intended to generate the ongoing knowledge and understandings of the human condition. This definition of democracy reinterpreted democracy as an ethical/moral endeavor rather than as solely a political act. In expanding democracy to be a moral/ethical as well as political act, Young's redefinition not only incorporated women, but also challenged the very definition of what constituted the political. Considering that women were at this time excluded from the public/political sphere by repositioning democratic life as moral/ethical, Young was able to create spaces for women to have a voice in democratic life. This reconceptualization provided the rationale for teachers being central to the democratic process. It was the ethical duty of educational leaders to model at every level this democratic process of reflection. In defining ethics as the "science of duty, of conduct" the emphasis is on actions, how we conduct ourselves in our daily life. Young (1902) maintains that ethics is not a set of rules to abide by, but that "all interpretations of truths pertaining to the higher nature must, however, from time to time be subjected to revision" (p. 11). The continual revisioning of knowledge is not something to be left solely to philosophers or to educational administrators. She maintains in *Ethics in the School* (1902),

The day has come when the teaching corps must, as a body, pass in review the customs of the school; must analyze those based on the morality of an institution which separated itself from the social whole; must reject those which develop a traditional morality for a brief period of life; must move in step with the time spirit, developing throughout the school those sympathetic and sterling qualities which make for righteousness all through life. (p. 12)

Young's vision of education as an ethics of social responsibility in which teachers as public intellectuals played a critical role was in stark contrast to the construction of the teacher embedded in the discourses of progressivism. At the heart of her analysis was the gendered nature of education that was antithetical to her understanding of democracy.

Gendered Experience

Young's unique pragmatist thought grew out of her experiences as a woman educator activist situated within the conflicting and contradictory gendered discourses of progressivism, both social efficiency and social reconstructionist. For Young, educational leadership was about creating schools as models of democracy in action. Central to this vision was the active involvement of all members of the school community in decision making. This vision was in stark contrast to the emerging discourse of social efficiency that has been described as one of centralization and bureaucratization which emphasized increased efficiency, standardization, and reliance on experts which reduced the teacher to a mere "factory hand" (Kliebard, 1986; Pinar, Reynolds, Slattery, & Taubman, 1995; Tyack, 1974). Within the social efficiency model, teachers were to implement the curricula designed by supposed experts. Consequently, teachers were denied any role in decision making. Social reconstructionist ideology, on the other hand, saw schools as miniature communities in which learning took place within the context of real world activities. In contrast to social efficiency with its emphasis on supposed "experts," the discourse of social reconstructionism maintained that learning should be more focused on the agency of the students in preparation for participation in a democratic society. Teachers were to act as facilitators of learning, not transmittors of knowledge. Although conceiving of the purposes of education very differently, both social reconstructionism and social efficiency were predicated on the assumption that women teachers' influence should be indirect. In the case of "social reconstructionism," women's agency was to be subjugated to the child, and in the case of "social efficiency," it was to be subjugated to the "expert" and "principal."

Young's dissertation (directed by John Dewey), completed in 1900, entitled "Isolation in the School" was an analysis and critique of the ideology of social efficiency. She claimed that the isolation of teachers resulting from centralization and bureaucratization functioned to disempower teachers (women) by removing their decision making power over curriculum and school policy and placing it into the hands of supposed "experts" (male). This separation reinforced dominant gender relations. When teachers were denied participation in decision making, Young warned that schools would develop a system comparable to a "great machine" (Reid, 1982: xxi). This mechanistic view of schools was antithetical to Young's pragmatist vision.

According to Jackie Blount (1998), the "premise of 'Isolation in the School' is that schools have become highly differentiated institutions where individuals are dehumanized and separated from their intelligence" (p. 167). Schools were differentiated along various lines including: grade levels, subject matters, administrative hierarchy from society, and from higher education. The reductionist nature of education resulted, according to Young (1900), in "parts that have been brought together mechanically, thus making the accepted conception of this great social institution that of an aggregation of independent units, rather than that of an organization whose successful operation depends upon a recognized inter-relation, as well as distinction, between its various members and their particular duties" (p. 7). Young's emphasis on interrelation as opposed to separation was central to her vision of schools as organic, real-world spaces in which students and teachers were first and foremost human beings engaged in relationships that were to further democracy. To reduce and separate, to decontextualize school from society or public from private or self from teacher/student was to hinder the process of democracy as well as reinforce dominant gender norms.

A particular gendered manifestation of this separation was the ideology of professionalism embedded in the discourse of social efficiency. The "professional" was expected to be objective, scientific, and gender neutral (thus, like a man). The degendering effect of "professionalism" was another form of separation that Young critiqued. The objectification of the teacher occurred in the division between what Young termed the professional and social self. The professional self, a subtext of social efficiency, promoted autonomy, objectivity, and rationality as the qualities of the teacher. This was in contrast to the social self, which Young saw as embodying a more holistic vision that acknowledged the relation of the self to others, the interaction of subject/object, the relationship of schools to democratic society, rather than a decontextualized notion of self. Although she considers the professional self as a subclass of the social self, it is the social self that should be at the forefront of the teacher. To separate out a different self is in essence to objectify oneself and reify a subject/object dualism. Young (1902) gives the following example:

> It is not uncommon to see a young woman with an attractive face and manner undergo a transformation equally surprising, upon entering the schoolroom for the work of the day. The corners of the mouth will take a downward direction; the eye will become alert, suspicious, reproving; even

the personal identity will be lost, and she will know and speak of herself in the third person during those hours when she should say with the Great Teacher, "Suffer little children to come unto me." She asks "Would it not be better to be a man or woman than to be the guardian of a professional self?" (p. 21)

The social self that becomes lost is the female self. In fact, Young points out how teachers participated in their own objectification and degendering when they talk of themselves in the "third person." Making themselves invisible by erasing their gender, teachers were complying with the assumed gender neutrality that was embedded in the discourse of professionalism (Bloom & Munro, 1995). Her reservations against a professional identity suggest a critique of the concept of professionalism, a discourse that was particularly gendered as male and in which women teachers were to give up a subject position. To suggest that the social self was to take precedence over the professional self was a way in which to critique the degendering of the teaching profession.

By claiming women's experience as a site of knowledge, Young contested the discourse of social efficiency which claimed bureaucratization and professionalism as the site of knowledge and the discourse of social reconstruction which claimed experience as gender neutral and the providence of the child. In advocating women teachers' right to be active agents in decision making and central to shaping democracy through their work in school, Young contested the control of education by experts (either progressives or those advocating social efficiency) through asserting that women's experiences as teachers were a site for generating knowledge. Claiming women's experience as an epistemological site threatened the normative gender ideologies embedded in both discourses which required the subjugation of women's knowledge. This subjugation of women as central to "progressive" ideology reflects how educational institutions "replaced traditional physical discipline with scientifically based ideas of 'normal behavior' as a means of promoting and controlling the development of 'docile citizens'" (Maher, 2001: 24). In seeing teachers as active meaning makers and thus having authority, Young suggests that central to women's work as teachers is their role as public intellectuals and pragmatists.

Although I have focused on Young, she was one of countless women who sought to shape democracy through shaping a pragmatic leadership style that embodied democratic practices. Laura Joanna Ghering, superintendent of the Kingfisher Schools in Oklahoma during the 1920s; Bertha Palmer, state superintendent of public instruction in Minnesota; Susannah Parrish, state superintendent of schools in Georgia from 1911 to 1918; Betsey Mix Cowles, superintendent of Canton school in Ohio from 1850 to 1855; Susan Dorsey, superintendent of schools in Los Angeles from 1920 to 1929; and Julia Richman, a district superintendent in New York City at the turn of the century, all worked to promote democratic education and saw schools as central to social reform (Blount, 1998).

African-American women educators, who acted as principals and administrated schools, were particularly galvanized to promote democracy during the height of Jim Crow. Some, such as Fannie Jackson Coppin and the Philadelphia Youth Institute, worked to establish schools for African-American youth. Others, such as Maria L. Baldwin, promoted democratic leadership by serving at schools which were primarily White. Maria Baldwin was principal at Boston's elite and primarily White Agassiz Grammar School. Lucy Craft Laney was founder of the Augusta, Georgia, Haines Normal and Industrial School, a multidimensional school that filled the need for African-American education. Young, although often depicted as an exemplar and extraordinary woman, was in fact one of many women educational pragmatist leaders whose vision of democracy was predicated on an understanding of experience as gendered, raced, and classed. At the heart of this leadership style was the central belief that schools must model democracies and that teachers were the primary leaders in decision making.

On the West Coast two women, Corinne Seeds (1889–1969) and Helen Heffernan (1896–1987), in particular stand out as educational women leaders who sought to enact the ideals of the progessive/pragmatist movement. Helen Heffernan was the head of elementary and rural education for the California Department of Education from 1926 to 1965 and Corrine Seeds was the principal of the laboratory school at the University of California at Los Angeles from 1925 to 1957. These women, according to Crocco, Munro, and Weiler (1999), built on the "accomplishments of an earlier generation of women," including Young and Addams, who had put forward a vision of teaching as challenging intellectual work (p. 84).

Seeds began her educational career as a teacher at a Los Angeles city evening school. These schools were part of the reform activities of progressive women educators and were directed at immigrant and poor families.[9] In 1916, she obtained her B.A. from Teachers College, Columbia University, where she studied with Dewey and Kilpatrick, and was deeply influenced by the educational philosophy of both. In 1925 she became principal of UCLA Laboratory School, a position she held until 1954. The school was part of the UCLA Teachers College and this gave Seeds an opportunity to engage not only in implementing progressive pedagogies but also to work in teacher training. In several articles published in the 1930s she articulated her vision of education.[10] Central to this vision was a democratic classroom in which children would discover and create knowledge rather than memorize information. Classrooms were to be as egalitarian as possible and be central to the building of a more democratic social order.

Heffernan, who had studied at the University of California, had been introduced to the scholarship of Mabel Carney of Teachers College who argued that the rural school was an ideal setting for the child-centered approach.[11] In her quest to establish progressive rural schools throughout California, she established state rural demonstration schools. Central to these schools was a vision of schools as models of democracy. Heffernan was adamant that "When equal opportunity, an equal chance for all the children of all the people shall be realized, then democracy will be firmly established" (Crocco, Munro, & Weiler, 1999: 88). Her work in rural education quickly attracted national attention, and in 1931 she was elected to head the Rural Supervisors Section of the National Education Association.

Heffernan and Seeds met at UCLA in the early 1930s and they began a ten-year period of collaboration, as well as a personal relationship. According to Crocco, Munro, and Weiler (1999), "together, they complemented each other, Seeds emphasizing the training of classroom teachers and the development of a progressive approach to social studies, and Heffernan encouraging democratic supervision and providing leadership for curricular innovation at the state level" (p. 98). This collaboration was exemplified during the summer courses they offered at UCLA for teachers and supervisors, which hundreds of teachers attended. The Laboratory School (University Elementary School) run by Seeds became a focal point of these courses where teachers could see actual progressive methods in practice.

The educational activism of Seeds and Heffernan was to come under attack in the 1940s for a number of reasons. When war broke out, Seeds continued to support a vision of democracy that was embedded in the people and not in blind allegiance to patriotism. As a consequence, she refused to make the flag salute a part of the daily school ritual, since she saw the children merely going through the motions, not truly understanding the significance. She saw this lack of the children's spirit as disrespectful to democracy. In addition, she voiced her opposition to the internment of Japanese Americans. When Japanese-American families were interned at the Santa Anita racetrack, she sent clothes, books, and school supplies. Her actions began to arouse suspicions about her "patriotism." Heffernan also was committed to upholding a vision of democracy throughout the war and included the education of Japanese-American children in camps as part of her responsibility. These activities, as well as their personal relationship, and a growing trend to "masculinize" teacher education programs at universities resulted in ongoing criticism of both Heffernan and Seeds with continued attempts to weaken their positions of influence. This masculinization of teacher education occurred as colleges of education began to shift to a more "scientific" research model that emphasized quantitative methods. The kind of qualitative, reflective practitioner research that characterized most laboratory and demonstration schools was criticized as not rigorous enough.[12]

Heffernan and Seeds were not unique in this growing trend of women educators who were seen as suspect or "un-American." Of course, World War I had resulted in Jane Addams being described by the FBI as the most dangerous woman in America due to her pacifist ideals. For many women pragmatists whose commitment to democracy was grounded not in blind patriotism, but in critical, reflective engagement in community as a means to empathetic understanding, the rhetoric of the war was a threat to democracy. Maintaining a progressive, pragmatist ideology throughout the war and through the period of McCarthyism was a difficult time for many educator activists.

The radical nature of many women educator activists work can be gauged by the public scrutiny of their activities during the "red scare" after World War II. Geraldine Clifford (1994) cites the case of two women teachers at Canoga Park High School in Los Angeles who were called to appear before the California State Senate Committee of Un-American Activities for being consistently friendly to the Soviet Union, unfairly criticizing the United States and trying to indoctrinate their students in foreign ideologies. Although both teachers were found innocent, the public scandal caused by these attacks brought teachers under even closer surveillance. The public perception of schools being infiltrated by communists functioned overtime to result in less public support for national educational organizations and teachers unions. Consequently, the organizing power of classroom teachers has decreased with more power being concentrated at the administrative level and at the state and federal level. According to Stuart Foster (1997), the "increasing virulent attacks on public education in the late 1940s and 1950s . . . would be a victory for arch conservatives [resulting in] reduction in tax support for public education, the maintenance of racially segregated schools, the removal of federal interference, the rejection of allegedly un-American instructional materials, and the passionate celebration of nationalist ideals" (p. 2). In response to these attacks on teachers, the National Education Assocation formed a Defense Commission which was designed to help teachers in their defenses. In the end, the defense of the teaching profession was difficult given the very influential political, business, and reactionary forces who headed the "red scare."

By the 1950s, pragmatist women educators whose vision of society had been shaped by their pragmatist beliefs in democratic education were going the "way of the buffalo." As Jackie Blount (1998) suggests,

> Although the turn-of-the-century women's movement had created enor-
> mous momentum favoring the ascent of women into school administration,
> a massive cultural shift extending from the economic depression of the 1930s
> through the Cold War effectively reversed the trend. Several factors
> contributed to this shift. First, the women's movement, which had been
> instrumental in propelling women into leadership positions, lost its focus and
> faded in the decades after passage of the suffrage amendment. A quietly
> brewing, yet powerful backlash movement further eroded organized efforts
> of women's groups. This backlash stigmatized women (and men) who
> crossed gender-appropriate lines of behavior. (p. 113)

Lastly, the hundreds of thousands of unemployed World War II veterans who were seeking civilian careers and education provided a space once again to reconstruct gender. More recently, women pragmatists' marginalization has been attributed to the "reductionist attempt to blame progressive educational theory and the education reforms of the 1960s for the current educational 'crisis' as defined by certain conservatives" (Stanley, 1992: 3). While conservatives have argued that progressives (the social reconstructionists) were too political, the marginalization of women pragmatists by curricular historians was accomplished because they have been interpreted as not political or theoretical enough. Ironically, in many cases, it was their political activism that resulted in a backlash against women pragmatists. Their unique understanding of democracy incorporated a clear pragmatist commitment to action and experience which was exemplified in numerous educational experiments.

Pragmatist Experiments

> Experience and experimental understanding dynamically interact with tradition and community to bring about an altered state of affairs thought to be more valuable.
>
> *(Charlene Seigfried, 1996)*

> No facts are sacred to me; none are profane; I simply experiment, an endless seeker, with no past at my back.
>
> *(Ralph Waldo Emerson, 1995)*

This quote by Emerson might very well have guided many of the women pragmatists who saw experimentation as the heart of social education. The pragmatist notion of experiment, however, must be distinguished from the detached, value-free positivist notion that came to replace it. The social experiments of women pragmatists were grounded in the fundamental belief that theory arises from experience. Theory and experience are two sides of the same coin; they are inextricably connected. This being the case, the concepts of objectivity and validity are not concepts that apply. Experience is not something that we can observe or detach ourselves from. Quite to the contrary, experience is not "out there" but we ourselves are formed within it. Experience is not a passive process but an interactive one. Consequently, when experience becomes the basis for reflection and action, the mode of inquiry must be one that is interactive. Pragmatist experimental methodology "sought to replace both the palliative sentimentalism of charity work and the destructiveness of technocratic arrogance" (Seigfried, 1996: 182).

Pragmatist experimentation challenged the notion of the "expert" by seeking the involvement of those who were directly affected by the social problems and issues of the day. For many educators that included not only the poor, the immigrants, or minorities, but also children themselves. Women pragmatists took for granted that the experiences of children were just as legitimate and important as those of adults. And, in fact, understanding the development of children, how they develop habits, become socialized, and learn morals was central to understanding how they develop as democratic citizens and what role education should play. Experimentation was not just a "method," but the heart of the ethics of democracy. Ongoing reflection and reconstruction of experience for the betterment of society was the basis of democracy. For women pragmatists, the central question became how this "way of life" developed in children.

Understanding the growth of children was the focus of women pragmatists' experiments as compared to that of male pragmatists (Hendry, 2008). The founding of experimental and laboratory schools by women pragmatists was a radical experiment in democracy. In contrast to some progressives, particularly the social reconstructionists, these experiments were attempts to base theory on experience. This necessitated that preconceived notions and theories be discarded. As Seigfried (1996) maintains, "feminist pragmatism rejects the *a priori* cookie-cutter model of knowledge and theory" (p. 263). From the point of view of many women pragmatists, the theories of social reconstructionists such as George Counts and Boyd Bode were more concerned with coherence and explanatory power. They sought to test whether situations modeled the theory, not whether social conditions actually were improved. For women pragmatists, the imposition of theory was in direct opposition to the central beliefs of pragmatism that theory arises out of experience. According to Seigfried (1996), they were often criticized by radicals (Counts) for "being reformists rather than revolutionary, as though radicalism is determined by adherence to absolutist theories rather than by recognition of the extent and quality of change required to reconstruct society" (p. 263). The many laboratory and demonstration schools at universities throughout the 1920s and 1930s are a testament to the experimentation done by women pragmatists and their influence of pragmatist philosophy.

The University School at Ohio State University, founded in 1932, was "perhaps the most experimental institution in the Eight-Year Study" (Pinar, Reynolds, Slattery, & Taubman, 1995: 157). Laura Zirbes (1884–1967), who had joined the faculty in 1928, established the elementary demonstration school that joined the secondary laboratory school to form the University School. Zirbes had begun her career (1903–1919) teaching immigrant children and quickly realized that the teacher manual she had been given was only getting in the way of her really teaching these children (Reid, 1993). In 1920 she accepted a position as an investigator in reading at Lincoln School, a well-known experimental elementary school affiliated with Teachers College. After four years, she became a lecturer at Teachers College while completing her B.A., M.A., and Ph.D. degrees. After completion, she began at Ohio State where she taught until 1954.

Zirbes's focus on experimentation (which included using scientific methods, action research, and multiple methods), children's experiences, and creativity as the heart of learning were central to her pedagogy, scholarship, and pragmatist philosophy. Most notable was her emphasis on the relationship between experimentation, creativity, and democracy. She saw these as inevitably interrelated and connected. Central to democracy was creativity, the ability to reimagine and revision daily lived experience, in more humane ways. And the way to stimulate creativity was through experimentation. Experimentation in reading methods (Moore, 1986; Zirbes, 1928), teacher education, and curriculum were central to the Laboratory School that she founded to demonstrate progressive methods at Ohio State. In her book *Spurs to Creative Teaching* (1959), she relates the relationship between democracy and creativity as one of learning how to live democratically and not in complacency:

> Living within the law is not good enough. Herd minded conformity is not enough. Getting by is worse. Worthy social living can be cultivated in school living during the so called growing years. (p. 70)

Cultivating democracy would be achieved by getting into "the act of democracy and getting other people into the act. Operate on it, not just talk about it. If it is a way of life, you walk in it" (p. 70). Zirbes was a prolific researcher and scholar, publishing over 100 articles and several books. She served as editor and on the editorial boards of numerous progressive journals as well as being involved in multiple professional organizations. In 1948, H.S. Truman conferred upon her the Woman of the Year Award calling her an outstanding teacher of teachers. Julie Teel (1996) suggests that Zirbes provides the earliest traces of the reconceptualization of the curriculum field. Paul Klohr was one of Zirbes's students and his student William F. Pinar has become one of the most prominent names associated with the reconceptualist movement.

Margaret Naumberg (1890–1983) founded the Walden School in New York City in 1914. She had studied "organic education" with Marietta Johnson in Fairhope, Alabama, during the summer of 1914. Like Johnson, Naumberg was concerned with the natural growth and development of the inner subjective life as central to social participation in a truly democratic, humanistic manner freed from the damages of impositions and ideologies that were not of one's own making. For Naumberg, curiosity, interest, imagination, individuality, and self-expression were central to fostering the democratic imagination. Naumberg, perhaps more than any other pragmatist exemplified the radical nature of pragmatism, its vision for social justice, as predicated on experience. Rather than be a process of "stuffing," education was for Naumberg a method for laying hold of the fundamental realities of life (Hinitz, 2002).

After attending Vasser for one year, Naumberg transferred to Barnard where she graduated with majors in philosophy and economics in 1912. She studied with Dewey, was president of the Socialist Club, and in the summer after her graduation went to study with Sidney and Beatrice Webb at the London School of Economics. She did not want to enter education, and only after realizing that she might construct a new plan with new foundations for radically altering schools did she consider education as a profession. Her first offer to teach came from Lillian

Wald who invited her to open a Montessori class at the Henry Street Settlement. Although an admirer of Montessori she felt that the materials did not stimulate anything unusual or creative. Naumberg and her close friend Caroyln Pratt, both part of a circle of avant-garde educators, also considered starting a school together. In May of 1916 she visited the Gary Schools in Indiana, which were well known in progressive education circles. During this trip she also visited the Francis W. Parker School in Chicago, considered the first "progressive" school. While in Chicago, she visited Jane Addams's Hull House and attended a "radical" party for Clarence Darrow (Hinitz, 2002).

During this time she also discovered Freudian teaching and the work of Carl Gustav Jung. Later in the 1920s she was also influenced by Eastern and mystical philosophies that prompted her to recognize the complexity of inner life. Self-realization was not only a cognitive, social, emotional, and aesthetic experience but also a psychological and spiritual one. Not only were students to engage in self-realization but the "Teachers must first be reeducated to know themselves as people, to uncover their unconscious motivations" (Hinitz, 2002: 42). She encouraged teachers who taught at Walden to undergo therapy.

The Walden School began as a modified Montessori kindergarten in 1914 on East 60th Street in New York City. It was named after Henry David Thoreau's *On Walden Pond* as a way to honor the democratic tradition of the New England Transcendentalists. In her own words, Naumberg (quoted in Hinitz, 2002), stated this tradition as:

> a current which asserts the rights of the individual against pressures for mass conformity, and the rights of minorities against the oppressions of majorities. In the area of social law it asserts the primacy of the law of conscience. In the area of socio-moral decisions, it questions systemizations and asserts the integrity of individual vision. (p. 42)

The Walden program was based on the "threefold nature of children, as organisms, needing a unified and balanced development of physical, emotional and intellectual powers" (p. 43). The nursery incorporated music, movement, and coordination as a means to help children get connected with their inner sense of rhythm. Of primary concern to Naumberg was maintaining inspiration in children, she saw this as the key to learning. The question that she was concerned with was "How were things that were inspirational maintained?" Naumberg was also one of the first to draw on analytic psychology to understand childhood development. Walden became a site for research in that the teachers and Naumberg sought the study of the unconscious through observation of children's play. They collected and kept data of the emotional development of children and published their findings. Working closely with parents the teachers sought to preserve in each child his or her own identity. While focusing on the self-realization of the individual, Walden also facilitated group socialization in which children engaged in cooperative activity. Naumberg's research exemplifies the pragmatist belief in experimentation and observation as central to the construction of knowledge. In this sense she was a forerunner in seeing teachers as researchers, and expecting them to engage in teaching as a continual form of inquiry. This focus on inquiry was the heart of pragmatist philosophy.

Teachers at Walden met on a regular basis to discuss emergent issues and to continue their own intellectual growth. Guest speakers, such as George Counts, were invited to discussions with the faculty. His visit in particular sparked further discussion among the faculty about the role of freedom, indoctrination, and socialization. Naumberg had been critical of the "project method" advocated by progressives as being too structured, not allowing enough independent group dynamics. The continual tension between the need for socialization for a new social order or the need for individual freedom of children to ensure the new social order were at the heart of teachers' deliberations at the Walden School as well as the larger educational community. For Naumberg, the revolution could not be imposed; it must emerge through children who had developed integrity from within as a prerequisite for "any sense of social consciousness in the real sense" (Hinitz, 2002: 51). The political nature of both Naumberg and Zirbes, with its focus on democracy, has been dismissed and misinterpreted as child-centeredness and individualistic. Alternatively, I would argue that they saw the development of children as self-realized individuals, able to direct their inner thoughts and habits—not indoctrination or standardized learning—as the most important stage in the political development of children. Central to this development was the role of creativity, imagination, and inspiration in constructing a democratic self. While marginalized by curriculum theorists and historians for being unpolitical, Naumberg and Zirbes were instead reimagining the political.

The tension between indoctrination and individual freedom as central to democracy would also be at the heart of the inquiry and deliberations of Margaret Naumberg's close friend, Carolyn Pratt (1867–1954), who opened the Play School, later known as The City and Country School, in New York's Greenwich Village in 1914. Born in upstate New York, Pratt began teaching at age 16 and later attended Teachers College, at Columbia University. While teaching at the Philadelphia Normal School for Girls, Carolyn met Helen Marot, a social investigator, writer, editor, and feminist, who also became her life partner. In 1899, they conducted an investigation of custom tailoring trades in Philadelphia. The deplorable realities of work conditions and home life among the urban poor prompted both women to commit themselves to social activism. They moved together to New York where Pratt worked in a small private school and two settlement houses.

In 1913, Pratt began her experimental school with children from working–class homes. While clearly drawing on the pragmatism of progressive philosophy, she did not want to be "placed in any category of educational philosophy or practice" (Hauser, 2002: 70). In her autobiography, *I Learn From Children*, she was adamant:

"My resistance to anything in the nature of a blueprint was instinctive and desperate. All my life I have fought against a formula. Once you set down a formula you are imprisoned by it" (Pratt, 1948: 67). Ironically, it was her refusal to be imprisoned by any system, blueprint or formula that has contributed to her being relegated to the margins of pragmatist philosophy and progressive educational history.

Pratt does not fit neatly into the dominant characterizations of progressivism as social efficiency, child-centeredness, or social reconstructionism. On the contrary, she charted out a unique feminist, pragmatist philosophy that was characterized by three central tenets: 1) play as critical to democracy; 2) social change as the continual reconstruction of experience; and 3) science as the emancipatory potential of democratic inquiry (Hendry, 2008). Her critique of Frobelian methods to which she had been introduced at Teachers College resulted in her designing "unit blocks" that were more open-ended and less restrictive than the more complex Frobelian blocks. According to Hauser (2002), Pratt wanted her "blocks to be tools for representing the experiences that children had, both inside and outside the classroom" (p. 68). Blocks were central to the "play" that formed the heart of Pratt's pedagogy. It was at the City and County School (originally named the Play School) that Pratt enacted her pragmatist philosophy and practice of play. All play activities had to be meaningful to the student, not the teacher. Children had to participate voluntarily and chose their projects rather than following a set curriculum. Pratt saw play as critical to creating a democratic society because children learned social interactions at the earliest age through play.

Like Naumberg's Walden School, the emphasis at City and Country School was on the creative expression of the children. This expression was seen as central to their developing strong habits of first-hand research through which they could learn to make sense of abstract forms, motor experiences, and bodily perceptions. This creative expression was developed in part through the use of the arts. "The arts were counter to both the superficial aestheticism of the Victorian Period and to the bleakness and spiritual aridity of the Industrial Revolution" (Hauser, 2002: 70). A pragmatic orientation was central to the curriculum. Practice was never solidified but was altered as experience and imagination were continually reflected upon. The focus on "learning from children" was not mere sentimentality, but a profound belief in reflecting on experience through observing children and their engagement with the world as central to the science of learning and the heart of social reform.

Lastly, among the experimenters to be discussed is Lucy Sprague Mitchell (1878–1967), founder of Bank Street College in New York. A commitment to democratic, inclusive education is still a driving force of the teacher education curriculum at Bank Street today (Field, 1999). Born in Chicago to a wealthy merchant family, several key events in her early life were to have a profound and lasting impact on her vision of education. The first were the Haymarket Riot of 1886 and the Pullman strike of 1894; second was her association with Jane Addams.

As a young teenager, she began regular visits to Hull House and fell "under the spell of Addams . . . who became a symbol of the real world, a world of work, and of people that she longed to reach" (p. 128). Lastly, she came into contact with scholars from the newly established University of Chicago, including John Dewey who was a major influence in her future choice of profession.

In 1900, Mitchell graduated with honors in philosophy from Radcliffe where she took courses from William James, Royce, George Santanya, Munsterberg, and George Herbert Palmer. Her search for her true vocation took many years and in the end she settled on early childhood education. In her autobiography, *Two Lives*, Mitchell (1953) recalled that

> public education is the most constructive attack on social problems, for it deals with children and the future. It requires experimentation in curriculum for children and in teacher education. It requires an understanding of our culture. It is the synthesis of all my interests, all my hopes for humanity. (p. 210)

Her decision to enter education reflected her pragmatist ideology wherein knowledge is of value only in so far that it makes a difference in the real world; experimentation is central to understanding and all knowledge is socially contingent. It was these basic foundations that converged in her founding of Bank Street School. In preparation for her newly found profession she took classes at Teachers College, Columbia University, where she attended the classes of Edward Thorndike and John Dewey. She read Dewey's *Democracy and Education*, and it was to shape much of her thinking about the role of schooling in a democratic society. She also spent several years working at Caroline Pratt's Play School where she was drawn to the experimental approach to teaching children. While teaching there, she began to clarify her understanding of children's development, especially the role of language and story in children's understanding of themselves, others, and their world. In 1921, she published *The Here and Now Story Book*, which focused on allowing children to explore their own environment. She went on to publish several other children's books. By focusing her work on the world of children and how they experience it, she became increasingly drawn to geography and its importance in children's lives. She was especially interested in children's understandings of the relationships between people and the earth. Her "tool maps" were an outgrowth of this work.

Mitchell's years of teaching eventually resulted in her turning her attention from teaching children to teaching teachers. Bank Street opened in 1930 and was essentially a cooperative school for experimental teachers. Mitchell (1953) recalled in her autobiography that the goals of the school were to:

> . . . help students develop a scientific attitude towards their work and toward life. To us this means an attitude of eager, alert observations; a constant questioning of the old procedure in light of new observations; a use of

the world as well as of books as source material; an experimental open-mindedness; and an effort to keep as reliable records as the situation permits in order to base the future upon actual knowledge of the experience of the past. (p. 470)

No other pragmatist woman educator exemplified the central tenet of "scientific method" as much as Mitchell. Basing knowledge and understanding on experience was not to be taken lightly. The central pragmatist tenet that "theory arises directly from and is accountable to experience" allowed women educators to trust in their own experiences (Seigfried, 1996: 57). But as Seigfried points out, "experience is not simply uncritically reproduced; it is interrogated as to its value for a richer, fuller, more expansive life. Therefore, the second pragmatist principle, deriving from the process character of reality, is the definition of knowledge as the outcome of experimentation according to ends-in-view" (p. 57). Experience and experimental understanding are engaged in an ongoing interaction that results in new understandings. And, as Seigfried points out "the pragmatist notion of experiment and hypothesis verification should not be confused with the detached, value-free positivist notion that eventually replaced it" (p. 57).

Mitchell's work as a pragmatist educator not only foreshadowed the "teacher as researcher" movement that emphasizes teachers' work as inquiry, but her research took seriously the children's experiences as a site of research—not as objects of study, but as co-participants in the quest to understand a complex and ever-changing world. Mitchell focused her child-centered teaching and teacher education programs on the basic premise that understanding how children make sense of language, place, and community and their interrelationships was essential to social reform.

The notion of experiment as central to the pragmatist project was particularly salient in regard to African-American women educators. The "Negro question" was at the forefront of progressive reform. For African-American women, the double burden of being Black and female created unique challenges in the desire for "racial uplift" through education (Taliaferro, 1998). Black women confronted extreme negative racial stereotypes. *Outlook* magazine in 1904 maintained that the Black woman has "the brain of a child and the passions of a woman, steeped in centuries of ignorance and savagery and wrapped about with immemorial vices" (Salem, 1990: 8). Critical to African-American educational experiments was the need to contest these stereotypes, as well as the complex racial ideologies embedded in dominant discourses of African-American education which focused on "vocational" education and "separate but equal" (Seigfried, 1996).

The "experimental" aspect of African-American schools founded by women such as Mary McLeod Bethune (1875–1955), founder of the Daytona Normal and Industrial Institute for Negro Girls in 1904, Nannie Helen Burroughs (1879–1961), who founded the National Training School for Women and Girls in 1909 in Washington, DC, and Janie Porter Barrett, who founded, in 1915, the Industrial Home for Delinquent Colored Girls in Virginia was the focus on creating spaces for education while negotiating the world of Jim Crow. While the schools founded by these women are often categorized as "vocational," they often deviated from Booker T. Washington's accommodationist model. According to Reynolds and Schramm (2002) "these African American women did not accommodate or compromise in their determination to visibly and vocally push for immediate and full inclusion of black citizens in all benefits of a democratic society" (p. 75). Contrary to the dominant images of Black women, these progressive educators sought to create spaces where Black women's role as central to "racial uplift" could be nurtured. Providing a holistic curriculum that interwove academic preparation, industrial training, religious emphasis, strict discipline, and racial pride, these schools contested the subordinate position that cultural scripts prescribed for Black women. I would argue that they were truly radical experiments in reshaping notions of race and gender. Like other pragmatist women educators, Bethune, Burroughs, and Barrett saw education as central to social change. Yet, true social justice would never be attained until social inequalities were combated. In this vein, these women were involved in a number of social movements, including women's suffrage, the anti-lynching movement, employment discrimination, and the National Association of Colored Women among others. Their commitment, like other pragmatist experimenters, was on basing theory in experience. In this case, the experience was that of Black men and women living not only under Jim Crow, but a growing scientific racism and eugenics movement in which "it was felt that a naturally inferior Black must always occupy a socially subservient position" (Watkins, 2001: 40). These experiences became the heart of Black women pragmatist educator's experiments in providing a counterdiscourse to the ideologies of the "white architects of Black education" (Watkins, 2001).

Relationship of Theory to Practice: Community and Cooperation

> A community school forgoes its separateness. It is influential because it belongs to its people. They share its ideals and its work. It takes from them and gives to them. There are no bounds as far as I can see to what it could accomplish in social reconstruction if it had enough wisdom and insight and devotion and energy. It demands all these for changes in living and learning of people is not produced by imparting information about different conditions or by gathering statistical data about what exists, but by creating with people, for people.
>
> *(Elsie Ripley Clapp, 1933)*[13]

Central to the pragmatist tradition was the belief that philosophy should have a direct bearing on social practices. In fact, the pragmatist belief that theory unrelated to practice is moribund did, according to Seigfried, inspire some of the more radical students of pragmatism to abandon purely conceptual philosophical analysis (W.E.B. Du Bois, being one, as well as C. Wright Mills). According to Seigfried (1996), women pragmatists were singular in adopting

> the radical position that scholars ought to be or become members of communities plagued by the problems their theories are supposed to solve. They uniquely intergrated their personal and private lives, deliberately putting themselves in experimental situations for the purpose of answering their own needs along with those of others. Their experiments were experiments in community living as well as in community problem solving. (p. 58)

The development of alternative, innovative education communities such as Hull House or Young's school democracies, teacher councils, and female reforms networks exemplifies this mode of pragmatic thought. The relation between theory and practice provided an ongoing dialectic that was characterized by an understanding of knowledge as intersubjective, situated, and contextual.

For a whole group of women pragmatists, this focus on community as the expression of democracy resulted in the founding of schools that were to reflect their deepest pragmatist convictions. Schools were to be community based, drawing on the historical, social, cultural experiences of that community to shape a unique and emergent curriculum that addressed the practical, social needs of its members. Many of these schools were not only for school-age children, but included adults of all ages. These women pragmatists envisioned schooling as life-long and as central to the ongoing learning and interaction that was necessary for democracy.

Historical research has focused for the most part on Northern schools that were progressive experiments. According to Sam Stack (2002), while "urban attempts at progressive education, such as the Dewey School at the University of Chicago, the Gary Schools in Gary, Indiana, and the Lincoln School at Teachers College, Columbia University, are well known, the rural applications, particularly those attempts below the Mason-Dixon line, have received little attention" (p. 116). Thus, I hope to disrupt the narrative that privileges the North as the exclusive site for community-based, progressive schools. Pragmatism was not a regional phenomenon, it was a national, and to some degree, international movement of women educator activists.[14] The diversity of schools founded by women is a testament to the pragmatist tradition in which "experience" was the foundation for "action." Put another way, each school was unique because it addressed specific historical and cultural needs. The range of schools is reflective of the truly democratic tradition that was fostered by pragmatist thought.

Elsie Ripley Clapp (1879–1965) was the founder of two community schools, the Roger Clark Ballard Memorial School in Jefferson County, Kentucky, from 1929 to 1934, and the Arthurdale School and Community Activities in Arthurdale,

West Virginia from 1934 to 1936. She published two books, *Community Schools in Action* (1939) and *The Use of Resources in Education* (1952), as well as numerous articles. From 1937 to 1939 she was the editor of *Progressive Education*, and was vice president of the Progressive Education Association (PEA) from 1933 to 1934, as well as serving on the PEA Advisory and Executive board from 1924 to 1936. In many ways, she exemplified this group of pragmatist women who sought to create a vision of schooling that embodied pragmatist principles while simultaneously being researchers, scholars, and activists, all the while being outside the academy. According to Stack (2002), Clapp's work was grounded in the belief that learning was "both an individual and a social process, grounded in human experience—the foundation of community and democracy as an ethical association" (p. 93). Born in New York, Clapp attended Vassar College for one year, leaving because she was disappointed by the lack of rigorous coursework. She went on to earn a B.A. in English at Barnard College in 1908 and a M.A. in Philosophy at Columbia in 1909. Although continuing her coursework at Columbia for her doctorates in both English and philosophy, she never completed either degree. During her time at Columbia she took at least 14 courses from Dewey and was his graduate assistant for 12 courses between 1911 and 1927. According to Seigfried (1996), Dewey is quite specific about Clapp's substantive contributions to his ideas and it is also clear from their letters that Clapp helped Dewey with the content of the course and not just grading papers.

Several events shaped her commitment to community education. While taking and teaching courses at Columbia she also gained experience teaching high school, being a principal, and in 1923–1924 taught 7th grade at the City and Country School begun by Caroline Pratt in 1914. In 1912 she had also been a member of the Committee on Children for Patterson Silk Worker's Strike Organization. This was her first experience of poverty and class conflict and the home visits she conducted resulted in her belief that cooperation between classes for a common cause was possible. In 1929, she was offered the principalship at George Rogers Clark Ballard Memorial School in Jefferson, Kentucky, where 75% of the students were considered poor rural students. Seeing an opportunity to put her abstract ideas of pragmatist/progressive education into practice, as well as considering the fact that Dewey had retired from teaching, she took the position. According to Seigfried (1996), Clapp said that the idea of a community school arose "partly from a longing that education really function in people's lives, and partly from a growing feeling about America, and an interest in using its cultures and resources and its regional differences. With us it needed the experience of work in a rural community to quicken our understanding of the school as a social institution that John Dewey had expressed forty years before" (p. 52).

As a social institution, the first step in building a community school was to develop a sense of trust between the community and the school. This could only be done by not assuming a preconceived notion of community, but through experience and observation that might be likened to a form of ethnographic research (not so much the scientific method as advocated by other progressives, including Dewey). Rather than focus on school curriculum, the pedagogy of the school became focused on understanding the children's real life experiences and culture. According to Stack (2002), the "essence of a community school had to be discovered by inquiry and questioning, coupled with a study of culture, history, belief, values, and the nature of labor. It was through the latter that Clapp began to build a community school" (p. 98). During the time that Clapp was principal, Ballard developed a new curriculum whose foundation was the cultural history of the area. Although much Native American history was excluded or stereotypical, the curriculum served to strengthen the community support for schooling and show how community school efforts could improve the lives of community members.[15]

Clapp's second experiment in putting pragmatism into practice was part of a larger experiment designed to address rural poverty during the Depression. After a visit by Eleanor Roosevelt to impoverished West Virginia, she called for federal aid to establish model communities in which people would be given 4–7 acres of land. Originally called the Reedsville Experimental Project, and later Arthurdale, this community provided the perfect setting to use the schools to restore community life, with the actual community being built physically around them. With the help of her advisory committee, which consisted of Eleanor Roosevelt, John Dewey, E.E. Agger, Lucy Sprague Mitchell, and W. Carson Ryan, Clapp designed the school aesthetically and geographically as a central facet in the lives of the people.

Like Ballard, the curriculum was designed to focus on real learning experiences that were connected to the vocational life of the community. In addition, the school linked culture with identity by drawing on the cultural heritage of the Appalachian culture, which was largely Scots–Irish, by integrating square dancing, fiddle playing, guitar playing, ballad singing, quilting, writing plays, dancing jigs, and playing the mouth harp (Stack, 2002). Central to the pragmatist orientation of the school was a commitment to embodying democracy through having a democratic school in which teachers, administrators, and community members were involved in the decision making process. Unfortunately, the school was short lived as an experiment. Federal funding was cut, industries did not develop, and the project became a target for Republicans who branded it is as socialist. In 1936 it came under local jurisdiction and reverted to a traditional curriculum. Despite being short lived this experiment is another testament to the attempts to put theory into practice.

The Moonlight Schools in Kentucky are another example of building democratic community in the South. Cora Wilson Stewart (1875–1958) opened these schools for illiterate adult mountain folk in Rowan County, Kentucky. Born to a middle-class professional family in Kentucky, Stewart attended Morehead Normal School for college preparatory training and teacher's course. While teaching she attended the National Normal University in Lebanon, Ohio, from 1892 to 1895.

In 1899 she graduated from Wilbur R. Smith Business College in Lexington, Kentucky, and by 1901 she had been elected the Rowan County school superintendent. She gained a reputation as a public speaker and focused her efforts on providing both a vocational education and classic liberal arts education to the mountain children.

From her position as a superintendent, Stewart emerged as a powerful public figure becoming the first woman president of the Kentucky Education Association. Her emphasis on education increasingly focused on literacy. She chaired the illiteracy section of the World Conference of Education Associations, conducted dozens of illiteracy conferences throughout the United States, served on the executive board of the National Education Association, and founded the National Illiteracy Crusade in 1926. In her book *Moonlight Schools for the Emancipation of Adult Illiterates* (1922), Stewart expressed her commitment to "emancipate from illiteracy all those enslaved in its bondage" (p. 9).

Because of a lack of public funding for literacy teaching, Stewart engaged public school teachers to teach in the evening. By 1913, 25 counties had started the schools, and by 1915, 19 states had adopted Stewart's model for anti-literacy campaigns (Reynolds & Schramm, 2002). Like other pragmatists, she drew on the experiences of the mountain people she was teaching as a starting point for her pedagogy of reading and writing, as well as bridging the home and school environment. She often referred to the young children as "our mountain jewels" and extolled the virtues of female youth of the hills in her lecture entitled "The Mountain Girl" (Nelms, 1997). Stewart understood the institutionalized prejudice against the education of adults, especially mountain folk whom she defended against popular stereotypes of being "inferior people" or "degenerate stock." To combat this prejudice she drew not only on the rhetoric of crusade, engaging a missionary zeal to convince women that it was their responsibility to teach, but also on the rhetoric of patriotism and democracy to defend every person's right to read and write. The underside of this rhetoric was its focus on mountain people as needing literacy because they were a "reservoir of strength and patriotism in the millions of pure Anglo-Saxon Americans" (Stewart, 1922: 5). The irony of engaging "nativist" rhetoric to promote the education of a disempowered group is a reminder of the complex racial world these women pragmatists negotiated and the contradictory subject identities they inhabited. Despite these limitations, Stewart's radical notion that adult education was a primary mechanism for social change was to create spaces in the future for a more inclusionary vision of adult education. The Opportunity Schools in South Carolina founded by Wil Lou Gray (1883–1984), patterned after the work of Cora Wilson Stewart, were extended to African-Americans when she began the "Opportunity School for Negros" at Seneca Junior College in 1936 and another at Voorhees Industrial School in 1936.[16] Likewise Myles Horton's Highlander Folk School, at which Septima Clark taught, also grew out of the work of Stewart. This legacy of adult education is a testament to the ongoing impact of these women pragmatists. Despite claims that progressive education failed or made no lasting impact, the literacy schools clearly shaped adult education throughout the 20th century and had at their roots pragmatist beliefs.

Contradictory postures were not only taken up by Whites, but also by African-American women pragmatists who engaged in the development of community schools. Charlotte Hawkins Brown (1883–1961), who founded the Alice Freeman Palmer Memorial Institute (Palmer Institute) for African-Americans in rural Sedalia, North Carolina, was considered "a school rule bound in method and controlling in philosophy" (Reynolds, 2002). In contrast to "progressive" ideology, her experiences and contributions might be excluded. However taken within the context of regional, social, and economic realities, her work has been seen as a "reform subgroup" (Kliebard, 1995). I would maintain that this analysis takes mainstream progressivism as the norm and functions to marginalize Brown and others' experiences which highlight the very nature of pragmatist philosophy as situated, contingent, and historically bound. Brown is a pragmatist specifically because she based her philosophy on the social, historical context in which she was situated. So, when Brown opened the Palmer institute in 1902, it was contingent on the context in which there were no provisions for the education of southern Black citizens (Anderson, 1988).

Although attending elementary and high school in Boston, Charlotte Brown returned to North Carolina, where she took a teaching job in McLeansville (just east of Greensboro) at the request of the American Missionary Association (AMA). When the AMA could no longer support the school, parents encouraged Charlotte to take it over. By 1922, the Palmer Institute became the only rural high school in Guilford county to receive accreditation. In 1924 it had grown to 214 students, mostly boarders, with property valued at $200,000 on over 300 acres (Reynolds & Schramm, 2002). At a time when most African-Americans either could not attend school or had no opportunity, the Palmer Institute with its nine-month school year and curriculum, which included English, math, physics, chemistry, French, Latin, history, and civics, was a location where social reform took a foothold (Reynolds, 2002). Not content just to teach, Brown, like the other pragmatist educators, saw education as only one piece of a larger vision of social reform. For her, this vision was one of "racial uplift." In 1912, she became the president of the North Carolina Federation of Negro Women's Clubs, an office she held until 1932. Her activism extended to active roles in the National Council of Colored Women and the International Council for Women of the Darker Races, and she also served on the advisory board of the National Urban League. She maintained relationships with other African-American educators, including Mary McLeod Bethune, Anna Julia Cooper, and Nannie Helen Burroughs. Long before Brown vs. Education, she was pushing for racial integration. She insisted that "the races needed to become aware of one another, and school was where that should start" (Reynolds, 2002: 13). Her book *Mammy: An Appeal to the Heart of the South*, recounting the trials of a former slave, was a form of literary activism designed to educate Whites as to the ills of racial prejudice.

The establishment of a school for African-Americans in the South at the height of Jim Crow was a testament to Brown's ingenuity in courting White benefactors in the North who sought a more accommodationist curriculum. A delicate balance, she often found herself at odds with the donors who wanted a more vocational curriculum. Brown did emphasize the social graces by insisting that there was one right way to speak, respond, sit, stand, walk, dress, and eat. At this time, Brown believed that proper etiquette was the "all important edge for blacks in improving their relationships with whites and convincing them of their right to equality" (Reynolds & Schramm, 2002: 53). Often depicted as accommodating, these strategies once again reflect the situated nature of subject identities and the ways in which identities are taken up in complex and contradictory ways. While vocational in nature, the curriculum was a means to "fill the gap between no opportunity and entry opportunity" (p. 74). Schools for Blacks, for the most part, were expected to follow the accommodationist model laid out by Booker T. Washington, which focused on "skills" education. Although seen by some as "acting White," for Brown and other African-American educators, whose actions were under scrutiny by a South deeply embedded in racism, as exemplified by Jim Crow and lynching, these strategies were a way to deflect suspicion in order to get on with the larger vision of providing education for social change. Creating educational opportunity for African-Americans in the South that stressed the equal rights of Blacks was a challenge to prevailing racial norms. For women the "double burden" of being both black and female made their negotiations of race/gender relations all the more complex.

White women, who were positioned differently in the South, had more leeway to "experiment" with pragmatist and progressive ideals.[17] One example of this is the School of Organic Education founded by Marietta Johnson (1864–1938) in 1909 in the socialist community of Fairhope, Alabama. Described by Lawrence Cremin (1961) as easily the most child-centered of the early experimental schools, it is ironically one of the most neglected in the history of education. When John and Evelyn Dewey visited the school as part of the *Schools of To-Morrow* report (1915), they reported that "under her direction the school has proved a success. Time and larger opportunities will undoubtedly correct the weak spots and discrepancies that are bound to appear while any school is in the experimental state" (p. 39). That the embodiment of Dewey's philosophy would manifest itself in a small Alabama town is testament to the sweeping influence that pragmatism and progressivism had at the turn of the century. That the School of Organic Education is still in existence today contests again the dominant narrative of the failure of progressivism.

Although originally from the Midwest, where she graduated in 1885 from the State Normal School at St. Cloud, Minnesota, Johnson went on to teach for five years and then take a position as "critic" teacher at Mankato State Normal School. Around 1901 she was introduced to two books that made her question what she considered to be her perfected teaching techniques. The first was *The Development of the Child* (1898) by Nathan Oppenheim and the second was Henderson's (1902) *Education and the Larger Life*. Oppenheim's book questioned dominant ideas about children as small adults. He argued that small children treated like adults would be permanently damaged and that a special environment was needed for children to encourage their development. Henderson's book emphasized treating each child as a complete organism, one comprised of body, mind, and spirit. These two books, as well as Dewey's *School and Society* (1900), provided the basis for her "awakening." She could not rest until she started a school.

Johnson's opportunity came when she, her husband, and son heard about the single-tax community founded on the ideas of Henry George, who wrote the late 19th-century bestseller *Progress and Poverty*. Believing it had a "Fair Hope" of succeeding as a single-tax experiment, the founders put into practice a model of cooperative individualism. Members of the community owned the land, but leased (this was the single tax) it from the city for 99 years, the goal being to control the gap between the rich and the poor by protecting against monopolies. The colony attracted attention as a socialist community and Upton Sinclair visited in 1909, as well as Dewey in 1913.

What was lacking as part of this community experiment was a school. Less than a month after moving to Fairhope, the 38-year-old Marietta took over the public elementary school. According to Newman (2002) Johnson's goal was for students to "cultivate 'inner, human' standards, the feeling of 'inner necessity' that developed in the absence of external demands" (p. 26). Johnson exemplified a truly child-centered approach to the degree that she rejected external, competitive standards as the guiding principles of education. Children at the Organic School did not read until they chose to, they determined the curriculum by their interests, there were absolutely no grades, and classes were organized around stages of child development. Steering young children away from books, she encouraged them to learn through direct experience in nature. There was no homework, no tests and students never received grades or report cards. In her 1938 book, *Thirty Years With An Idea*, she reflected that "since life—growth—education—are synonymous, why try to measure education? This is no doubt due to our general commercialization. Since money is the false measure of industry, we have fallen into the error of rating growth by the acquisition of facts—attainment of skills" (p. 18). The arts as well as vocational skills and physical activity were integrated into the curriculum. Committed to creating a school that was a model of democracy, Johnson worked hard to establish an egalitarian climate. Children of all social classes attended as well as disabled students. However, no African-Americans attended the school. As the school progressed even the boundaries between the school and the community faded.

As word of this experiment spread, Johnson was able to secure large donors and she engaged in public lectures around the country. She conducted the Fairhope Summer School in Greenwich, New York every summer for 20 years and was director of the "Organic School North" in Edgewood, Connecticut. After his visit in 1913, Dewey's (1915) praise for her school in *Schools of To-Morrow*, where he declared it a success, in part due to the fact that his son Sabino, who attended school there for a week, did not want to leave, catapulted her into national fame. Followers of her methods founded nine satellite schools, her initiative prompted the founding of the Progressive Education Association (PEA) in 1919, of which she was a founding member, and she became an international star, speaking at numerous conferences abroad (Newman, 2002). Her influence was to shape many other experimental schools including that of Margaret Naumberg. The obscurity of her as a philosopher and her pragmatic approach to education was in part due to her characterization as a "play schooler" by the social reconstructionists who seized leadership of the PEA in the 1930s. Their reluctance or inability to see that Johnson's pedagogy and beliefs about children were political, in that they were part of her vision for social reform has resulted in her exclusion as a serious pragmatist philosopher or social reconstructionist. The social reconstructionists—George S. Counts, Harold O. Rugg, and Theodore Brameld—according to Stanley (1992) were

> concerned with using the schools to challenge directly the dominant social order and to achieve specific changes in our social, cultural, and economic institutions. Since socialization was essential to being human, the reconstructionists believed that we should use education to socialize our young in ways calculated to expand and reinforce a democratic culture. (p. 8)

Marietta Johnson and Elsie Clapp, as well as other "child-centered" progressives (Naumberg, Pratt, Mitchell) saw this type of socialization as indoctrination that resulted in regimented and conformist youth. They saw no difference between social reconstructionists and the more traditional approaches to education formalized through social efficiency—both resulted in youth who were not prepared for active participation in democracy. Alternatively, these women pragmatists focused on the "child's interests and the enrichment of his powers of observation [and] believed they were contributing to the creation of citizens with scientific attitudes capable of handling new problems as they arose. In this sense they believed they were helping to create a new society of independent, free-thinking individuals" (p. 7). These women pragmatists lived in that in-between space of having a social vision of democracy while simultaneously opposing any form of indoctrination. Stanley summarizes:

> While they did promote democracy, this was seen as an imposition of a process and not a content of fixed truths to be learned. One sense of this approach to education is captured in Marietta Johnson's (1926) comment that "childhood is for itself and not a preparation for adult life." (p. 349)

As someone who was committed to knowledge as experience, to disrupting the boundaries between school and society, and who saw children's real-world experiences of democracy in school as central to shaping their vision of society, Johnson was clearly a pragmatist in the truest sense. Like many other women pragmatists engaged in radical experiments, I continue to question why they remain on the margins of curriculum and educational history. How might we re-imagine progressive educational history? What spaces for conversation would emerge if the tale of progressivism were not anchored by deeply gendered constructs of subjectivity and identity? What makes it possible to tell the narrative of progressivism in the ways that we do?

Reflections

The exclusion of women pragmatist philosophers is deeply troubling. What has perhaps been most neglected is their commitment to pragmatism as a means to further social justice. All of these women shared a commitment to embodying the ideals of democracy as a living process. This process was driven by the central tenets of pragmatism—experience, experiment, and community. These are interrelated concepts that fold into one another and are in continual conversation. Most importantly, this is a cyclical process that never ends. Their experiences as women, as educators, as social reformers shaped pragmatism in unique ways.

First and foremost was their theorizing as to the ways in which experience was gendered, raced, and classed. Experience is not a universal concept, nor is it an individual one. Experience is the consequence of social relations. Experience is not an end in and of itself. It is the starting point for reflection and experimentation for action. Experimentation is the commitment to draw on the knowledge and experiences of those whose social problems are being investigated. True experimentation requires that ideologies and theories be put aside. The usefulness of theory is ultimately answerable to those whose lives are supposed to be bettered by it (Seigfried, 1996). Women educator pragmatists, who have often been characterized as "apolitical" for not having been theoretical enough, were in essence embodying a social ethics of democracy in which the imposition of any theoretical construct was considered a form of indoctrination and thus undemocratic. In fact, the truly radical nature of their work has been marginalized, particularly the work of African-American women of this period, whose vision of social equality cut against the grain of America's social fabric. Rarely is their work included in the narratives of curriculum history and theory as a form of theory, and never as pragmatist. Lastly, the focus on community was a challenge to the cherished national and cultural ideal of individualism. Their belief that all knowledge is embedded in networks of relationships that are socially and culturally contingent shifted the focus of democracy from the rhetoric of individualism to a vision of "cooperative intelligence" (Seigfried, 1996). Democracy was a not a form of government, but a way of life.

Although much knowledge of these women and their ideas has been obscured, there is a continuing legacy of women and men educator activists committed to a vision of democracy who draw on the legacy of these women, including the scholarship of Margaret Crocco, Wendi Kohli, Janice Jipson, Patti Lather, Janet Miller, Elizabeth Ellsworth, Jessie Goodman, Jennifer Gore, Mimi Orner, Kathleen Casey, Kathleen Weiler, and Sandra Hollingsworth. In addition there is an ongoing struggle to define what constitutes democratic leadership as exemplified by the work of Becky Ropers-Huilman, Jackie Blount, Diane Dunlap, Kate Rousmaniere, and others. Thus, I would contest narratives that maintain that "progressivism" had no lasting impact. The work of these educators is a testament to a continuing vision of education as the heart of a more democratic and more just society. In our rewriting of educational history and curriculum theory, there must be room for more than one vision of social education. Rather than continue to construct a narrative of "struggle" which functions to perpetuate the "family plot" of reproduction and exclusion, pragmatism can provide a vision for embracing the multiple ways in which educators experience and make sense of their roles as change agents. At the heart of pragmatism is a refusal to embrace any unitary, single ideology. Keeping multiple, contradictory ideologies in "play" (Doll, 2002) is what pragmatism calls us to do. It is our democratic obligation and what keeps alive the conversation that is democracy.

7

THE FUTURE OF THE PAST

Fellow Educators—are we not lost?
Do we know where we are,
Remember where we have been,
Or foresee where we are going?

(Dwayne Huebner, 1999)

Curriculum is a moving form. That is why we have trouble capturing it, fixing it into language, lodging it in our matrix.

(Madeline Grumet, 1988)

To remember where we have been as a way to re-imagine the future is the task of curriculum. This requires getting "lost"—losing a sense of order, linearity, and progress in order to embrace movement, complexity, and cacophony. There is no ending to the past. What I have presented here is incomplete and partial. There are many curriculums, and many ways of knowing. The quest for an absolute understanding of knowledge is an illusive one. It is almost impossible to see clearly our own deeply embedded assumptions about knowledge, learning, and education without having some distance, some point outside ourselves. History can provide an Archimedean point—a positionality in which we are situated like a stranger in a new land. Becoming the stranger induces new perspectives and also stirs us to remember home, but home is never quite the same.

I could not have anticipated the connections, the disruptions, and the threads that would emerge from my journey through space and time. I am again reminded that for the ancients history was not a sequence of events that were linked casually but was expressed as repetition. Continually engaging in the act of remembering—this is what makes us human. This memory work has reminded me of the profound ways in which humanity has struggled to claim themselves as "knowers." Beginning with the earliest creation stories that reveal the struggle to understand our place in the cosmos, humans have sought to "inquire" into how they shape and are shaped by the universe. In many ways we have not moved far from the original questions asked by humans. Are we born of a physical (material) world or of a metaphysical (divine) world? Are the two incommensurable?

What is clear across time is the human propensity for inquiry. What can be known? How do we come to know? Who can be a knower? The earliest human beings understood the cosmos as paradoxical, unknowable, and chaotic. Central to the epistemological worldview was the key notion of balance that entailed embracing life and death, earth and heaven, the feminine and masculine divine. From the beginning knowledge was gendered. By examining the subject positions and identities made im/possible through gender, I have come to a deeper appreciation of the ways in which gender has always structured and been structured by power relations. The profoundly diverse ways in which women such as Sappho, Mary Magdalene, Hildegard of Bingen, Christine de Pizan, Anne Hutchinson, Henriette Delille, and Jane Addams were able to assert themselves as knowers signifies not only the fluidity of gender, but also the ongoing curricular struggle to construct and legitimate themselves as knowers.

However, what was not apparent to me at the outset of this study was that in "engendering" history, bringing into existence the relationship between history and curriculum, the very concept of gender would take on new meaning. Gender, as a construct, looking through space and time, is only possible in relationship to other constructs—notions of time, space, race, class, religion, history, and place. Consequently, while my journey began with a focus on gender, through looking historically it is obvious to me now that gender, like history, is not a fact or a theoretical construct with absolute explanatory power. To assert that all history is the history of patriarchy or class struggle is to mistake this as doctrine and to neglect the necessity of plurality of interpretations. Holding multiple and often contradictory interpretations is what becomes the generative process of history. To focus solely on a gender analysis suffers like all other theoretical constructs in that it is a closed system. To take up a gendered analysis is also to realize its limitations, which then in turn simultaneously opens the way for new possibilities. The paradox of this curriculum theorizing is that there must be a capacity to hold multiple and contradictory worldviews. To seek a totalizing theory is to "cut" off inquiry. The heart of wisdom, on the other hand, is to remain open to unknowing.

How might we become more comfortable with "unknowing" history and gender? I return again to the central premises of this book—that an engendered history is one that seeks *re-membrance* and representation, *reflexivity* and linearity, and *responsibility* and truth. These 3 Rs are based on an epistemology of ethics that is predicated not on curriculum history as a discipline, but on history as a way of life grounded in an ethics of relationality. Re-membering, reflexivity, and responsibility are central to this ethics.

Re-membrance

> Someone, I say, will remember us in the future.
>
> *(Sappho, 640 BCE)*

> I found that the two foundations of Memory—first, its importance in interpreting and appeasing life for the individual, and second its activity as a selective agency in social reorganization—were not mutually exclusive, and at moments seemed to support each other.
>
> *(Jane Addams, 1916)*

I began this book with the above quote from Sappho. From the moment I read this quote some 15 years ago, I knew it would mark the beginning of this work. The first time I read these words, "someone will remember us in the future" I was struck by the haunting human desire not to be forgotten. I felt called across time to respond. My response has been long in coming. In part because I have struggled so much to try to "get it right"—to represent with some accuracy the life and philosophy of Sappho as well as those of others. I finally realized that I could not do this. I could never capture the "life" of Sappho. Her poetry is illusive, mysterious, and passionate—that is what makes it so powerful. For Sappho, ethics emerged from passion and love, not reason and logic. While I cannot re-present Sappho, I can remember that her work, her curriculum theorizing posited a worldview in which knowledge could not be reduced to "representation." Opening this space of memory, this rupture can prompt us to reconsider the multiple ways in which humans have understood knowledge.

As Jane Addams reminds me, though, the role of memory is not one of mere remembering, but one of reorganization. Re-membering is a relational ethics that connects us across space and time to those ties that remind us of our humanity. The memory of Sappho in and of itself is a call to "reclaim" her in the narratives of curriculum history. However, in remembering her, in making her present, I see the world differently. I am emboldened to ask my students why we don't speak more of "love" in education. What might a pedagogy of "love" or "passion" entail? or "How might we think of learning as an erotic act?" Re-membering Sappho is critical to asking new questions, rethinking taken-for-granted assumptions about learning, knowing, and education. The power of remembering (as opposed to representation) is the force that it has to reorganize our way of being in the world and our relations to others.

Reflexivity

While linearity or other modes of temporality provide one way in which to conceptualize history, the use of time to structure the human condition is only one way in which to understand the human story. For Aristotle, God was timeless and did not reveal himself in history. Accordingly, he dismissed history as a mere illusion that deflected from gaining a more serious truth. History was inferior to philosophy because philosophy had no beginning, middle, and end. For the Greeks, history was more trivial than poetry or myth. History described what happened (the particular) and poetry (the universal) what might be. Greek tragedies did not represent "truth" or "facts" but were meant to elicit certain human emotions as a means to re-experience the human condition and be transformed. History as linear time in which there is a past (literally bracketed) prohibits a reflexive experiencing of history in which re-connecting becomes a transformative experience. The past is not an object, but a whole system of relationships in which we cannot take apart the whole (past, present, future), but in which the whole (history) is greater than the parts.

To read history reflexively will require the suspension of chronological readings of curriculum in which history progresses from a supposed "Golden Age" with an inevitable decline into the "Dark Ages" and once again to "Enlightenment." Suspending linearity and progress provides a space in which Hilda of Whitby, Hildegard of Bingen, Mechthild of Magdeburg, and Teresa of Avila can be called from the "dark" to join the conversation. How does the transgender theorizing of medieval women religious intersect with contemporary gender, feminist, and queer theory? How does the body as a site of knowing transcend time and space? How does the holistic cosmology theorized by medieval women religious intersect with current ecological worldviews? Much like medieval women religious, contemporary curriculum theorists also suggest the complex and often paradoxical ways in which subject identities are constructed through memory as embodied in space and place, as well as through discourses, ideologies, and power relations. Eugenia Whitlock (2007) who identifies as a White, female, lesbian, working-class, liberal, fundamentalist Christian, teacher educator suggests that her queer fundamentalism "reveals a complexity of being-in-place from which to question dominant, constricting conventions" (p. 85). It is the spaces of contradiction, paradox, and "unknowing" that move us to spaces that are generative.

The reflexive moment is one in which subjectivities are continually being constituted in relation across time, space, and history. Experience, while grounded in lived social relations, is embedded in history and memory. As Jane Addams ultimately believed "experience is nothing but memory" (Seigfried, 2002: xx). Thus, our understandings of self and other are deeply implicated in memory. Memory as reflexivity, as recursion is not only what establishes connections but it is central to resisting the logic of identification or representation. History as a web of relationships, or a social ethics, defies the logic of linear time and knowledge as representation.

Responsibility

History as responsibility is our response to the call of the Muses. To open ourselves to the infinite relationships and connections that are present in history is taunting. This necessitates a truly "cosmopolitan" curriculum (Pinar, 2009). The current "presentist" tendency, in which history is mere nostalgia, is a response to "fear"—

fear of the unknown. Like dominant constructions of curriculum, that focus on control and order, history has remained in the past as an icon, as an object, something that is dead. Our responsibility as curriculum theorists is to "bring out" the dead—to "respond" and engage in conversation with the past.

To assume that we can go it alone, without the stories and wisdom of those who came before us, is to sever our human relations. We are our relationships. Ironically, as the Dalai Lama (2005) suggests, "any belief in an objective reality grounded in the assumption of intrinsic, independent existence is untenable" (p. 46). He explains this irony. To possess an independent existence would mean that things and events are somehow complete and entirely self-contained; nothing would have the capacity to interact. However, we do interact and therefore we are not independent (although this is the story we tell ourselves and it is, of course, deeply gendered). According to the Dalai Lama,

> Everything is composed of dependently related events, of continuously interacting phenomena with no fixed, immutable essence, which are themselves in constantly changing dynamic relations. Things and events are "empty" in that they do not possess any immutable essence, intrinsic reality, or absolute being that affords independence. (p. 47)

While most of us relate to the world as if it did have an enduring intrinsic reality (the story of history), it does not. In fact, our responsibility might be to "let go" and "empty" history of "truth" as a means to embrace inquiry as a dynamic process of relationships.

It is this broader understanding of the role of curriculum history as one of "responsibility" that this book has sought to articulate. It was not so long ago (the beginning of the 20th century) that history was seen as critical to the new discipline of education. In fact, both history and philosophy were seen as providing the frameworks for a "science" of education (Lagemann, 2000: 73–75). Ironically, one way in which the field eventually legitimated itself was to "cut" itself off from the past, from history. Education has been reduced to method, rather than a form of inquiry, to a corporate enterprise rather than a humanistic one, and to an individual endeavor rather than one of communion. Learning and research is no longer considered a sacred act but a utilitarian one (Hendry, 2010). Rather than being understood as both a practical (*episteme*) and poetic (*gnosis*) undertaking, education has become a purely technical endeavor. Scholars in education who train as philosophers, historians, and curriculum theorists are marginalized as not "scientific," as too "political," and not "practical" enough. The deintellectualization and ahistorical nature of education make the future devoid of a past. What identities are made possible or impossible when we embrace this type of presentism? This engendering will be left to a new field of scholars—scholars whose identities are unknown to me. I cannot imagine how the field will be transformed, I can only hope that someone will respond to the call.

NOTES

Introduction

1   See Seigfried (1996) and Doll (1993). Due to the increasing dominance of positivist views of science, much of the research by pragmatists such as Lucy Sprague Mitchell, Elsie Clapp, and Carolyn Pratt is not considered legitimate research and has consequently been excluded from histories of educational research.

2   Dewey articulated this vision in his 1929 book, *The Sources of a Science of Education*, in which he expressed that "the command of scientific methods liberates individuals; it enables them to see new problems, devise new procedures and, in general, makes for diversification rather than for set uniformity" (p. 12).

3   Drawing on the work of Michel Serres (1995), Denise Egea-Kuehne (2006) deconstructs the notion of linearity as central to "reason" and notions of history.

4   Mnemosyne and Zeus slept together for nine consecutive nights and thereby created the nine Muses. These nine Muses were the first "curriculum" or life course.

Chapter 1

1   Foucault's notions of archaeology and genealogy undertake to dismantle the hold of humanism on history by positing the unitary subject of traditional history as a product of discourse.

2   I would like to delineate the history of curriculum theory from the history of teaching and education. Although these fields are interrelated, the history of teaching and education is primarily concerned with the history of the profession itself and its role in shaping what we consider the institution of schooling. The history of curriculum theory is more specifically concerned with the question of how education (more general than schooling) shapes and is shaped by ideology and culture. Women's symbolic relegation to nature versus culture (Rosaldo & Lamphere, 1974) has necessarily excluded them from being taken seriously as curriculum theorists. In other words, although much is written about the history of women and teaching, little consideration has been given to women curriculum theorists or how the history of curriculum theory itself constitutes gender.

3 As Hannah Arendt (1954) maintains, history is itself a concept that must be historicized. Thus, modernist history with its emphasis on development and progress and objectivity is distinct from ancient history in which the poet and historian were not distinguished. Martin (1986) reminds us that until the end of the 18th century, history was considered part of literature and drew its methods primarily from classical rhetoric.

4 I draw here on the work of Said (1989) and Spivak (1988), who show how identities in the West are always dependent on the construction of binaries—colonizer and colonized, White and Black, male and female, etc.

5 I do not want to dismiss the importance of historical work done on these individual women; without it we would not even be having this discussion. However, to "add" them as exemplars of women progressives without deconstructing the dominant historical narrative is to potentially reproduce the very categories of subjectivity and agency that contributed to their exclusion in the first place (Crocco, Munro, & Weiler, 1999).

6 However, although experience can never be achieved, I am reluctant to give up a material world. As Mark Freeman (1993) suggests, furniture only exists through language, but that doesn't keep him from bumping up against it.

7 For further discussion of this "paralysis" of poststructuralism due to the loss of the subject and consequently agency, see Nancy Hartsock (1990). My concern with these critiques is that agency and subjectivity continue to be embedded in notions of power as unitary and graspable (Bloom & Munro, 1995; Munro, 1998b). When power continues to be conceptualized in these ways, the multiplicities of ways in which agency and power are enacted are obscured.

8 Like Jameson (1981), I am skeptical of whether the popular notion that history is text means that the "referent" does not exist.

9 Remembrance, Mnemosyne, was regarded with such reverence by the Greeks since it guaranteed their immortality that it was made the mother of Muses. Mnemosyne was a Titan goddess, the sister of Kronos and Oceanus, the mother of the Muses, she presided over the poetic function. In Homer, the narrator of the *mythoi* was the poet, the *aoidos*, who was society's bearer of tradition and educator.

10 Several curriculum histories (Schubert, 1986) do situate curriculum within a larger historical perspective by tracing curriculum history back through the Greeks, etc. However, this tracing is conspicuously male, White, and Western.

11 That this is called the democratization of education is a misrepresentation when we consider that at the end of this time period Blacks and women were still severely restricted in their access to public education. What, then, makes it possible for us to tell this story, why are we so invested in this fiction?

12 I do not want to romanticize Beecher as a new heroine. Beecher engaged dominant ideologies in complex ways which functioned in contradictory ways. Her engaging of dominant racial ideologies to support the influx of women into teaching certainly functioned in oppressive ways.

13 There are several exceptions to this genre of "good daughter" history—the work of Ellen Lagemann (1985) on Jane Addams, Kathryn Sklar (1973) on Catharine Beecher, Joyce Antler (1987) on Lucy Sprague Mitchell, Carolyn Steedman (1989) on Margaret McMillan, and Jane Roland Martin (1985) on Charlotte Perkins Gilman. However, this work is rarely analyzed in relation to the history of curriculum.

14 The work of Mary Jo Deegan (1990) and Smith and Smith (1994) are an exception, yet most discussions of pragmatism do not include Young (Kliebard, 1992b; Stanley, 1992). Cremin (1961) also notes that Young was not merely carrying out Dewey's idea but was, in fact, central to crystallizing Dewey's ideas.

15 The following are only examples of her work: *Scientific Method in Education* (1903), Chicago: University of Chicago Press; *Some Types of Modern Educational Theory* (1909), Chicago: University of Chicago Press; Democracy and Education (July 6, 1916), *Journal of Education*.

16 Constructing history as the tale between social efficiency and progressivism is reductionist in the sense that it obscures the micropractices of power and resistance. Reese (1986) provides a more complex, dialectic portrayal of progressivism.

17 Deleuze and Guattari (1987). Terms such as schizoanalysis, rhizomatics, pragmatics, digrammatism, cartography, micropolitics are used in order to prevent their position from stabilizing in an ideology, method, or single metaphor. Privileging botanical metaphors, they employ the term rhizome to designate the decentered lines that constitute multiplicities. Rhizomatic seeks to extricate roots and foundations, to thwart unities and brake dichotomies, and to spread our roots and branches, thereby pluralizing and disseminating, producing differences and multiplicities, making new connections. Rhizomes are nonhierarchical systems of deterritorialized lines that connect with other lines in random and unregulated relationships.

18 In fact, Young led the campaign for women's suffrage in Illinois. In June 1913, she was pictured with Jane Addams and Julia Lathrop, two other Chicago social reformers, with a caption that read "Three reasons why Illinois women won the vote" (Smith & Smith, 1994: 307).

19 When heterosexuality is one of the ways in which men's power over women is maintained, the spinster or lesbian functions as a threat to that power. See Khayatt (1992) and Oram (1989).

20 Bowers (1987) maintains that the discourse of liberalism is part of a political lineage going back to John Stuart Mill, Jeremy Bentham, John Locke, and Thomas Hobbes.

21 The phrase "warring extremes" is used by Kliebard (1992b: 154) to describe the tension between Dewey and Tyler. Pinar, Reynolds, Slattery, and Taubman (1995: 127) use the term a "call to arms."

22 Recent curriculum theorists have critiqued the monolithic and idealistic view of Dewey as a social reconstructionist and, in fact, argue that Dewey's views were representative of an effort to maintain the status quo. See Hlebowitsh and Wraga (1995) for a review of these critiques.

23 According to Prawat (1995), Dewey rejected the either/or nature of the child-centered versus the subject-centered debate. In fact, Prawat argues that Dewey has been misread as an advocate of child-centered or project-based approaches to education.

24 Stanley's only reference to a specific "child-centered" educator is Marietta Johnson. Dewey, however, is distanced from the child-centered faction of progressivism when Stanley (1992) suggests that the social reconstructionists "posed a direct challenge to the child-centered progressivism who tended to dominate the Progressive Education Association (PEA) through the 1920s" (p. 7). Stanley points out that Dewey himself spoke out against the child-centered contingent of the PEA, because of the wide range of social problems that this approach tended to ignore (pp. 6–8).

25 In fact, taking up the discourse of child-centeredness might have functioned as both a political and theoretical move to counteract the gender-neutral ideologies of progressivism. Taking into account prevalent gender norms and expectations, the child-centeredness discourse also provided many women an acceptable way to enter the public sphere of education as a way to reshape it. Thus, taking up this ideology probably worked in complex and contradictory ways.

26 I would like to thank Philip Bennett and Wendy Kohli for their thoughtful readings of ongoing drafts of this work. A special thanks to Douglas McKnight for his comments and careful editing.

Chapter 2

1 600 CE is when state systems emerge that have as central to their legitimation a written code. For example, in China Confucianism emerges in 600 CE, in 345 CE Christianity

is codified in the Nicene Creed. Although "laws" had been written prior to this, Hammarabi's code or the ten commandments, these written laws were still enmeshed in mythic stories, they were not seen as independent of a divine or mythic connection. In contrast, those codified belief systems in the early Middle Ages function as man-made, although perhaps shaped by beliefs about God and the divine, they are clearly seen as separate from "revelation" and in fact gain their power from being conceived out of reason.

2 "Goddess" has such diverse connotations, and within popular culture is a New Age term, that I will use instead of the term female creator. The earliest understandings of creation were not understood as the result of both male and female. Women were seen as "the" creators of life through some mysterious process. Consequently, it is not surprising that the earliest creation stories have female figures as the creator.

3 The snake or serpent is often associated with the goddess and symbolizes the power of regeneration. In later stories the association of the serpent with evil (as in the biblical story of Adam and Eve) is a way to delegitimate the goddess.

4 Molly Quinn (2001) draws on Heidegger to underscore how current technocratic notions of education have forgotten "Being" and lost the very question of the meaning of Being in human consciousness.

5 Thomas Merton (1968) refers to this as the struggle between the "true self," the self that works in union with the divine, and the "false self" which is the self that goes it alone without God.

6 Consequently, like Berman (2000), I am reluctant to suggest that there was a goddess age, where women ruled, etc. Although the work of anthropologists such as Gumpta have maintained this thesis, I am more cautious because it seems we are imposing today's culturally understood gender concepts to a radically different time.

7 Although the Hebrew term Kabbalah simply means tradition, the scholar Gershom Scholem has explained that those who take the path of Kabbalah seek to know God "not through dogmatic theology, but through living experience and intuition" (Pagels, 2003: 94).

8 Her influence is still present in the shape of the challah bread which are the braids of her hair (Edwards, 1991).

9 The sacred sexual rites engaged in by both men and women were enactments of the sacred marriage in which "human copulation was seen as the localized expression of the cosmic Heaven—Earth, the great fertility machine created by the gods, who were themselves the archetypal—and highly sexed—engenders of all that is" (Cahill 1998: 39). "Prostitutes" is the contemporary name given to women and men who engaged in ritual sex that honored the cycle of life and death.

10 Christianity was not a unified belief system until 325 CE when Constantine convened the Council of Nicea.

11 Sophia was also an important mythical figure for Jewish Gnostics, such as Philo, a Jewish-Hellenistic philosopher based in Alexandria (25 BCE–50 CE).

12 Sparta also educated its women but for the purposes of the state. Women from Lesbos, on the other hand, could find a measure of cultural education within Sappho's circle of women, women who voluntarily lived separate from men.

13 Another Greek woman of note was Aspasia of Miletus (5th century BCE) who came from what is now Turkey. She arrived from Turkey in Athens brilliantly educated. Aspasia could ignore the traditional enclosure of the female body. Her reputation as a rheterotician and philosopher was memorialized by Plato and Cicero. She clearly represented the intelligentsia of Periclean Athens (as well as being his lover).

14 Philo reconciled this tension by saying that God had two dimensions—his essence (*ousia*) which was beyond comprehension, and what he called powers or "energies" which represented his activities in the world.

15 These scholars include Elisabeth Schussler Fiorenza, Susanne Heine, Elaine Pagels, Rosemary Radford Ruether, Leonard Swidler, Ben Witherington III, and Carla Ricci.

16 Meister Eckhardt in his work *The Clouds of Unknowing* also exemplifies this type of epistemology.

Chapter 3

1 According to Colish (1997), Augustine maintained that mysticism provided only a temporary union with the divine. He saw that sustained contact with God was possible only through Christ, prayer, and the sacraments of the Church.
2 This was particularly the case in the work of St. Thomas Aquinas.
3 This shift had political as well as theological reasons. This was a period in which the Church was being increasingly criticized for its corruption and elitism. To counteract this, the focus on the human experience of Christ was seen as allowing the ordinary person a way to relate to the Church and find meaning.
4 Mysticism in this chapter is focused on Western forms. Mysticism is found in all major religions—Kabbalah (Judaism), Sufis (Islam), as well as Eastern forms of Zen and Buddhism. According to Karen Armstrong (1993), there are several characteristics that are shared by all mystical traditions—"it is a subjective experience that involves an interior journey, not a perception of an objective fact outside the self; it is undertaken through the image-making part of the mind—often called the imagination—rather than through the more cerebral, logical faculty" (p. 219).
5 Carolyn Bynum (1992) in fact suggests that medieval women religious did not develop a religious subculture motivated by the need to counter the stereotypes of women as fleshy, weak, irrational, and disorderly. She maintains this because women's religiosity overlapped with men's. In other words, both men and women shared mystical experiences, Eucharistic piety, and devotion to the human Christ. Thus, the behavior was not particularly gendered. She maintains that women religious were not motivated to elevate or redeem the female gender, but that these women theologians saw women as a symbol of humanity, where humanity was understood as physicality. She argues that because women are unable to propose their experience as dominant, they will quite naturally couch their perception in terms of "humanity" (p. 177).
6 Lerner (1993) suggests that these female figures have their roots in the ancient pre-Christian goddesses. Sophia is similar to the representation of the Hellenistic Sophia and the ancient Near Eastern Mother Goddess. Male and female medieval scholars alike drew on these figures, Lady Philosophy in Boethius' *Consolation*, Queen Sapientia in Prudentius' *Psychomachia*, and the learned bride in Martianus Capella's *On the Marriage of Philology and Mercury*.
7 She has had a reemergence and renaissance, particularly in Germany where her music, books, recipes, and health products are being sold. Her ecological worldview is one that speaks to many in contemporary society.
8 For Bernard, this also extends to our relationships with others; there is no knowledge of God without love of neighbor.
9 The majority of monasteries for women in Norfolk and Suffolk were founded in the mid to late 12th century, a time of great expansion of female monasticism in England (Gilchrist & Olivia, 1993).
10 The primary informal religious community was the Beguines. They flourished in the Low Countries in the late Middle Ages. The Beguines devoted themselves to caring for the sick and poor, combining prayer and personal austerity with social action in a way that made them attractive to the lower classes but a threat to the ecclesiastical establishment, whose wealth and too frequent unconcern they repudiated by word and example. Consequently, they were suspected of heresy and in the 14th century were fiercely persecuted on the continent.
11 Their daily lives were marked by a continual routine of prayer and meditation. Food and clothing were to be simple.

12 There was something of a revival of solitary life beginning in the 11ᵗʰ century. However, rather than isolate themselves totally from humanity, they removed themselves to solitary places in towns, being of the world but not in it.

13 The Lollards insisted that the rulers of the Catholic Church were overstepping the powers granted to them in the New Testament, thus barring men and women from experiencing the inner truth of the gospel.

14 Current theorizing, which suggests the body as a site of disciplining gender boundaries, must be set aside. Control of the body in medieval times was not the rejection of the physical or repression of sexuality but signaled the elevation of the body as the means of accessing the divine. For Foucault (1977), the body is ultimately the site of discipline and regulation. Yet, this only makes sense when the body is seen as something negative, something bad. For Julian and other mystics, the reclaiming of the body, through illness, enclosure, self-flagellation, and anorexia, is not punishment for being bad, but as a means to access the divine.

15 On one level this is no surprise. Female bodies were behaving as they were supposed to. For medieval thinkers, women were associated with the body. And the body signified the irrational, lust, emotion, weakness, while the mind signified male, reason, and strength. However, what we must consider is that these gender dichotomies (which we now associate with misogyny) take on different meanings within this historical context.

16 Medieval biologists thought that the mother blood fed the child in the womb and then, transmitted into breast milk, fed the baby outside the womb (Bynum, 1992: 214).

17 Traditionally, by feminists, the body is seen as a site of patriarchic oppression. Accordingly, it also becomes the potential focus of liberation. Liberation means control of the body by women, rather than men.

18 According to Cohen (1957), St. Teresa's autobiography is, after *Don Quixote*, the most widely read prose classic in Spain.

Chapter 4

1 Pizan's Muses, Reason, Rectitude, and Justice, reflect the emerging humanist understandings of education grounded in the analytical-referential discourse of modern science. This is in contrast to the ancient educational concepts of Nature, Art, and Practice which were promoted by Plato, Isocrates, and Plutarch. See Triche (2004) for further elaboration.

2 The feudal period is also marked by a different conception of education. As Craig Kridel (1979) maintains, "the feudal system of government, lead by its 'chivalrous warrior,' had disdain for the 'bookish learning' of the clerics, and viewed scholarship as an example of the "pen invading the sword" (p. 95).

3 This chapter will focus on the education of women. However, educating men to be men—in other words, to be subservient to the state—required strict discipline and was gendered through the use of the "rod." While not discussed here, see Pinar (2006) for his discussion of "enlightenment" pedagogies, especially those of Locke.

4 While "contract" is often understood as political or social category, Margaret Cavendish theorized the notion of passion as central to contract.

5 Some of these women included Judith Drake, Lady Mary Chudleigh, Lady Mary Wortley Montagu, and Elizabeth Elstob (Lerner, 1993).

6 I would maintain that this was not even a Renaissance for men. Given that social relations shifted to make men subordinate to the state, this also functioned as a site of colonization. How the formation of gender relations in the Renaissance disadvantaged both men and women is important to understand the profound impact this had on ideas regarding education.

7 While reason was emerging as the privileged way of knowing, and was used to construct women as "irrational" and emotional, the ideology of reason was not hegemonic.

Giambattista Vico, an 18th-century philosopher, was an anti-Cartesian thinker. According to Littleford (1979), Vico argued that while "rational processes, although of crucial importance for modern man, are secondary and derived; they originated from and must constantly return to the more primary processes of poetic imagination, intuition, and sensing" (p. 55). Thus, the concepts of reason/imagination were dependent on gender for their construction. The construction of man and woman along this dichotomy was central to the colonization of both men and women.

8 Merle Curti (1955) has called John Locke "America's Philosopher."

9 Brent Davis (2004) draws on Foucault to suggest that ironically it is during the "Enlightenment" that schools emerge as sites in which students are always under the watchful gaze of the teacher. The emphasis on surveillance is a tradition that continues to manifest itself in classrooms today through metaphors such as control, management, discipline, etc. Another extension of this discipline and surveillance occurred through school supervision. Ministries of education were formed in the modern nation-states to ensure that teachers were following the state-approved syllabi.

10 Wollstonecraft, after returning to London from Ireland, became a member of a "cosmopolitan London-based group which included Henry Fuseli, the Swiss Painter, Joseph Priestly, the famous chemist and radical in politics and theology, William Godwin, the political philosopher, the poet William Blake and Thomas Paine, the international patriot" (Brody, 2004: xvi).

11 Wollstonecraft argued much for the economic independence of women. The kind of skilled labor in which women had engaged during the late medieval and guilded age was now being done by machines. Women's traditional economic function was being displaced by a woman totally dependent on her husband.

12 *Letters on Education* was based in part on her earlier work *A Treatise on the Immutability of Moral Truth*, published in 1783, in which she articulates her metaphysical position on the nature of God and the correlation between God's nature and the nature of the human being. She maintains that both male and female have been created in the image of one deity. As a consequence, she does not talk about masculine or feminine but uses terms to describe attributes of both sexes. Wholeness or integration, rather than equality is the focus of her philosophy.

13 While I focus on the Quakers as an example of the Protestant Reformation, there were many sects or groups that formed—the English Congregationalists or Separatists, the Calvinists, the German Baptists (exemplified by Katherine Zell), the Dutch Anabaptists (exemplified by Elizabeth Dirk and martyr Elizabeth Munstdorp), the Huguenots, the French Prostestants (martyr Hellen Stirke).

14 Several women, including Anne Askew, who were Protestant reformers were burnt at the stake when their "rhetorical" strategies were not compelling to inquisitors.

15 In 16th-century England, the king's agents disbanded all religious communities of women.

16 And, although Protestant women did preach, their ministerial roles were closely scrutinized and in some cases sanctioned by death.

17 While the education would be universal, it would be differentiated. Class relations of the 17th century were reproduced within the convent through the designation of classes of nuns, including the choir and lay nuns.

18 This epistemological stance is ultimately the foundation of American education. As McKnight (2003) notes, these foundations have gone mostly unexcavated although they were implemented not only in every Puritan school, but also at the first American university, Harvard.

19 By caste system, I mean the stratification or grouping of students into remedial, special education, basic, regular, and gifted and talented. These groupings have become so normalized that they are seen as inevitable and not as a social construction. See Anyon (1983), Apple (1979), McNeil (1986), and Spring (2004) for an elaboration of this normalization.

20 I use the term the "tree of life" in contrast to the "tree of knowledge."

21 The debate over what constitutes literacy and for what purposes literacy is to be used continues today in the wars over phonics and whole language (Nelson, 1996).

22 French Catholic women were not alone in their vision of a "New Eden." Spanish colonizers also sought to reshape the world along more universalist lines. So Juana Ines de la Cruz (1648–1695) was the Creole daughter of Spanish man and native-born Spanish woman or Creole. Known as "the tenth muse" she became a nun and was a writer and educator. She taught adults through her poems, hymns, plays, and essays to question dominant norms for women and women's education in the New World.

23 Free People of Color (FPC) were the result of sexual relations among European settlers, African slaves, and Native Americans during the period of French rule in Louisiana (1718–1768). These relations resulted in a third race of people who were neither White nor Black and neither slave nor completely free (Martin, 2000).

24 The literacy rates and cultural achievements of FPC suggest a culture in which education was highly valued. The literary, artistic and educational achievements of this group refute dominant stereotypes of Blacks in the antebellum era (see Kein, 2000; Lowe, 2005). Their focus on education as a form of liberation as well as a means to contest the institution of slavery is often neglected in traditional curriculum histories of education.

25 Clearly, as mentioned throughout the chapter, there were male theorists who did not embody this distrust of women or relegate them to the margins of domesticity; however, their philosophies have also been excluded from the dominant narrative of history as a means to ensure the tidy story of "enlightenment."

Chapter 5

1 Several curriculum histories have presented alternative interpretations of progressivism which deconstruct the dominant narrative of this period as one of progress and inherently liberatory including Anderson (1988), Bowers (1987), Crocco, Munro, & Weiler (1999), Reese (1986), and Walkerdine (1990).

2 Ironically, research studies that relied on testing were used by feminists during this time to show that men and women did not differ in their mental endowments. Leta Hollingsworth, a student of Thorndike's at Teachers College, was at the forefront of this use of testing (Rosenberg, 2004).

3 For a further discussion of how the body, through physical education and sport, became a site of regulation for manliness, see Azzarito, Munro, & Solmon (2004).

4 This chapter will focus on the settlement house movement at the expense of the women's club movement, although the club movement was also an alternative site of education and to some degree sought to deconstruct social categories of race, class, and gender. For further insights into the role of women's clubs as reshaping society, see Crocco, Munro, & Weiler (1999), Salem (1990), and Woody (1929).

5 Focusing on two women is problematic because their work, ideas, and lives were shaped by a much larger network of activists. In Chicago this network included not only Addams and Wells, but also Margaret Haley (1861–1939), Catherine Goggin (1854–1916), and Ella Flagg Young (1845–1918). All five of these women articulated a central role for women educators in shaping society along more democratic lines. Haley and Goggin organized women teachers into a union (Chicago Teachers' Federation) and built community networks that bridged class and ethnic divisions, creating a strong infra-structure for the promotion of women's rights. Teachers in the Chicago Teachers' Federation (CTF), led by Haley and Goggin, allied in 1902 with the Chicago Federation of Labor as well as with the Illinois Women's Alliance. Young, a Chicago public school principal and educational administrator, worked to organize schools as model democracies in which women's work as teachers was central to social reform. Clearly,

Addams and Wells were not two lonely heroines. However, in order to provide a rich thick description and interpretation of their complex ideas regarding citizenship it is necessary to focus solely on their work.

6 Addams's focus on the "lived experience of every day life" is well articulated in her book *The Long Road of Woman's Memory* (1916).

7 Young (1995: 104) suggests that without conceptualizing women as a group in some sense, it is not possible to conceptualize oppression as a systematic, structured, institutional process.

8 Charlotte Perkins Gilman rejected suffrage, believing that equal relations between the sexes would emerge only when economic inequalities, such as women's use as domestic slaves, were redressed. Mary Ritter Beard, although an ardent suffragist, also questioned investing energy in a political reform that left the foundations of American society untouched and brought women into a political culture defined by men for men. Simple-minded slogans calling for equality, she insisted, denied the power and force of the moral community of women. The militant call for absolute equality, Beard believed, denied the existence and value of female culture.

9 Gerda Lerner (1993: 13) suggests that the "historiographic emphasis on the organized women's movement reflects traditional interest in organized political activity in the public realm."

10 J. Addams, *A Modern Lear: Jane Addams' Response to the Pullman Strike of 1894* (Chicago: University of Chicago Press, 1994), p. 20. The original response appeared in *Survey, 29* (November 2, 1912): 131–137.

11 Addams's sympathy with Marxist thought was evident in her support of the Russian Revolution. This support resulted in her labeling by the United States government as the "most dangerous woman" in America, as noted in Deegan (1990: 7).

12 In this regard, Addams differed dramatically from her contemporaries at the University of Chicago who relied on a "social-technological" analysis of social relations; see Deegan (1990).

13 Jill Conway suggests that the failure to see women's activism for what it is—a real departure from women's domesticity—indicates the controlling power of the stereotypes of the female temperament. These stereotypes continued, according to Conway, unaltered from the 1870s to the 1930s; see Conway (1971: 166).

14 Tolstoy was a continuing influence throughout Addams's life, as evidenced by her ongoing study of him through the 1930s, when she compared his ideas with those of Gandhi.

Chapter 6

1 Taken from Smith (1979: xii). *Chicago Record Herald*, December 22, 1913, p. 1.

2 Social efficiency as promoted by David Snedden believed that schools should "classify and train the children of the rank and file to meet the needs of society" (Ravitch, 2000: 82). According to Ravitch, the differentiation of curriculum required preparing students for various roles to meet society's needs and undermined equal access to a liberal arts curriculum that served to "equalize" education as well as provide a curriculum grounded in academic core subjects. Social efficiency thus undermined an "equal" and democratic education by advocating that the child's future occupation should define their education.

3 While there is not space in this particular chapter to develop the notion of the unique writing style of women pragmatists, I would argue that their writing was also a reflection of their pragmatist belief. For the most part the books and essays they wrote were reflections on their experiences and included autobiography as a primary genre for intellectual thought. This would be in line with a pragmatist understanding of research as reflection and beginning with experience rather than abstraction.

4 How educational historians define "progressivism" is varied and open to much debate. Ravitch (2000) maintains that progressive education was characterized by education professors who saw themselves as reformers of a deeply conservative field—one that focused on an elite, college preparatory, outdated academic curriculum—that needed to be liberated from tradition and guided by modern science. Progressivism led to a range of ideas and movements, including mental testing, child-centered, social efficiency, and social reconstructionsts. While quite diverse in their underlying assumptions, they represented "progress" in relation to the "traditional" college-bound curriculum that had dominated the 19th century. While all these movements could be considered "progressive," the designation has increasingly been understood to apply to the child-centered and social reconstructionist movements, whereas social efficiency and mental testing has been characterized as social engineering and even described as part of the eugenics movement (Winfield, 2007).

5 This quote is from a series of lectures delivered by James at the Lowell Institute in Boston in November and December, 1906, and in January, 1907, at Columbia University in New York. These lectures are collected in T. Crofts & P. Smith (1955) *William James: Pragmatism*, New York: Dover Publications.

6 See seminal texts such as R.B. Goodman (Ed.) (1995) *Pragmatism: A Contemporary Reader*, New York: Routledge, for histories of pragmatism that do not include any women philosophers.

7 In fact, Young led the campaign for women's suffrage in Illinois. In June 1913, she was pictured with Jane Addams and Julia Lathrop, two other Chicago social reformers, with a caption that read "Three reasons why Illinois women won the vote" (Smith & Smith, 1994: 307).

8 Seigfried (1996: 68) points out that in 1900 women students outnumbered men in the departments of philosophy (which included psychology and pedagogy), history, sociology, Greek, Latin, the modern languages, and English.

9 According to Crocco, Munro, and Weiler (1999), these schools had been deeply influenced by the settlement house movement.

10 C. Seeds (1934) "An Interpretation of the Integrated Program in the Elementary School." *California Journal of Elementary Education*, *3(2)*, 89–98; C. Seeds (1934) "Democratic Thinking and Living in the Classroom." *Educational Methods*, *14*, 57–63.

11 Mabel Carney has been another neglected woman pragmatist.

12 Ironically, this type of action research would reappear in the 1990s as a means to improve teacher education (see Connelly & Clandinin, 1988; Goodson, 1992; Schubert, 1991.

13 Taken from "A Rural School in Kentucky" by Elsie Ripley Clapp. *Progressive Education, 10* (March, 1933), 128.

14 Time will not permit me to include a whole section on the international pragmatist movement. However, some of the more familiar names would be Sylvia Ashton Warner, Maria Montessori, and Susan Fairhurst Brierly Isaacs (Hall, 2002).

15 There have been several critiques of Clapp's failure to address racial diversity. See Dan Perlstein, "Community and Democracy in American Schools: Arthurdale and the Fate of Progressive Education," *Teachers College Record* (Summer 1996), 625–650.

16 Wil Lou Gray was a graduate of Vanderbilt and also received her Masters degree from Columbia where she studied with progressive scholars, including James Harvey Robinson, Charles Beard, Frederick Jackson, and Carl Becker. Her studies at Columbia shaped her belief that history was a continuous human process and that knowledge should be made accessible to ordinary men and women. The Opportunity Schools were based on the pragmatist premise that all knowledge is constructed from experience. She drew on the experiences of the mill workers to shape her curriculum and moreover recognized that the problems of poverty and illiteracy are always grounded in the experiences of race, class, and gender.

17 Not only were Southern White women progressives situated differently due to their

class and race, but they were situated differently in regards to Northern Progressives. Fraser, Saunders, and Wakelyn (1985) maintain that Southern women had to confront the expectation that they were to be "ladies" and thus unfit for the rigors of public life, as well as having to be cautious around racial issues.

REFERENCES

Adams, T.D. (1990). *Telling lies in modern American autobiography*. Chapel Hill: University of North Carolina Press.

Addams, J. (1895). *Hull-House maps and papers: A presentation of nationalities and wages in a congested district of Chicago, together with comments and essays on problems growing out of social conditions*. New York: Thomas Y. Cromwell & Co.

Addams, J. (1902). *Democracy and social ethics*. New York: Macmillan.

Addams, J. (1909). *The spirit of youth*. New York: Macmillan.

Addams, J. (1910). *Twenty years at Hull-House*. New York: Macmillan.

Addams, J. (1911). *Newer ideals of peace*. New York: Macmillan.

Addams, J. (1916). *The long road of woman's memory*. New York: Macmillan.

Addams, J. (1930). *The second twenty years at Hull-House*. New York: Macmillan.

Anderson, B.S. & Zinsser, J.P. (1988). *A history of their own*. New York: Harper & Row.

Anderson, J. (1988). *Education of Blacks in the South, 1860–1935*. Chapel Hill: University of North Carolina Press.

Ankersmit, F.R. (1998). Historiography and postmodernism. In B. Fay, P. Pomper, & R.T. Vann (Eds.), *History and theory: Contemporary readings* (pp. 175–192). Malden, MA: Blackwell Press.

Antler, J. (1987). *Lucy Sprague Mitchell: The making of a modern woman*. New Haven, CT: Yale University Press.

Anyon, J. (1983). Intersections of gender and class: Accommodation and resistance by working class and affluent females to contradictory sex-role ideologies. In S. Walker & L. Barton (Eds.), *Gender, class and education*. Sussex, UK: Falmer Press.

Apple, M. (1979). *Ideology and curriculum*. London: Routledge & Kegan Paul.

Aptheker, B. (1977). *Lynching and rape: An exchange of views*. San Jose, CA: The American Institute of Marxist Studies.

Arendt, H. (1954). *Between past and future*. New York: Viking Press.

Armstrong, K. (1993). *A history of God: The 4,000-year quest of Judaism, Christianity and Islam*. New York: Ballantine Books.

Arnot, M. & Dillabough, J. (Eds.). (2000). *Challenging democracy*. London: Routledge.

Aronowitz, S. & Giroux, H. (1985). *Education under siege*. South Hadley, MA: Bergin & Garvey.

Asher, N. (2002). (En)gendering a hybrid consciousness. *Journal of Curriculum Theorizing, 18(4)*, 81–92.

Asher, N . (2005). At the interstices: Engaging postcolonial and feminist perspectives for a multicultural education pedagogy in the South. *Teachers College Record, 107(5)*, 1079–1106.

Asher, N. (2010). Decolonizing curriculum. In E. Malewski (Ed.), *Curriculum studies handbook: The next moment* (pp. 393–401). New York: Routledge.

Association of Early Childhood Education. (1972). *Dauntless women in education*. Washington, DC: Association of Childhood Education International.

Autio, T. (2009). From gnosticism to globalization: Rationality, trans-Atlantic curriculum discourse, and the problem of instrumentalism. In B. Baker (Ed.), *New curriculum history* (pp. 69–95). Rotterdam, The Netherlands: Sense Publishers.

Azzarito, L., Munro, P., & Solmon, M. (2004). Unsettling the body: The institution-alization of physical activity at the turn of the 20th century. *Quest, 56(4)*, 377–396.

Bailyn, B. (1960). *Education in the forming of American society*. Chapel Hill: University of North Carolina Press.

Baker, B. (1998). "Childhood" in the emergence and spread of U.S. public schools. In T. Popkewitz & M. Brennan (Eds.), *Foucault's challenge: Discourse, knowledge and power in education* (pp. 117–143). New York: Teachers College Press.

Baker, B. (2001). *In perpetual motion*. New York: Peter Lang.

Baker, B. (2009a). Borders, belonging, beyond: New curriculum history. In B. Baker (Ed.), *New curriculum histories* (pp. ix–xxxv). Rotterdam, The Netherlands: Sense Publishers.

Baker, B. (2009b). Western world-forming? Animal magnetism, curriculum history, and the social projects of modernity. In B. Baker (Ed.), *New curriculum histories* (pp. 25–68). Rotterdam, The Netherlands: Sense Publishers.

Baker, B. & Heyning, K. (2004). Dangerous coagulations? Research, education and a traveling Foucault. In B. Baker & K. Heyning (Eds.), *Dangerous coagulations: The uses of Foucault in the study of education* (pp. 1–84). New York: Peter Lang.

Baker, P. (1990). The domestication of politics: Women and American political society. In E.C. DuBois & L. Ruiz (Eds.), *Unequal sisters: A multicultural reader in U.S. women's history* (pp. 66–91). New York: Routledge.

Bauer, N. (1996). Abbess Hilda of Whitby: All Britain was lit by her splendor. In M. Schmitt & L. Kulzer (Eds.), *Medieval women monastics* (pp.13–33). Collegeville, MN: Liturgical Press.

Beale, H. (1975). The education of negroes before the Civil War. In. J. Barnard & D. Burner (Eds.), *The American experience in education* (pp. 85–97). New York: New Viewpoints.

Becker, C. (1935). *Everyman his own historian*. New York: Appleton-Century-Crofts.

Bederman, G. (1995a). *Manliness & civilization: A cultural history of gender and race in the United States, 1880–1917*. Chicago: University of Chicago Press.

Bederman, G. (1995b). "Civilization," the decline of middle-class manliness, and Ida B. Wells's antilynching campaign (1892–94). In D.C. Hine, W. King, & L. Reed (Eds.), *"We specialize in the wholly impossible": A reader in black women's history* (pp. 407–432). Brooklyn, NY: Carlson.

Beer, F. (1992). *Women and mystical experience in the Middle Ages*. Suffolk, UK: Boydell Press.

Berman, M. (2000). *Wandering God*. New York: SUNY Press.

Bernstein, B. (1975). *Class, codes and control*. London: Routledge & Kegan Paul.

Biesta, G. (1994). The identity of the body. In M.S. Katz (Ed.), *Philosophy of education*. (pp. 223–232). Urbana, IL: Philosophy of Education Society.

Block, A. (2004). *Talmud, curriculum and the practical*. New York: Peter Lang.

Bloom, L. (1998). The politics of difference and multicultural feminism: Reconceptualizing education for democracy. *Theory and Research in Social Education, 26*, 30–49.

Bloom, L. & Munro, P. (1995). Conflicts of selves: Non-unitary subjectivity in women administrators' life history narratives. In A. Hatch & R. Wisniewski (Eds.), *Life history and narrative* (pp. 99–113). London: Falmer Press.

Blount, J. (1998). *Destined to rule the schools: Women and the superintendency, 1873–1995.* New York: SUNY Press.

Bock, G. & James, S. (Eds.). (1992). *Beyond equality and difference: Citizenship, feminist politics, and female subjectivity.* London: Routledge.

Bordo, S. (1993). *Unbearable weight.* Los Angeles: University of California Press.

Bowen, L. (1913). *The colored people of Chicago.* Chicago: Juvenile Protective Association.

Bowers, C. (1987). *Elements of a post-liberal theory of education.* New York: Teachers College Press.

Bowles, S. & Gintis, H. (1976). *Schooling in capitalist America.* New York: Basic Books.

Britzman, D. (1998). *Lost subjects, contested objects.* New York: SUNY Press.

Brody, M. (Ed.). (2004). *Mary Wollstonecraft: A vindication of the rights of women.* London: Penguin Books.

Broudy, H. (1988). Aesthetics and curriculum. In W. Pinar (Ed.), *Contemporary curriculum discourses* (pp. 332–342). Scottsdale, AZ: Gorsuch Scarisbrick.

Brown, V.B. (1995). Jane Addams, progressivism, and woman suffrage. In M. Wheeler (Ed.), *One woman, one vote: Rediscovering the woman suffrage movement* (pp. 179–202). Troutdale, OR: Newsage Press.

Butler, J. (1990). *Gender trouble: Feminism and the subversion of identity.* New York: Routledge.

Butler, J. (1993). *Bodies that matter: On the discursive limits of "sex."* New York and London: Routledge.

Bynum, C. (1992). *Fragmentation and redemption: Essays on gender and the human body in medieval religion.* New York: Zone Books.

Cahill, T. (1998). *The gifts of the Jews: How a tribe of desert nomads changed the way everyone thinks and feels.* New York: Anchor Books.

Carr, E.H. (1962). *What is history?* London: Macmillan.

Cherryholmes, C. (1999). *Reading pragmatism.* New York: Teachers College Press.

Chomsky, N. (2007). *Failed states.* New York: Henry Holt.

Clapp, E.R. (1939). *Community schools in action.* New York: Viking.

Clapp, E.R. (1952). *The use of resources in education.* New York: Harper & Row.

Clark, E. (1997). "By all the conduct of their lives": A laywoman's confraternity in New Orleans, 1730–1744. *The William and Mary Quarterly, LIV(4)*, 769–794.

Clark, E. (1998). A new world community: The New Orleans Ursulines and colonial society, 1727–1803. Ph.D., Tulane University, New Orleans, LA.

Clark, E. (2007). *Masterless mistresses: The New Orleans Ursulines and the development of a new world society, 1727–1834.* Chapel Hill: University of North Carolina Press.

Clark, E. & Gould, V. (2002). The feminine face of Afro-Catholicism in New Orleans, 1727–1852. *The William and Mary Quarterly, 59(2)*, 409–448.

Clay, R.M. (1914). *The hermits and anchorites of England.* London: Methuen.

Clifford, G. (1989). Man/woman/teacher: Gender, family and career in American educational history. In D. Warren (Ed.), *American teachers: Histories of a profession at work* (pp. 293–343). New York: Macmillan.

Clifford, G. (1994). The quest for perfection: Case studies in the political lives of American women teachers. A paper presented at Indiana University, Bloomington.

Coburn, C. & Smith, M. (1999). *Spirited lives: How nuns shaped Catholic culture and American life, 1836–1920.* Chapel Hill: University of North Carolina Press.

Cohen, J.M. (Translator). (1957). *The life of St. Teresa of Avila by herself.* London: Penguin Books.

Cohen, S. (1999). *Challenging orthodoxies.* New York: Peter Lang.

Cole, E. & Coultrap-McQuin, S. (1992). *Explorations in feminist ethics.* Bloomington: Indiana University Press.

Colish, M.L. (1997). *Medieval foundations of the Western intellectual tradition.* New Haven, CT: Yale University Press.

Collins, G. (2003). *America's women.* New York: HarperCollins.

Connelly, F.M. & Clandinin, D.J. (1988). *Teachers as curriculum planners: Narratives of experience.* New York: Teachers College Press.

Conway, J.K. (1971). Women reformers and American culture, 1870–1930. *Journal of Social History, 5(2),* 164–177.

Cook, B. (1977). Female support networks and political activism: Lillian Wald, Crystal Eastman, Emma Goldman. *Chrysalis, 3,* 43–61.

Cooper, A.J. (1892). *A voice from the South.* Xenia, OH: Aldine Printing House.

Corbin, H. (Translated by N. Pearson). (1990). *Spiritual body and celestial earth: From Mazdean Iran to Shi'ite Iran.* London: I.B. Tauris.

Cormack, P. & Green, B. (2009). Re-reading the historical record: Curriculum history and the linguistic turn. In B. Baker (Ed.), *New curriculum histories* (pp. 223–236). Rotterdam, The Netherlands: Sense Publishers.

Counts, G.S. (1932). *Dare the schools build a new social order?* New York: John Day.

Cremin, L. (1961). *The transformation of the school.* New York: Alfred A. Knopf.

Crocco, M., Munro, P., & Weiler, K. (1999). *Pedagogies of resistance: Women educator activists, 1860–1960.* New York: Teachers College Press.

Cruz, C. & McClaren, P. (2002). Queer bodies and configurations: Toward a critical pedagogy of the body. In S. Shapiro & S. Shapiro (Eds.), *Body movements: Pedagogy, politics and social change* (pp. 187–208). Cresskill, NJ: Hampton Press.

Cubberley, E.P. (1909). *Changing conceptions of education.* Boston: Houghton Mifflin.

Curti, M. (1935). *The social ideas of American educators.* New York: Charles Scribner's Sons.

Curti, M. (1955*). Probing our past.* New York: Harper.

Dalai Lama (2005). *The universe in a single atom: The convergence of science and spirituality.* New York: Broadway Books.

Davis, A.D. (1967). *Spearheads for reform: The social settlements and the progressive movement, 1890–1914.* New York: Oxford University Press.

Davis, B. (2004). *Inventions of teaching: A genealogy.* Mahwah, NJ: Lawrence Erlbaum.

Davis, N. (1965). City women and religious change. In N. Davis (Ed.), *Society and culture in early modern France* (pp. 65–96). Stanford, CA: Stanford University Press.

de Pizan, C. (Translated by Earl Jeffrey Richards). (1405 [1982]). *The book of the city of ladies.* New York: Persea Books.

Deegan, M. (1990). *Jane Addams and the men of the Chicago School, 1892–1918.* New Brunswick, Canada: Transaction Books.

Deleuze, G. & Guattari, F. (1987). *A thousand plateaus.* Minneapolis: University of Minnesota Press.

Dewey, J. (1894). John Dewey to Alice Chipman Dewey, October 9. John Dewey Papers.

Dewey, J. (1900). *School and society.* Chicago: University of Chicago Press.

Dewey, J. (1916). *Democracy and education.* New York: Macmillan.

Dewey. J. (1928). Progressive education and the science of education. *Progressive Education, 5(3)*, 197–294.

Dewey, J. (1929). *The sources of a science of education*. New York: Horace Liveright.

Dewey, J. and Dewey, E. (1915). *Schools of to-morrow*. New York: E.P. Dutton.

Dieker, A. (1996). Mechthild of Hackeborn: Song of love. In M. Schmitt & L. Kulzer (Eds.), *Medieval women monastics: Wisdom's wellsprings* (pp. 231–244). Collegeville, MN: Liturgical Press.

Doll, M. (2000). *Like letters in running water: A mythopoetics of curriculum*. Mahwah, NJ: Lawrence Erlbaum.

Doll, W.E. (1993). *A post-modern perspective on curriculum*. New York: Teachers College Press.

Doll, W.E. (2002). Ghosts and the curriculum. In W.E. Doll & N. Gough (Eds.), *Curriculum visions* (pp. 23–70). New York: Peter Lang.

Doll. W.E. (2005). The culture of method. In W.E. Doll, J.M. Fleener, D. Trueit, & J. St. Julien (Eds.), *Chaos, complexity, curriculum and culture* (pp. 21–76). New York: Peter Lang.

Douglas, M. (1999). *Leviticus as literature*. Oxford: Oxford University Press.

Dronke, P. (1984). *Women writers of the Middle Ages*. Cambridge: Cambridge University Press.

Duster, A. (1970). *Crusade for justice: The autobiography of Ida B. Wells*. Chicago: University of Chicago Press.

Edwards, C.M. (1991). *The storyteller's goddess*. San Francisco: HarperCollins.

Egea-Kuehne, D. (2006). The humanities and Serre's "new organization of knowledge." *International Journal of the Humanities, 3(3)*, 131–138.

Eisenstein, Z.R. (1994). *The color of gender: Reimaging democracy*. Berkeley: University of California Press.

Eisler, R. (1988). *The chalice and the blade*. San Francisco: HarperCollins.

Elshtain, J. (2002). *Jane Addams and the dream of American democracy*. New York: Basic Books.

Emerson, R.W. (1995). Circles. In R. Goodman (Ed.), *A contemporary reader* (pp. 25–33). New York: Routledge.

Engels, F. (Ed. E. Leacock). (1884 [1972]). *The origin of the family, private property, and the state*. New York: International Publishers.

Eppert, C. (2007). Fear, fictions of character and Buddhist insights. In C. Eppert & H. Wang (Eds.), *Cross-cultural studies in curriculum: Eastern thought, educational insights* (pp. 55–109). Mahwah, NJ: Lawrence Erlbaum.

Fanon, F. (1967). *Black skin, white masks*. New York: Grove Weidenfeld.

Farrell, J.C. (1967). *Beloved lady: A history of Jane Addams' ideas on reform and peace*. Baltimore, MD: Johns Hopkins University Press.

Fell, M. (1667). *Women's speaking justified, proved and allowed by scripture*. London.

Felman, S. (1992). Education and crisis, or the vicissitudes of teaching. In S. Felman & D. Laub (Eds.), *Testimony: Crisis of witnessing in literature, psychoanalysis, and history* (pp. 1–56). New York: Routledge.

Field, S. (1999). Lucy Sprague Mitchell: Teacher, geographer, and teacher educator. In M. Crocco & O.L. Davis (Eds.), *"Bending the future to their will": Civic women, social education and democracy* (pp. 125–148). Lanham, MD: Rowman & Littlefield.

Fiorenza, E.S. (1983). *In memory of her: A feminist theological reconstruction of Christian origins*. New York: Crossroads.

Flax, J. (1990). *Thinking fragments: Psychoanalysis, feminism, and postmodernism in the contemporary west*. Berkeley: University of California Press.

Fleener, J. (2005). Chaos, complexity, curriculum and culture: Setting up the conversation. In W.E. Doll, J.M. Fleener, D. Trueit, & J. St. Julien (Eds.), *Chaos, complexity, curriculum and culture* (pp. 1–20). New York: Peter Lang.

Flinders, C.L. (1993). *Enduring grace: Living portraits of seven women mystics*. San Francisco: HarperCollins.

Foster, S. (1997). Red alert!: The National Education Association confronts the "red scare" in American public schools, 1947–1954. Paper presented at the Annual Conference of the American Educational Research Association, Chicago. March.

Foucault, M. (Ed. D.F. Bouchard). (1977). *Language, counter-memory, practice*. Ithaca, NY: Cornell University Press.

Foucault, M. (1980). *Power/knowledge: Selected interviews and other writings, 1972–77*. New York: Pantheon.

Fraser, N. (1996). Equality, difference, and radical democracy. In E. Trend (Ed.), *Radical democracy: Identity, citizenship, and the state*. New York: Routledge.

Fraser, W., Saunders, R., & Wakelyn, J. (1985). *The web of Southern social relations: Women, family, and education*. Athens: University of Georgia Press.

Freeman, M. (1993). *Rewriting the self: History, memory, narrative*. New York: Routledge.

Friedman, S. (1995). Making history: Reflections on feminism, narrative and desire. In D. Elam & R. Weigman (Eds.), *Feminism beside itself* (pp. 11–53). New York: Routledge.

Garrison, J. (1997). *Dewey and Eros: Wisdom and desire in the art of teaching*. New York: Teachers College Press.

Gawronski, R. (1995). *Word and silence: Hans Urs von Balthasar and the spiritual encounter between East and West*. Grand Rapids, MI: William B. Eerdmans.

Gilchrist, R. & Olivia, M. (1993). *Religious women in medieval East Anglia: History and archaeology c. 1110–1540*. Norwich, UK: University of East Anglia, Centre of East Anglian Studies.

Gilmore, L. (1994). *Autobiographic: A feminist theory of women's representation*. Ithaca, NY: Cornell University Press.

Gimbutas, M. (1991). *The civilization of the goddess*. San Francisco: HarperCollins.

Giroux. H.A. (1983). *Theory and resistance in education*. South Hadley, MA: Bergin & Garvey.

Glenn, C. (1997). *Rhetoric retold*. Carbondale: Southern Illinois University Press.

Goodman, J. (1995). Change without difference: School restructuring in historical perspective. *Harvard Educational Review, 65(1)*, 1–29.

Goodson, I. (Ed.). (1992). *Studying teachers' lives*. New York: Teachers College Press.

Goodson, I. (1997). *The changing curriculum*. New York: Peter Lang.

Gordon, L. (1990). *Gender and higher education in the progressive era*. New Haven, CT: Yale University Press.

Graham, P. (1967). *Progressive education: From Arcady to Academe*. New York: Teachers College Press.

Greene, G. (1993). Looking at history. In G. Greene & C. Kahn (Eds.), *Changing subjects: The making of feminist literary criticism*. London: Routledge.

Griffin, P. (1998). *Strong women, deep closets. Lesbians and homophobia in sport*. Champaign, IL: Human Kinetics.

Grumet, M. (1988). *Bitter milk*. Amherst: University of Massachusetts Press.

Guillory, N. (2010). (A) Troubling curriculum: Public pedagogies of black women rappers. In E. Malewski (Ed.), *Curriculum studies handbook* (pp. 209–222). New York: Routledge.

Gusfield, J.R. (1986). *Symbolic crusade: Status politics and the American temperance movement*. Urbana: University of Illinois Press.

Hall, G.M. (2005). Historical memory, consciousness, and conscience. In B.G. Bond (Ed.), *French colonial Louisiana and the Atlantic world* (pp. 291–310). Baton Rouge: Louisiana State University Press.

Hall, J. (2002). From Susan Isaacs to Lilian Weber and Deborah Meier: A progressive legacy in England and the United States. In A. Sadovnik & S. Semel (Eds.), *Founding mothers and others* (pp. 237–252). New York: Palgrave.

Hardt, M. & Negri, A. (2004). *Multitude: War and democracy in the age of empire*. New York: Penguin Books.

Harris, T. (1991). *Selected works of Ida B. Wells-Barnett*. New York: Oxford University Press.

Hartsock, N. (1990). Foucault on power: A theory for women? In L. Nicholson (Ed.), *Feminism/postmodernism* (pp. 157–175). New York: Routledge.

Haskins, S. (1993). *Mary Magdalen: Myth and metaphor*. New York: Harcourt Brace & Company.

Hauser, M. (2002). Caroline Pratt and the city and country schools. In A. Sadovnik & S. Semel (Eds.), *Founding mothers and others* (pp. 61–76). New York: Palgrave.

Held, V. (2005). *The ethics of care: Personal, political and global*. New York: Oxford University Press.

Hendry, P. (2005). Disrupting the subject: Julian of Norwich and embodied knowing. *Journal of Curriculum Theorizing, 21(1)*, 95–108.

Hendry, P. (2007). Engendering wisdom: Listening to Kuan Yin and Julian of Norwich. In C. Eppert and H. Wang (Eds.), *Cross-cultural studies in curriculum: Eastern thought, educational insights* (pp. 207–227). New York: Lawrence Erlbaum.

Hendry, P. (2008). Learning from Caroline Pratt. *Journal of the Advancement of Curriculum Studies, 4*, 1–16.

Hendry, P. (2010). Narrative as inquiry. *The Journal of Educational Research, 103(2)*, 72–80.

Hendry, P. (in press). Problems of memory, history and social change: The case of Jane Addams. In D. Schafsma (Ed.), *The Jane Addams reader*. New York: Teachers College Press.

Heschel, A.J. (1959). *Between God and man: An interpretation of Judaism*. New York: Free Press.

Hinitz, B. (2002). Margaret Naumberg and the Walden School. In A. Sadovnik & S. Semel (Eds.), *Founding mothers and others* (pp. 37–60). New York: Palgrave.

Hlebowitsh, P. and Wraga, W. (1995). Social class analysis in the early progressive tradition. *Curriculum Inquiry, 25(1)*, 7–21.

Huebner, D. (1975). Curriculum as concerns for man's temporality. In W.F. Pinar (Ed.), *Curriculum studies: The reconceptualization* (pp. 318–331). Berkeley, CA: McCutchan Publishing.

Huebner, D. (1999). Education and spirituality. In V. Hillis (Ed.), *The lure of the transcendent*. Hillsdale, NJ: Lawrence Erlbaum.

Jaggar, A. (1989). Love and knowledge: Emotion in feminist epistemology. In A. Jaggar & S. Bordo (Eds.), *Gender/body/knowledge: Feminist reconstructions of being and knowing*. New Brunswick, NJ and London: Rutgers University Press.

Jambet, C. (1983). *La Logique des Orientaux*. Paris: Editions du Seuil.

James, W. (1902 [1982]). *The varieties of religious experience*. London: Penguin Classics.

James, W. (1907 [1995]). *Pragmatism*. New York: Dover Publications.

Jameson, F. (1981). *The political unconscious: Narrative as a socially symbolic act*. Ithaca, NY: Cornell University Press.

Jantzen, G.M. (1995). *Power, gender, and Christian mysticism*. Cambridge: Cambridge University Press.

Jaramillo, N. (2010). Response to Nichole A. Guillory: The politics of patriarchal discourse: A feminist rap. In E. Malewski (Ed.), *Curriculum studies handbook* (pp. 223–227). New York: Routledge.

Jardine, L. (1999). Woman humanists: Education for what? In L. Huston (Ed.), *Feminism and Renaissance studies* (pp. 48–81). Oxford: Oxford University Press.

Johnson, M. (1938 [1974]). *Thirty years with an idea*. Tuscaloosa: University of Alabama Press.

Juster, S. (1994). *Disorderly women: Sexual politics and Evangelicalism in revolutionary New England*. Ithaca, NY: Cornell University Press.

Kaestle, C. (1983). *Pillars of the republic*. New York: Hill & Wang.

Kasson, J.F. (2001). *Houdini, Tarzan and the perfect man: The white male body and the challenge of modernity in America*. New York: Hill & Wang.

Katz, M. (1968). *The irony of school reform*. Cambridge, MA: Harvard University Press.

Kein, S. (Ed.). (2000). *Creole: The history and legacy of Louisiana's free people of color*. Baton Rouge: LSU Press.

Kelly, G. (1993). *Women, writing and revolution, 1790–1827*. Oxford: Clarendon Press.

Kelly, J. (1984). *Women, history, theory*. Chicago: University of Chicago Press.

Kelly, J. (1999). Did women have a renaissance? In L. Hutson (Ed.), *Feminism and renaissance studies* (pp. 21–47). Oxford: Oxford University Press.

Kerber, L. (1980). *Women of the republic: Intellect and ideology in revolutionary America*. Chapel Hill: University of North Carolina Press.

Kerber, L. (1983). *The impact of women on American education*. U.S. Department of Education, Women's Educational Equity Act Program. Newton, MA: WEEA Publishing Center.

Khayatt, M. (1992). *Lesbian teachers: An invisible presence*. New York: SUNY Press.

Kimmel, M.S. (1996). *Manhood in America: A cultural history*. New York: Free Press.

King, K. (2003). *The gospel of Mary of Magdala: Jesus and the first woman apostle*. Santa Rosa, CA: Polebridge Press.

Kliebard, H. (1986). *The struggle for the American curriculum: 1890–1958*. London and Boston: Routledge & Kegan Paul.

Kliebard, H. (1992a). Constructing a history of the American curriculum. In P. Jackson (Ed.), *Handbook of curriculum research* (pp. 157–184). New York: Macmillan.

Kliebard, H. (1992b). *Forging the American curriculum: Essays in curriculum history and theory*. New York: Routledge.

Kliebard, H. (1995). *The struggle for American curriculum*. New York: Routledge.

Knight, L. (2005). *Citizen: Jane Addams and the struggle for democracy*. Chicago: University of Chicago Press.

Knupfer, A.M. (1996). *Toward a tenderer humanity and a nobler womanhood*. New York: New York University Press.

Kohli, W. & Munro, P. (1995). Poststructural interrogations and interrogating poststructuralism: Two feminist tales. Paper presented at the annual Conference of Curriculum Theorizing, Sewanee, TN, October.

Kridel, C. (1979). Castiglione and Elyot: Early curriculum theorists. *Journal of Curriculum Theorizing, 1(2)*, 89–99.

Kridel, C. & Bullough, R. (2007). *Stories of the eight-year study*. New York: SUNY Press.

Krug, E.A. (1964). *The shaping of the American high school*. New York: Harper & Row.

Lagemann, E. (1985). *Jane Addams on education*. New York: Oxford University Press.

Lagemann, E. (1989). The plural worlds of educational research. *History of Education Quarterly, 29(2)*, 185–214.

Lagemann, E. (2000). *An elusive science: The troubling history of education research.* Chicago: University of Chicago Press.

Landes, J. (1988). *Women and the public sphere in the age of the French Revolution.* Ithaca, NY: Cornell University Press.

Lao Tzu (Translated by Victor H. Mair). (1990). *Tao te ching.* New York: Bantam Books.

LaPlante, E. (2004). *American Jezebel: The uncommon life of Anne Hutchinson, the woman who defied the Puritans.* San Francisco: HarperCollins.

Larabee, D. (2010). How Dewey lost: The victory of David Snedden and social efficiency in the reform of American education. Revised version of a paper presented at the conference on "Pragmatism as the Reticle of Modernization: Concepts, Contexts, Critiques," Centro Stefano Fanscini, Monte Verita, Ascona, Switzerland, September, 2008.

Lasch-Quinn, E. (1993). *Black neighbors: Race and the limits of reform in the American settlement house movement, 1890–1945.* Chapel Hill: University of North Carolina Press.

Laslett, B., Brenner, J., & Arat, Y. (1995). *Rethinking the political: Gender, resistance, and the state.* Chicago: University of Chicago Press.

Lather, P. (1991). *Getting smart: Feminist research and pedagogy within the postmodern.* New York: Routledge.

Leloup, J. (2002). *The gospel of Mary Magdalene.* Rochester, VT: Inner Traditions.

Lemert, C. & Bhan, E. (1998). *The voice of Anna Julia Cooper.* Lanham, MD: Rowman & Littlefield.

Lerner, G. (1986). *The creation of patriarchy.* Oxford: Oxford University Press.

Lerner, G. (1993). *The creation of a feminist consciousness.* New York: Oxford University Press.

Lesko, N. (1998). A phenomenological reflection on Maxine Greene's pedagogy. In W. Pinar (Ed.), *The passionate mind of Maxine Greene* (pp. 238–246). Bristol, PA: Falmer Press.

Lewis, D. (Translator). (1997). *The life of St. Teresa of Jesus written by herself.* Rockford, IL: Tan Books and Publishers.

Linde, C. (1993). *Life stories: The creation of coherence.* New York: Oxford University Press.

Lissak, R.S. (1989). *Pluralism & progressives: Hull House and the new immigrants,* Chicago: University of Chicago Press.

Littleford, M. (1979). Vico and curriculum studies. *Journal of Curriculum Theorizing, 1(2),* 54–64.

Long, T. (1995). Julian of Norwich's "Christ as Mother" and medieval constructions of gender. Paper presented at the Madison Conference on English Studies, James Madison University, Harrisonburg, Virginia.

Lowe, J. (Ed.). (2005). *Bridging southern cultures.* Baton Rouge: LSU Press.

MacIntyre, A. (1984). *After virtue: A study in the oral theory.* Notre Dame, IN: University of Notre Dame Press.

Macrine, S. (2002). Pedagogical bondage: Body bound and gagged in a techno-rational world. In S. Shapiro & S. Shapiro (Eds.), *Body movements: Pedagogy, politics and social change* (pp. 133–146). Cresskill, NJ: Hampton Press.

Maher, F. (2001). John Dewey, progressive education and feminist pedagogies: Issues in gender and authority. In K. Weiler (Ed.), *Feminist engagements* (pp. 13–32). New York: Routledge.

Margolis, J. (1993). *The flux of history and the flux of science.* Berkeley: University of California Press.

Marshall, J.D. (1995). Putting the political back into autonomy. In W. Kohli (Ed.), *Critical conversations in philosophy of education* (pp. 364–378). New York: Routledge.

Martin, J. (2000). *Placage* and the Louisiana *Gens de Couleur Libre*. In S. Kein (Ed.), *Creole* (pp. 57–70). Baton Rouge: LSU Press.

Martin, J. & Goodman, J. (2004). *Women and education, 1800–1980*. New York: Palgrave.

Martin, J.R. (1985). *Reclaiming a conversation*. New Haven, CT: Yale University Press.

Martin, W. (1986). *Recent theories of narrative*. Ithaca, NY: Cornell University Press.

McCarthy, C. (1998). The uses of culture: Canon formation, postcolonial literature, and the multicultural project. In W.F. Pinar (Ed.), *Curriculum: Toward new identities* (pp. 253–263). New York: Garland Publishers.

McKnight, D. (2003). *Schooling, the Puritan imperative, and the molding of an American national identity: Education's "errand in the wilderness."* Hillsdale, NJ: Lawrence Erlbaum.

McManis, J. (1916). *Ella Flagg Young and a half-century of the Chicago public schools*. Chicago: A.C. McCluurg & Co.

McNeil, L. (1986). *Contradictions of control*. London: Routledge & Kegan Paul.

Mead, G.H. (1914). A heckling school board and an educational stateswoman. *Survey, 31*, 443–444.

Medwick, C. (1999). *Teresa of Avila: The progress of a soul*. New York: Alfred A. Knopf.

Menand, L. (2001). *The metaphysical club*. New York: Farrar, Straus & Giroux.

Merton, T. (1968). *Zen and the birds of appetite*. New York: New Directions Books.

Miller, D. (1997). *City of the century*. New York: Touchstone.

Mills, C.W. (1964). *Sociology and pragmatism*. New York: Paine-Whitman.

Minh-ha, T. (1991). *When the moon waxes red*. New York: Routledge.

Mitchell, L.S. (1953). *Two lives: The story of Wesley Clair Mitchell and myself*. New York: Simon & Schuster.

Moi, T. (1986). *The Kristeva reader*. New York: Columbia University Press.

Moore, D.W. (1986) Laura Zirbes and progressive reading instruction. *The Elementary School Journal, 86(5)*, 663–672.

Morris, M. (2008). *Teaching through the ill body*. Rotterdam, The Netherlands: Sense Publishers.

Mouffe, C. (1995). Feminism, citizenship, and radical democratic politics. In L. Nicholson & S. Seidman (Eds.), *Social postmodernism: Beyond identity politics*. Cambridge: Cambridge University Press.

Munro, P. (1995a). Educators as activists: Five women from Chicago. *Social Education, 59(5)*, 274–278.

Munro, P. (1995b). Speculations: Negotiating a feminist supervision identity In J. Jipson, P. Munro, S. Victor, K. Froude Jones, & G. Freed-Rowland, *Repositioning feminism and education: Perspectives on educating for social change* (pp. 97–114). Westport, CT: Bergin & Garvey.

Munro, P. (1995c). "Widening the circle": Jane Addams, gender and the definition of social education. A paper presented at the National Council for the Social Studies. Chicago.

Munro, P. (1998a). Resisting resistance: Stories women teachers tell. *Journal of Curriculum Theorizing, 12(1)*, 16–28.

Munro, P. (1998b). *Subject to fiction: Women teachers' life history narratives and the cultural politics of resistance*. Buckingham, UK: Open University Press.

Munro, P. (1999). "Widening the circle": Jane Addams, gender and the re/definition of democracy. In M. Crocco & O.L. Davis (Eds.), *"Bending the future to their will": Civic women, social education and democracy* (pp. 73–92). Boulder, CO: Rowman & Littlefield.

Murphy, M. (1990). *Blackboard Unions: The AFT and the NEA, 1900–1980*. Ithaca, NY: Cornell University Press.

Murray, J.S. (1798). *The Gleaner* (3 vols.). Boston, MA.

Nelms, W. (1997). *Cora Wilson Stewart: Crusader against illiteracy*. Hillsborough, NC: McFarland Press.

Nelson, N. (1996). *The constructivist metaphor: Reading, writing, and the making of meaning*. New York: Academic Press.

Newman B. (1987). *Sister of Wisdom: St. Hildegard's theology of the feminine*. Berkeley: University of California Press.

Newman, J.W. (2002). Marietta Johnson and the Organic School. In A. Sadovnik & S. Semel (Eds.), *Founding mothers and others: Women educational leaders during the Progressive era* (pp. 19–36). New York: Palgrave.

Ng-a-fook, N. (2006). *An indigenous curriculum of place*. New York: Peter Lang.

Noddings, N. (1992). Social studies and feminism. *Theory and Research in Social Education, XX(3)*, 230–241.

Noddings, N. (2002). *Starting at home: Caring and social policy*. Berkeley: University of California Press.

Oden, A. (1994). *In her words: Women's writing in the history of Christian thought*. Nashville, TN: Abingdon Press.

Okin, S. (1989). *Justice, gender and the family*. New York: Basic Books.

Ong, W. (1982). *Orality and literacy*. London: Methuen.

Oram, A. (1989). Embittered, sexless or homosexual: Attacks on spinster teachers 1918–1939. In G. Angerman, A. Bennema, V. Keunen, V. Pucls, & J. ZirkZee (Eds.), *Current issues in woman's history* (pp. 183–202). London: Routledge.

Orner, M. (2002). Working up our appetites: Pedagogical encounters and the relentless pursuit of thinness. In S. Shapiro & S. Shapiro (Eds.), *Body movements: Pedagogy, politics and social change* (pp. 265–282). Cresskill, NJ: Hampton Press.

Paddle, S. (1995). Writing against the clock: Theorizing current feminist histories. *Melbourne Studies in Education, 29(1)*, 1–11.

Pagano, J. (1990). *Exiles and communities: Teaching in the patriarchal wilderness*. Albany: SUNY Press.

Pagels, E. (1979). *The gnostic gospels*. New York: Vintage Books.

Pagels, E. (2003). *Beyond belief: The secret gospel of Thomas*. New York: Random House.

Pateman, C. (1992). Equality, difference, subordination: The politics of motherhood and women's citizenship. In G. Bock & S. James (Eds.), *Beyond equality and difference*. London: Routledge.

Perry, T., Steele, C., & Hilliard III, A. (2003). *Young, gifted and black*. Boston: Beacon Press.

Petroff, E.A. (1994). *Body and soul: Essays on medieval women and mysticism*. New York: Oxford University Press.

Pinar, W.F. (1983). Curriculum as gender text: Notes on reproduction, resistance and male–male relations. *Journal of Curriculum Theorizing, 5(1)*, 26–52.

Pinar, W.F. (2001). *The gender of racial politics and violence in America*. New York: Peter Lang.

Pinar, W.F. (2002). The medicated body: Drugs and dasein. In S. Shapiro & S. Shapiro (Eds.), *Body movement: Pedagogy, politics and social change* (pp. 283–316). Cresskill, NJ: Hampton Press.

Pinar, W.F. (2006). *The synoptic test today and other essays: Curriculum development after the reconceptualization*. New York: Peter Lang.

Pinar, W.F. (2009). *The worldliness of a cosmopolitan education: Passionate lives in public service*. New York: Routledge.

Pinar, W.F., Reynolds, W., Slattery, P., & Taubman, P. (1995). *Understanding curriculum*. New York: Peter Lang.

Plaskow, J. & Christ, C. (Eds.), (1989). *Weaving the visions: New patterns in female spirituality.* San Francisco: HarperCollins.

Polakow, V. (1993). *Lives on the edge: Single mothers and their children in the other America.* Chicago: University of Chicago Press.

Polkinghorne, D. (1988). *Narrative knowing and the human sciences.* Albany: SUNY Press.

Popkewitz, T. & Brennan, M. (1998). Restructuring of social and political theory in education: Foucault and a social epistemology of school practices. In T. Popkewitz & M. Brennan (Eds.), *Foucault's challenge: Discourse, knowledge and power in education* (pp. 3–38). New York: Teachers College Press.

Popper, K. (1958). *The poverty of historicism.* London: Routledge.

Popular Memory Group. (1992). Popular memory: Theory, politics, method. In R. Johnson, G. McLennan, B. Schwarz, & D. Sutton (Eds.), *Making histories* (pp. 205–252). Minneapolis: University of Minnesota Press.

Porche-Frilot, D. (2006*). Propelled by faith: Henriette Delille and the literary practices of Black women religious in antebellum New Orleans.* Baton Rouge: LSU Press.

Porche-Frilot, D. & Hendry, P.M. (2010). "Whatever diversity of shade may appear": Catholic women religious educators in Louisiana, 1727–1862. *Catholic Southwest: A Journal of History and Culture, 21,* 34–62.

Portelli, A. (1991). *The death of Luigi Trastulli and other stories.* Albany: SUNY Press.

Pratt, C. (1948). *I learn from children.* New York: Harper & Row.

Prawat, R.S. (1995). Misreading Dewey: Reform, projects, and the language game. *Educational Researcher, 24(7),* 13–22.

Prentice, A. & Theobald, M. (1991). *Women who taught: Perspectives on the history of women and teaching.* Toronto: University of Toronto Press.

Procknow, H. (2007). Nietzsche and education: Giving birth as a condition of teaching. In P. Garramone (Chair), *The curriculum and the presence of the body.* Session conducted at the American Educational Research Association Conference, Chicago, April.

Putnam, J. (1996). Mechthild of Magdeburg: Poet and mystic. In M. Schmitt & L. Kulzer (Eds.), *Medieval women monastics: Wisdom's wellsprings* (pp. 271–230). Collegeville, MN: Liturgical Press.

Quinn, M. (2001). *Going out, not knowing whither.* New York: Peter Lang.

Rapley, E. (1990). *The Devotes: Women and church in seventeenth-century France.* Montreal: McGill-Queen's University Press.

Ravitch, D. (1974). *The great school wars: New York City, 1805–1973.* New York: Basic Books.

Ravitch, D. (2000). *Left back: A century of battles over school reform.* New York: Simon & Schuster.

Reese, W.J. (1986). *Power and the promise of school reform: Grassroots movements during the progressive era.* Boston: Routledge & Kegan Paul.

Reid, R.L. (1982). *Battleground: The autobiography of Margaret Haley.* Urbana: University of Illinois Press.

Reid, T. (1993). Toward creative teaching: The life and career of Laura Zirbes. Columbia: University of South Carolina, College of Education, unpublished doctoral dissertation.

Reynolds, K.C. (2002). Charlotte Hawkins Brown and the Palmer Institute. In A. Sadovnik & S. Semel (Eds.), *Founding mothers and others.* Basingstoke, UK: Palgrave Macmillan.

Reynolds, K.C. & Schramm, S.L. (2002). *Separate sisterhood: Women who shaped southern education in the progressive era.* New York: Peter Lang.

Ricoeur, P. (1976). *Interpretation theory: Discourse and the surplus of meaning.* Fort Worth: Texas Christian University Press.

Riley, D. (1989). *"Am I that name?": Feminism and the category of women in history.* Champaign: University of Illinois Press.

Robenstine, C. (1992). French colonial policy and the education of women and minorities: Louisiana in the early eighteenth century. *History of Education Quarterly, 32(2)*, 193–211.

Roelker, N. (1972). The appeal of Calvinism to French noblewomen in the sixteenth century. *Journal of Interdisciplinary History, 2*, 391–418.

Rorty, R. (1991). *Essays on Heidegger and others: Philosophical papers, Vol. II.* Cambridge: Cambridge University Press.

Rosaldo, M. & Lamphere, L. (1974). *Women, culture and society.* Palo Alto, CA: Stanford University Press.

Rosenberg, R. (2004). *Changing the subject.* New York: Columbia University Press.

Rousmaniere, K. (2005). *Citizen teacher: The life and leadership of Margaret Haley.* New York: SUNY Press.

Rudnick, L. (1991). A feminist American success myth: Jane Addams's twenty years at Hull House. In F. Howe (Ed.), *Tradition and talents in women* (pp. 145–167). Urbana: University of Illinois Press.

Ruether, R. (2005). *Goddesses and the divine feminine: A Western religious history.* Berkeley: University of California Press.

Ryan, M. (1979). *Womanhood in America.* New York: New Viewpoints.

Said, E. (1989). Representing the colonized. *Critical Inquiry, 15*, 205–225.

Salem, D. (1990). *To better our world: Black women in organized reform, 1890–1920.* New York: Carlson Publishing.

Salu, M.B. (1955). *The ancrene riwle.* Exeter, UK: University of Exeter Press.

Salverson, J. (2000). Anxiety and contact in attending to a play about land mines. In R. Simon, S. Rosenberg, & C. Eppert (Eds.), *Between hope and despair.* Lanham, MD: Rowman & Littlefield.

Sawyer, D. (1996). *Women and religion in the first Christian centuries.* London: Routledge.

Schechter, P.A. (1998). "All the intensity of my nature": Ida B. Wells, anger and politics. *Radical History Review, 70*, 48–77.

Schubert, W. (1986). *Curriculum: Prospective, paradigm, and possibility.* New York: Macmillan.

Schubert, W.H. (1991). Teacher lore: A basis for understanding praxis. In C. Witherall & N. Noddings (Eds.), *Stories lives tell.* New York: Teachers College Press.

Schwab, J.J. (1971). The practical: Arts of the eclectic. *School Review, 79*, 493–542.

Schwab, J.J. (1977). Translating scholarship into curriculum. In S. Fox & G. Rosenfield (Eds.), *Science, curriculum, and liberal education.* Chicago: University of Chicago Press.

Scott, A.F. (1993). *Natural allies.* Urbana: University of Illinois Press.

Scott, J. (1987). Women's history and the rewriting of history. In C. Farnham (Ed.), *The impact of feminist research in the academy* (pp. 34–52). Bloomington: Indiana University Press.

Scott, J. (1989). Gender: A useful category of historical analysis. In E. Weed (Ed.), *Coming to terms: Feminism, theory, politics.* New York: Routledge.

Seigfried, C.H. (1996). *Pragmatism and feminism: Reweaving the social fabric.* Chicago: University of Chicago Press.

Seigfried, C.H. (2002). *The long road of woman's memory/Jane Addams: Introduction by Charlene Haddock Seigfried.* Urbana: University of Illinois Press.

Selden, S. (1999). *Inheriting shame: The story of eugenics and racism in America.* New York: Teachers College Press.

Serres. M. (1982). *Hermes: Literature, science, philosophy*. Baltimore, MD and London: The Johns Hopkins University Press.

Serres, M. with Latour, B. (Translated by R. Lapidus). (1995). *Conversations of science, culture and time*. Ann Arbor: University of Michigan Press.

Shapiro, S. (2002). The life-world, body movements and new forms of emancipatory politics. In S. Shapiro & S. Shapiro (Eds.), *Body movement: Pedagogy, politics and social change* (pp. 1–24). Cresskill, NJ: Hampton Press.

Simon, R., Rosenberg, S., & Eppert, C. (2000) *Between hope and despair: Pedagogy and the remembrance of historical trauma*. Boston: Rowman & Littlefield.

Sklar, K. (1973). *Catharine Beecher: A study in American domesticity*. New Haven, CT: Yale University Press.

Sklar, K. (1990). Hull House in the 1890's: A community of women reformers. In C. Dubois & V. Ruiz (Eds.), *Unequal sisters: A multicultural reader in U.S. women's history* (pp. 109–122). New York: Routledge.

Sklar, K. (1995). *Florence Kelley and the nation's work: The rise of women's political culture 1830–1900*. New Haven, CT: Yale University Press.

Smith, B. (1995). Gender, objectivity, and the rise of scientific history. In W. Natter, T.R. Schatizki, & J.P. Jones III (Eds.), *Objectivity and its other* (pp. 51–66). New York: Guilford Press.

Smith, J.K. (1979). *Ella Flagg Young: Portrait of a leader*. Ames, IO: Educational Studies Press.

Smith, S. (2002). *Nursing as social responsibility: Implication for democracy from the life perspective of Lavinia Lloyd Dock*. Baton Rouge: LSU Press.

Smith, G. & Smith J. (1994). *Lives in education: A narrative of people and ideas*. New York: St. Martin's Press.

Spearing, E. (2002). *Medieval writings on female spirituality*. New York: Penguin Press.

Spivak, G. (1988). *In other words: Essays in cultural politics*. New York: Routledge.

Spring, J. (2004). *American education*. Boston: McGraw Hill.

Springgay, S. & Freedman, D. (2010). Sleeping with cake and other touchable encounters: Performing a bodied curriculum. In E. Malewski (Ed.), *Curriculum studies handbook* (pp. 228–239). New York: Routledge.

Stack, S. (2002). Elsie Ripley Clapp and the Arthurdale schools. In A. Sandovik & S. Semmel (Eds.), *Founding mothers and others: Women educational leaders during the progressive era* (pp. 93–110). New York: Palgrave.

Stanley, William B. (1992). *Curriculum for Utopia: Social reconstructionism and critical pedagogy in the postmodern era*. Albany: SUNY Press.

Starr, M. (Translation). (2003). *The interior castle*. New York: Riverhead Books.

Stebner, E.J. (1997). *The women of Hull House*. Albany: SUNY Press.

Steedman, C. (1989). *Childhood culture and class in Britain: Margaret McMillan, 1860–1931*. New Brunswick, NJ: Rutgers University Press.

Sterling, D. (1979). *Black foremothers: Three lives*. New York: The Feminist Press.

Stewart, C.W. (1922). *Moonlight schools for the emancipation of adult illiterates*. New York: Dutton.

Stone, L. (1996). Feminist political theory: Contributions to a conception of citizenship. *Theory and research in social education, xxiv(1)*, 36–53.

Stone, M. (1979). *Ancient mirrors of womanhood*. Boston: Beacon Press.

Taliaferro, D. (1998). Education for liberation as African American folk theory. Unpublished dissertation. Baton Rouge: Louisiana State University.

Teel, J. (1996). Laura Zirbes (1884–1967): An absent presence in the history of curriculum thought. Unpublished paper.

Titone, C. (1999). Catherine Macaulay: The mere production of art. In C. Titone & K. Maloney (Eds.), *Women's philosophies of education: Thinking through our mothers.* Upper Saddle River, NJ: Prentice Hall.

Triche, S. (2004). On two historical sources for a theory of curriculum: Gabriel Harvey's rhetor (1575/1577) and William Ames's technometry (1633). Paper presented at the American Association for the Advancement of Curriculum Studies Conference, San Diego, CA, April.

Trolander, J. (1987). *Professionalism and social change: From the settlement house movement to neighborhood centers, 1886 to the present.* New York: Columbia University Press.

Trousdale, A. (2007). Women in the early Christian church. Unpublished manuscript.

Trueit, D. (2006). Play which is more than play. *Complicity: An International Journal of Complexity and Education, 3(1),* 97–104.

Tyack, D. (1974). *The one best system.* Cambridge, MA: Harvard University Press.

Urban, W. (2002). Charles Williams and the National Education Association. In A. Sadovnik & S. Semel (Eds.), *Founding mothers and others: Women educational leaders during the progressive era* (pp. 201–216). New York: Palgrave.

Vernant, J.P. (1983). *Myth and thought among the Greeks.* London: Routledge & Kegan Paul.

Waithe, M.E. (1987). *A history of women philosophers.* Dordrecht, The Netherlands: Martinus Nijhoff.

Walkerdine, V. (1990). *Schoolgirl fictions.* New York: Verso.

Ware, V. (1996). *Beyond the pale: White women, racism, and history.* London: Verso.

Watkins, W.H. (2001). *The white architects of black education.* New York: Teachers College Press.

Wear, D. (1994). *Literary anatomies: Women's bodies and health in literature.* New York: SUNY Press.

Weaver, J. (2010). The posthuman condition: A complicated conversation. In E. Malewski (Ed.), *Curriculum studies handbook* (pp. 190–200). New York: Routledge.

Weiler, K. (1988). *Women teaching for social change.* South Hadley, MA: Bergin & Garvey.

Weiler, K. (2000). No women wanted on the social frontier: Gender, citizenship and progressive education. In M. Arnot & J. Dillabough (Eds.), *Challenging democracy* (pp. 122–137). London: Routledge.

Weiler, K. (2005). What can we learn from progressive education? *Radical Teacher, 69,* 4–9.

Wells, I.B. (1901). Lynching and the excuse for it. *The Independent,* May 16.

Wells, I.B. (Ed. M. Duster). (1970). *Crusade for justice: The autobiography of Ida B. Wells.* Chicago: University of Chicago Press.

Wertheimer, B. (1977). *We were there: The story of working women in America.* New York: Pantheon.

West, C. (1989). *The American evasion of philosophy: A genealogy of pragmatism.* Madison: University of Wisconsin Press.

Westphal, S. (1994). Stories of gender. In C. MacDonald & G. Wihl (Eds.), *Transformations in personhood and culture after theory: The languages of history, aesthetics and ethics* (pp. 153–164). University Park: Pennsylvania State University Press.

White, H. (1978). *Metahistory.* Baltimore, MD: The Johns Hopkins University Press.

Whitlock, E. (2007). *This corner of Canaan.* New York: Peter Lang.

Whitson, A. & Stanley, W. (1996). Re-minding education for democracy. In W. Parker (Ed.), *Educating the democratic mind.* Albany: SUNY Press.

Winfield, A. (2007). *Eugenics and education.* New York: Peter Lang.

Wolters, C. (1966). *Julian of Norwich: Revelations of divine love*. Harmondsworth, UK: Penguin.

Woody, T. (1929). *A history of women's education in the United States*. New York: Science Press.

Young, E.F. (1900). *Isolation in the school*. Chicago: University of Chicago Press.

Young, E.F. (1902). *Ethics in the school*. Chicago: University of Chicago Press.

Young, E.F. (1903). *Scientific method in education*. Chicago: University of Chicago Press.

Young, I.M. (1995). Gender as seriality: Thinking about women as a social collective. In B. Laslett, J. Brenner, & Y. Arat (Eds.), *Rethinking the political: Gender, resistance and the state* (pp. 99–124). Chicago: University of Chicago Press.

Young, R. (1990). *White mythologies: Writing history and the west*. New York: Routledge.

Zirbes, L. (1928). Progressive practice in reading. *Progressive Education, 5*, 99–103.

Zirbes, L. (1959). *Spurs to creative teaching*. New York: G.P. Putnam's Sons.

INDEX